Corporate Social Responsibility

Second Edition

Richard N. Farmer
Indiana University

W. Dickerson Hogue
Indiana University

Lexington Books
D.C. Heath and Company/Lexington, Massachusetts/Torc

D1399890

Library of Congress Cataloging in Publication Data

Farmer, Richard N.
  Corporate social responsibility.

  1. Industry—Social aspects—United States. I. Hogue,
W. Dickerson (Walter Dickerson) II. Title
HD60.5.U5F35   1985   658.4'08   84–40848
ISBN 0–669–10293–8 (pbk. : alk. paper)

Published simultaneously in Canada
Printed in the United States of America on acid-free paper
International Standard Book Number: 0–669–10293–8
Library of Congress Catalog Card Number: 84–40848

To Helen and Jean

Contents

Figures and Tables

Figures

Tables

Preface

What are big corporations? How should society control them and get them to take the right action? How do we know what action is right? Can an action be right?

Much has been written and said about the problems of corporate social responsibility. Everyone seems concerned. This may be partly because large firms are very powerful and influential: they provide millions of jobs; they produce needed goods and services; they provide various forms of satisfaction for workers and others; they earn profits for shareholders; they support education and other good works; and they also create problems by polluting the air and water. They are admired, envied, hated, feared—and frequently despaired by both admirers and critics.

This book is intended to be used in courses dealing with business ethics, corporate social responsibility, and relations between business and society. In it we focus only on the role of the large corporation in society. Our viewpoint is that of a manager in such a corporation. How should he or she respond to the various social demands the corporation faces? One could analyze the corporation according to the perceived needs and demands of a particular group—for example, women or Chicanos and equal employment opportunities, or government and pollution cleanup. Although significant and important, these aspects are considered here only as they are perceived and reacted to by managers in large firms. The general question of social responsibility is much broader than this book.

To avoid losing a corporate manager's viewpoint or being diverted to questions of personal ethics, we first present an overview of the major questions of ethical and social responsibility that face large firms. In chapter 2 we classify the participants in these issues and create a structure to show where they fit into the corporate picture. This structure will help you think about the problems in corporate social responsibility that are given in chapters 5 through 13. These incidents, or short cases, are based on a fictitious, but typical, large American conglomerate called Servex Consolidated Industries. Servex has several operating divisions, several levels of managers, and a multitude of problems—along with profits. This company's annual report is presented in chapter 3, and in chapter 4 various articles about the firm and its management are given. You can use these chapters to study Servex much as you would study any publicly owned corporation. Later as you work through an incident, you will probably want to refer to the annual report and articles to find out more about the managers and obtain useful data.

There are no right answers to the incidents in this book. As in the real world, what one person or group wants is usually not what all other people or groups want. How should management respond? You must first figure out what the ethical and economic issues are and then decide what should be done. Remember that what seems right to you may not seem so to someone else. Your aim should be not to set down corporate policy, but to decide exactly why you want the company to do something. It is not enough to decide that a certain course of action is required. You must justify this action ethically, socially, and financially.

All the incidents represent real situations. They illustrate the classic principle that there is no such thing as a free lunch: any significant action is likely to help some people, hurt others, and be acceptable or distasteful to still others. When a course of action is both obvious and gainful to everyone, it is not a problem. Unfortunately, the world is seldom structured so neatly. We must constantly make choices about who is hurt, who gains, and how much.

We have extensively revised this second edition, bringing the text up to date. We have added ten new cases and dropped a few which are no longer relevant. While most ethical questions are at least as old as the Bible, laws do change, and things once illegal or questionable are now proper. Attitudes also change, and several new cases suggest problems which have become more significant recently, such as racism in South Africa and the new situations created when large numbers of professional women enter management. The basic format of the book remains unchanged, since it is useful to explore social responsibility within an integrated framework, such as the Servex corporation.

We thank Skip McGoun, who read the entire book and made some valuable comments. In spite of his excellent advice, along with comments from hundreds of others who have read the first edition, we continue on our own way, so any errors, omissions, or other problems in this book are our responsibility entirely.

1
What is
Corporate Social Responsibility?

S ome people say that high corporate profits are evil. According to them, to be socially responsible a firm must voluntarily spend much of what would otherwise be profits and taxes to benefit parties other than its stockholders, managers, and sometimes workers. The percentage of profits to be spent and the projects on which they should be spent are matters that such advocates cannot agree on. Nevertheless, they all think that actions by a firm to further its own profits cannot be socially responsible.

From a Historical Viewpoint

For most of its history, the United States was much poorer than it is today. It was enough for companies to produce goods as efficiently as possible, while obeying laws such as observing valid contracts and paying taxes promptly. Firms had the social responsibility of getting the productive job done, and the ultimate test was the market. If the firm could sell its goods or services at prices high enough to make a profit and survive, then its social obligation was fulfilled.

Really big companies, such as we are now familiar with, began to appear in the 1870s. As they grew, the activities they engaged in to make money and produce goods and services began significantly to affect many parts of society. If major corporations, as a matter of policy, refused to hire blacks, then blacks were likely to be cut off entirely from many social and economic activities. When a major firm built a paper mill that dumped hundreds of tons of junk into the same river every day, social impact could be very great and very bad. If a few large firms conspired to raise prices, then a great many customers were exploited.

Government Control

Not long after large companies began to appear, furious debate began as to whether they were doing the right things. As early as the 1890s, our government passed laws attempting to control major corporations. These laws dealt with, among other things, the formation of trusts, use of child labor, and safety in various industries. From 1900 through 1920 such legislation continued, often extending and refining the controls. The New Deal of the 1930s saw a major extention of social controls into many fields, including labor protection, banking reform, and public utility controls. Each piece of legislation was accompanied by passionate debate on the issue itself, on the ethics of such change, and on control.

By legally controlling large corporations, we have insisted that they be responsible to the entire society, not just to their stockholders, managers, or workers. We now have antitrust laws, consumer-protection laws, requirements-to-serve laws. (The telephone company must give you a phone, if you are willing to pay for it, even though the company may feel that your phone will cost more than you actually pay.) All these rules, regulations, and laws require major companies to serve society better.

In the last forty years, the big corporations have steadily expanded, growing a bit faster than the total economy. Increased control has not wiped out big firms or even noticeably slowed them down. Therefore, people tend to feel these firms can handle yet more social responsibilities.

In the past, people have expected firms to make profits—and, to a certain extent they still do. But increasingly, some people are asking companies to sacrifice some of their profits in order to do more than just provide useful goods and services. "If you're so smart, why aren't you rich?" can be translated nowadays into "If you corporations are so capable and efficient, why aren't you solving important human problems, instead of only making soup and soap and sailboats?" If a firm does a good job, people expect more. What more a person expects depends on his or her values and ethics, but many people feel that they are being shortchanged by firms. Corporations are evil in some way because they have not used their tremendous power to do something that needs to be done.

Whatever large firms do to help solve social problems, someone will certainly want them to do more. If corporations are required to provide safe food, why not safe cars? If safe cars, why not safe bicycles and hair dryers? If they are expected to give money to charities, why not more money, to different charities? Anyone who thinks for a few minutes about what any private company is doing can easily come up with a few pet ideas about additional things it should do. And this is really what corporate social responsibility is all about. People expect firms not only to perform the traditional function of providing goods and services to all citizens who are willing to pay for them, but also to help society solve its problems. If these things are generally seen as desirable, and the firm does them, then it is socially responsible. If the firm does not, then some people may feel it is irresponsible. Merely saying that a firm is doing good, however, does not necessarily mean that all people agree that it is behaving responsibly.

Current discussions about how to make big firms behave responsibly have shifted emphasis somewhat from earlier days: pollution, hiring of minority groups and women, and consumer protection have replaced monopoly control, protection of workers, and adequate wages as major issues. Various groups or individuals perceive that evil is being done and attempt to get support for some kind of control. An issue is raised, supported, debated, and perhaps eventually passed into law—and the large firms have one more control to deal with.

A Company's View of Its Social Responsibility

If something that people want done does not cost a corporation anything by hurting its profits and if a lot of people want it done, then a corporation is probably already doing it. In fact, the corporation may even see it as profitable to take the action, since the goodwill of the public can only add to its profit. Hence, some factories fly the American flag in front of the building; some put United Fund posters on their bulletin boards; and some include get-out-and-vote messages in company publications. Companies are happy to take these socially responsible actions if they feel that the majority of the public approves and if the cost is negligible.

Just because a few concerned citizens feel that a company should do something does not mean that it will. Through force of law, administrative decision in government, and a variety of other means, society puts pressure on large corporations to behave responsibly; but this ordinarily occurs only after a general consensus has clearly emerged. The corporation must decide not only what the general consensus is but also what would be a socially responsible action and when to take it.

Maximization of Profit

Taking a socially responsible action presents a problem primarily when it will, in the company's view, decrease its profitability. If a company considers not only its profits, but also the needs of society, acting responsibly becomes a question of whether the company's objective of maximizing its profit* should always take precedence over objectives that seem to some people important for society. Even if a company feels that it is more profitable not to hire new employees over age forty, should it do so? Even if a company's profits would suffer, should it reduce smoke emissions to a level below what the law demands?

---

*To maximize profit is (1) to cause an optimum mixture of maximized short-, medium-, and long-term profits; (2) to cause the greatest possible increase in the value of the company's common stock. Although we believe that the second definition is true, we prefer to use the first definition, because it emphasizes the time dimensions profits have.

Distribution of Costs

From the economist's viewpoint, the problem of corporate responsibility is a matter of distribution of costs: Who is to bear how much of the costs of society's actions, including corporate actions? Stated this way, costs include not only money costs but also human, or social, costs, such as frustration with machinery that does not work, poor health from breathing foul air, and lack of choice in consumer goods.

Big and Little

Discussions of corporate social responsibility typically center on large corporations. The top 5000 or so major American firms produce over half of the total gross national product. With few exceptions, these firms are managed by professionals and owned by stockholders. Their shares are sold on major stock markets, and all have over 1000 employees. The rest of the American economy consists of about 9,000,000 companies, most of which are proprietorships and partnerships that are visible only to their owners, employees, and current customers. Joe's Shoe Store, with an owner and one or two employees, typically is responsible to society only in minimal ways, such as providing economic retail services to its few customers. Most people do not expect Joe to do much toward carrying the costs of antipollution campaigns, to contribute heavily to educational funds, or to lead businesses in working toward similar socially desirable goals.

Throughout this book, the large corporation's role will be stressed from the standpoint of corporate management. Social issues that do not directly involve such companies will not be covered in detail. Problems such as the proper role of welfare programs or what to do about drug abuse, while critical, belong to a broader context than this book. We are concerned here with the smaller but critical question: How can large firms be socially responsible and yet satisfy their many clienteles and their workers and managers?

A Definition of Corporate Social Responsibility

The following definition of corporate social responsibility is the one we will work with in this book.

Socially responsible actions by a corporation are actions that, when judged by *society in the future,* are seen to have been of maximum help in providing *necessary amounts of desired goods and services at minimum financial and social costs, distributed as equitably as possible.*

The italicized phrases in this definition are crucial, but they are difficult to apply in any practical way or in a particular context. Who can speak for society as it is now, much less as it will be in the future? Who can know how society will assess the relative values of providing goods and services, minimizing costs, and distributing the costs equitably? Who can decide how costs should be distributed among the nations, races, sexes, age groups, economic classes, occupations, and similar groups?

In this chapter and the next you will become familiar with the meaning of this definition, especially as we discuss the costs of corporate actions. You will come to see how complex the issues are and recognize that there are no simple solutions. Each person must arrive at his or her own answers after careful consideration of the many aspects of corporate social responsibility.

The basic problem in defining corporate social responsibility is that socially responsible actions necessarily reflect moral values, the substance of which cannot be determined apart from particular situations. What are society's needs? In what order of priority? Who will pay the costs of meeting them? Just because one group wants a particular action taken does not mean that others do or even that the action is socially responsible. In the end, someone has to establish a corporate goal system that makes social as well as economic sense. If firms are to be socially responsible, some goal system is needed to suggest what society wants them to do.

Goal Systems

What are firms for? As we have seen, their traditional function has been to supply desired material goods and services to individuals and organizations at the lowest possible financial cost. With time, however, other diverse tasks have been assigned to firms by society, often in quite casual ways. For example, oil and cigarette companies have often been legislated into becoming de facto tax collectors for various levels of government. Firms are legally required to give workers certain benefits such as pensions and safe working conditions. Products must meet various criteria of safety and quality, even though these requirements may raise the financial costs of producing the products. Firms are legally required to participate in various social programs, such as eliminating discrimination on the basis of race or sex. Tax laws make it possible to use tax-free funds to support charitable works and good causes, such as the local Community Chest or a university.

Most people who have thought about corporate goals argue that firms should be doing something that they are not doing or are doing badly: making workers happy, paying higher wages and salaries, eliminating racism and poverty, supporting (or ignoring) local and federal governments' points of view on domestic and foreign issues, solving the housing shortage, training hard-core unemployed, pressing colleges and universities to do or not to do

Figure 1-1. Goal Systems of Firms

certain things, helping to reform various kinds of public administration, eliminating pollution—to name a few possible goals. Of course, many of these goals are contradictory. Your view of university reform might be diametrically opposed to ours, and no firm can support both views simultaneously. There is also the problem that a stockholder may be angered if funds that might have gone to him are used to support a college he does not even like.

Figure 1-1 shows a continuum of corporate goals ranging from pure profit maximization to socially oriented action. Although theoretically a firm's goals could fit anywhere along the continuum, the goals of most firms tend to cluster at four points.

Point I: Profits

Of the approximately 9 million private firms in the United States, perhaps 8,990,000 still pursue the traditional goal of maximizing profits. These firms tend to be small, little known, and financially pressed. They are occasionally run by people who care only about the success of their own business. The international import-export trade is another example of this goal orientation, as are also small Western European firms.

Point II: Profits and Social Goals

At point II, some firms at least seem to be interested in such generally accepted ideas as eliminating discrimination, helping students and educational institutions, supporting local charities with man-hour or cash contributions. The goals of most larger American (and Western European) firms *appear* to fall on the continuum about here. Larger Japanese firms may also have such a goal system.

Point III: Social Goals and Profits

As social goals become far more important than profits, firms reach point III: they pay relatively little attention to profits and a great deal of attention to social goals. Often, such firms are content only to break even on cash inflows and outflows, as long as their social goals are realized. One large U.S. firm whose announced policy is at point III (or at least nearer III than II) is the Rockefeller-sponsored International Basic Economy Corporation (IBEC), which has businesses in many countries outside the United States.

Point III firms are very rare in the United States. Only publicly owned businesses such as transit systems, the Tennessee Valley Authority, and the post office can afford this goal orientation. The publicly owned transit companies in larger cities put first such goals as saving cities, helping revitalize downtown sections, and assisting planners in getting people to live in certain areas. If these social goals really are more important to the company than profits, then money losses will probably grow very rapidly, as they have in many American cities. These firms are not necessarily poorly managed or inefficient; they just have goals other than making profits. Similarly, the U.S. postal system in the early 1970's was established as a state-owned firm with a point III goal system. It will be interesting to see whether it, too, tends to have losses that grow rapidly.

Privately owned U.S. companies that attempt to let social goals come before profits tend to go bankrupt rather quickly. Even IBEC has announced what sounds like a shift of policy slightly towards point II. The reason is simple: if a manager for a firm with a point III goal orientation can either visit a key client to get a new contract or attend a fund-raising dinner for a cause supported by his firm, he is likely to go to the dinner. If he worked for a company that emphasized profits, he would try to get the contract. After five or ten years of business neglect, a privately owned firm with a point III goal system may not have much business to worry about.

Major examples of firms with point III goal systems are found abroad. Some Japanese and Western European public utilities operate this way, although from our observations, most of them (including British Airways, the French National Railways, and the German State Railways) are beginning to drift back to point II. If profits do not matter much in a firm's goal system, then the activities of its managers may even tend to generate money losses. After a while, a public sponsor finds that the bill is too big and forces a restructuring of the goal system, back at least partway to point II. Many Soviet public firms, however, still operate at about point III, by order of the state planning groups.

Point IV: Social Goals

Firms with point IV goal systems are very difficult to find, since they may have no output at all. A certain publicly owned firm in the Middle East existed for ten years without producing any salable goods. Its managers and workers were very well paid; its company housing was a model of efficiency and beauty; its medical clinic was one of the best in the country. The plan for the firm included producing superior goods at low prices—at some future time. If, however, they never got around to actual production, that was all right as long as they were achieving their primary goals.

Obviously, such a firm must have a wealthy financial sponsor who is willing to provide the operating funds. Only governments are likely to have enough resources to subsidize these enterprises, which are not only materially and financially unproductive but also parasitic: the well-paid workers and managers consume items other firms produce; the company doctors and nurses provide this group with services that they therefore cannot provide another group. Nevertheless, such firms appeared in China during the Great Leap Forward and may still be found in neutralist countries such as India.

U.S. Firms and Their Goals

What is the goal system of most U.S. firms? What should it be? Many people criticize U.S. firms for being too profit-oriented and feel that they should put some social goals ahead of their profit goals. Some people think that a substantial number of large U.S. companies have already done this. After all, the top executives of several large companies have said that social goals should rank ahead of profits; dozens of large firms have set up factories in ghettos, hired the hard-core unemployed as trainees, and even announced in their annual reports that their goal is to serve the U.S. public better. These actions are cited as proof that the goal systems of some firms are at point II or even point III.

Being and Seeming: Goals and Motives

Probably a number of U.S. firms have adopted as company policy (with the agreement of their top management) a goal system whereby they will divert to socially constructive actions part of what would otherwise have been profits and taxes. There are, however, many reasons why a company might, for example, announce that it will spend $1,000,000 on summer employment of teenagers.

1. The firm does in fact have a company policy that part of its earnings should be diverted from profits and taxes to socially desirable actions. Management has decided that, of all the money-losing but socially desirable actions they might take, summer employment of teenagers is the most desirable.
2. The firm sees the summer employment of teenagers as a profitable action. They may even customarily employ teenagers as seasonal laborers, perhaps on summer construction jobs.

3. One of the firm's managers has deep personal sympathy with unemployed teenagers or is under pressure from his wife or wants to be recognized publicly as a humanitarian. He makes the announcement about summer hiring even though it is a personal decision not in accord with company policy and later defends it to company headquarters as a profitable action: "Community pressure was so great that I felt it necessary to . . ."

4. The firm is controlled by one person or by a small group of people and their families. These people are personally very well off and view the company as an extension of their own personalities. When they make the announcement about summer employment, it is really as a personal contribution to charity.

5. The firm is well managed, but under great pressure from the mayor, the police chief, the governor, and many other powerful people both in and out of government to do something to avoid a "hot summer" of riots. Management objectively decides that any company money lost through teenage summer employment will be more than offset by money gained through the goodwill of city and state officials and other powerful people—that is, the action will be profitable.

6. The company's public-relations chief feels that the announcement will generate much goodwill among the public in general and create an image of the company as interested in the welfare of the community. (Public utilities and life insurance companies, whose profits depend heavily on general public goodwill, are particularly likely to emphasize community service in their announcements and advertisements.) The company would therefore be likely to attract and keep a better grade of employee. Management considers the loss ($10,000 before tax or $5000 after tax) objectively and decides that, in view of the excellent publicity it will buy, the action will be profitable.

The authors of this text disagree on whether a large, successful U.S. company can or should have as its company policy a goal system at point II. One author feels that it can; the other feels that profit maximization is the only workable position—seeming exceptions occur because of extraneous motives as in the example above. No doubt opinions of any large groups of students will also be divided on this subject.

Some Tough Questions

Should profit maximization or socially desirable action come first in a company's policies? A person might ask the proponent of profits how he justifies putting profits ahead of goals such as 100 percent clean milk, 100 percent pure water, and equal job opportunities. He might answer with the following argument: society assigns roles, industry's role is to supply goods, and profit orientation leads to the "best" supply of goods; anyway society can always change the rules through legislation. If you were to point out to him that, in reality, the profit system does not work perfectly, perhaps not even well, he might say that no other system works any better, implying that human frailties are bound to ruin any attempt at perfection.

What if a system of corporate social responsibility were put to the test? Suppose that society decided to establish such a system by raising federal taxes on corporate profit and returning to the corporation a certain percentage of the taxes collected from it—with the stipulation that this money be spent on whatever it decided was socially responsible, not including options that would specifically benefit its stockholders. In this situation there would be three basic questions that would have to be answered by anyone who advocates that corporations finance socially responsible actions with at least part of what would otherwise be profits and taxes.

First, what percentage of corporate profit should be spent on socially responsible actions that contribute nothing to future corporate profit? Under the present system of corporate taxation, 46 percent of profits goes to the federal government, and other substantial percentages go to state and local governments. Presumably, these public agencies spend the collected monies on socially responsible actions. How much of the remaining percentage of profit should also go in this direction?

Second, who in the corporation are you willing to trust to decide how to spend the money? Will you go along with whatever the top management of the corporation decides? If, politically, you lean to the left and top management decides to spend $350 million a year in support of the John Birch Society, what would you do? If you lean to the political right and top management spends $350 million a year to create a giant bank of personal data on every individual in the United States, what would you do?

In the 1930s, the majority of German (and Italian) industrialists looked at their politically atomized, economically depressed, and apparently leaderless country and sincerely felt that the socially responsible thing for them to do was to support a single, strong, modern political party. They followed through on their thinking with strong corporate support of the infant Nazi (and Fascist) party—to their grief and the world's.

Third, when a manager is appointed by a small group to manage their property, what gives him the right to dispose of it in ways not approved by them and to diminish the security and opportunities of suppliers and employees? In the case of the International Basic Economy Corporation or of a state-owned firm, a manager is appointed with everyone's understanding that profit maximization is not to be his primary goal. More important, he understands more or less exactly what his primary goals are. In more typical U.S. firms, both the law and the tacit general understanding specify that managers are entrusted with the job of maximizing profit through legal activities. What gives him the right to violate that trust?

These questions are extremely difficult to answer, and yet they must be answered by anyone claiming to hold a rational view of how corporations should act to be socially responsible.

Profits and Esthetics

Many critics of U.S. firms say that economic growth is not the only important aspect of society. There are, in addition, ethical considerations, religious and artistic values, educational options, and many other things that cannot be measured by any economic or business accounting. These critics suggest that the material wealth of the United States is large enough that such non-economic items can and should take precedence over increasing an already enormous production of goods and services.

The question of whether further economic growth is desirable seems to us to require two qualifications. First, is economic growth desirable even if it seriously threatens the health or survival of the human race or a large fraction of it? Our answer is clearly no. If oil slicks cover too many hundreds of thousands of square miles of ocean, threatening to prevent the entire human race from having enough oxygen to breathe, then we must stop the oil slicks even at the cost of stopping economic growth. Second, is economic growth desirable even if it destroys or diminishes certain esthetic aspects that many of us cherish? Virgin forests, landscapes unmarred by factories and empty beer cans, a sky clear enough that one can see the stars at night, a mountain stream full of trout—these are all highly valued by many people. Silence (at least the absence of banging, screeching, whining machinery) is a blessing to many. The ideal society for many people would be one in which spiritual, artistic, and intellectual values are held to be superior to material values.

From our observation, only an articulate but small part of the total society values esthetics more than material things. The people who say that further economic growth is undesirable are usually the ones who already have enough material possessions. Over two-thirds of the world population live in undeveloped countries that have average per capita incomes about one-fifth to one-twentieth the size of the U.S. average. Overwhelmingly, they want more of the material things economic growth can provide. Even in the United States and other industrialized nations, the vast majority of the people seem to us to want more material things; they can be counted on to vote for a new oil refinery or factory rather than for the preservation of a rare stretch of coastline. At this level the question as to whether economic growth is desirable now becomes: Is it more important to provide a small minority with the esthetic delights they want or to provide the vast majority with more of the material things they want? Our answer cannot be so unequivocal as before.

In the United States, private firms are faced with the need to produce something that someone will pay for: they must make at least some profits to ensure their long-term survival. In demanding that firms behave more responsibly, we are asking that they adopt a different goal system. If they do change, who decides whether they have changed for the better? It is very difficult to measure precisely the extent to which many worthwhile social goals are achieved. If firm X makes a million dollars in net profit, we have a pretty good idea of what this means. But if a survey indicates that firm X's workers are "less happy" than firm Y's, how do we decide how much to spend on making them more happy? Questions like this are extremely difficult to answer and, given the finiteness of resources, an answer such as "enough" is meaningless.

Finite Resources and Infinite Goals

While potential social demands for what needs doing are infinite, resources are finite. Every society has to find ways to ration scarce resources. Many Americans born after World War II have known affluence all their lives and therefore find it difficult to believe that resources are limited. If resources were in truth infinite, then people who denied resources to others in need of them would be very cruel.

Yet resources are limited—especially those such as skilled labor, managerial talent, school buildings, and hospitals. We could easily spend $50 billion a year (about 4 percent of total national income) for the next fifty years on rebuilding New York City alone. Improving rapid transit for the fifty largest American cities, at current costs, could use up all increases in national income every year for the next twenty years. Putting an additional 10 percent of eighteen-year-olds in college at present quality levels would take at least another 5 percent of increases in national income. Providing perfect medical care for all Americans is simply impossible for the next twenty years because of the lack of skilled doctors and other medical personnel. On account of the scarcity of resources, something desirable may have to give way to something more desirable, and highly desirable things may have to be done less than completely.

Setting Priorities

What are our goals, in order of their importance? Assigning priorities rationally is difficult and confusing, especially when the human problems that are involved touch our emotions deeply. It is hard for any of us to decide individually what human problems should be dealt with and how thoroughly. Your view of the proper priorities is certain to be objectionable—perhaps violently so—to many others who have as much right to their views as you to yours. How then can we arrive at a consensus for the goals of society as a whole?

One way to assign priorities is to neglect to think about or discuss them.

Some people cannot set priorities even when circumstances urgently demand that goals be ranked in some order of importance. They may assume that resources are infinite and therefore not recognize the need for priorities; such people are likely to criticize goal setters, rationers, and cost allocators for not doing everything anyone wants done or for doing the wrong thing.

But there may be no right thing. Consider the following crisis situation. It is late at night. A mother and her child have been seriously injured in an auto accident and brought to the emergency room of the local hospital. The intern on duty quickly examines them and concludes that he can save only one life. Which one? There is no time to obtain more medical resources to help him with both patients. He hesitates a moment, then turns to the child. The mother dies, but the child is saved.

A cynic might accuse the intern of murder, of letting a person die. An idealist might feel that the child had a potential value greater than the adult had and therefore approve the intern's decision. (Of course, the child might grow up to be a murderer, while his mother had in fact been a brilliant poet. The intern could not know this, but even so, would it have made any difference?) Another idealist might note that there should have been two doctors on duty. If the hospital administrator pointed out that there are not enough doctors to staff every such facility with two doctors around the clock, he would probably be dismissed as an evil man, trying to save money at the expense of human life. This last point begs the question: an additional doctor might not have been able to save other people if more had been in need of immediate help there that night. How should one determine the optimum rationing of scarce resources?

Rationing Resources

The apportionment of scarce resources is the crux of the problem of social responsibility. A firm might give large amounts to several charities, to stockholders, or to universities but, because of its limited resources, might not give enough to satisfy any of them. Dividing the money equally among all applicants is not a good solution, since many other charities and universities want donations and fulfilling their requests would eventually reduce each recipient's share to near-zero. Who is to decide who gets what, or even whether a firm should give at all and how much in total?

Point I with its profitability criterion is the simplest rationing system: the firm that produces something for which people are willing to pay an above-cost price is able to buy resources. Point III and point IV firms (and to a certain extent point II firms) have much trouble rationing their resources. Because their goal systems tend to be diffuse, these firms are never sure what to do with their resources. If workers are well paid, they could always be better paid. If one passenger train serves some people, two could serve more, and on and on. Colleges and universities face similar problems: which is better—a new gymnasium, a new chemistry lab, or four new professors of philosophy? If, as a manager or university president, you have no clear idea of what you are trying to achieve, you may as well toss coins. If you do a little bit toward a hundred goals, you are in danger of wasting much of your resources and having little to show for any of them. If you do express clearly what you are trying to do, many of your financial sponsors may withdraw their support because they feel your priorities should be different.

Bearing the Costs

How do we divide among specific members of present and future society the costs of the resources we have assigned? Who pays how much, in what way, and when?

Americans often comment on the excellence of European passenger trains compared with the rather undependable and dirty American ones. European state-owned railways have been run, however, in accordance with the goal of providing good service at almost any cost. If Americans were willing to give railroads almost endless amounts of money (and hence command over real, scarce resources), American trains could be among the best in the world. A train ticket might then cost someone—the taxpayers or the customers—twice as much as it now does, with the increase going to provide service and comfort for the customer, not profit to the company.

The deficits incurred by European railroads are borne by taxpayers. Some advantages (monetary and otherwise) may accrue to all people through government subsidies to railroads: reduced need for new highways and less pollution, which may in turn lead to both tangible gains (less dirty clothing and lung disease) and intangible gains (more sunshine and cleaner air). In businesses where the gains go beyond the typical profit-and-loss calculations for private, profit-making firms, democratic government is likely to cover the costs so that all the people may enjoy the benefits.

There is a danger, however, Suppose that almost no one rides the expensive, beautiful trains provided by the taxpayers. If the people prefer to use their private cars, a railroad deficit as well as traffic pollution and congestion may result. Government can again step in and tax cars off the road or ban them from certain areas, as has already been done in some European countries. But citizens can also go elsewhere or vote for other politicians at the next election. The railroads will then need still more money to run better trains to attract more customers, who may not be attracted.

There is another danger in that some people who might have worked in industries that produce things people are willing to pay a lot for are hired instead by the railroad to produce beautifully appointed, fast, punctual trains, which few people ride. Not only do taxes climb higher and higher to cover railroad deficits, but also other industries suffer a loss of talent because of the attempt to perfect the railroads. Things people are willing to pay for become scarce, because there are no profitability signals to tell firms to produce them. Even if there are signals, firms cannot get the materials, people, and other resources to produce the desired things. Exports may start lagging because foreigners are not interested in paying prices high enough to allow the achievement of the social-welfare goals of a foreign country. Price inflation inside the country may begin or accelerate. In short, reaching for perfection without profitability restraints is likely to produce things no one wants at the prices charged, while many things people do want are not available at reasonable prices.

If nonprofit-oriented output is a small percentage of total output, the overall loss is small. But when a really significant part of economic activity is carried out by firms with no efficiency or profitability orientation, then economic growth slows or stops.

Externalities

Much of an economist's thinking about distribution of the cost of corporate actions is involved with the concept of *externalities*. As used in economics, this term refers to the costs that are borne by persons outside the organization creating them. A classic case is a company that dumps its industrial wastes in a nearby river. A city downstream that uses this river for its supply of drinking water therefore has additional costs in treating the water. From the point of view of the firm, its disposal solution is cheap and efficient: to do anything else would cost more money. The company has not, however, eliminated the costs of disposal. It has merely made them externality costs by shifting them to someone who is not directly involved in generating them.

Other examples of externalities include extra cleaning costs for people as a result of smoke and other pollutants in the air as well as traffic congestion costs near big companies at starting and quitting times. In some cases, the costs can be very high. Several million auto owners may pollute the air so much that more and more people die of respiratory diseases and lung cancer.

Past, Present, and Future

Many activities that entail externality costs begin in ways that do not seem dangerous. When autos were first introduced, they were hailed as a depolluting factor in cities, since they quickly eliminated most horse manure and urine from the streets. Similarly, it seemed sanitary and reasonable to dump sewage and industrial wastes into broad, fast-flowing rivers, where they would quickly be carried out of sight and free towns from potential infectious diseases. In the last century, when America was lightly populated and had relatively little industry, dumping industrial wastes seemed to be the only sensible choice. Later, when population density rose and most people earned their living as corporate employees, the externality costs resulting from this practice became clear: air, water, and noise pollution. By this time, however, firms were locked into certain cost patterns. If one firm tried to depollute (that is, accepted its externality costs) and competitors did not, then it would likely face bankruptcy.

Our society has tended to ignore externality costs. This lack of awareness is especially evident in our handling of the costs of extracting raw materials. For many years we have been cutting down seemingly limitless forests, digging coal, pumping oil, and mining nickel ore. We have been aware of some of the externalities, such as smoke from a nickel smelter that kills all vegetation within twenty miles. We are becoming aware of externalities such as the cost of reclaiming a landscape scarred by the strip-mining of coal. We have yet to deal with externality costs created by the irreplaceability of many of the materials we use. The oil company and the redwood lumbering company do not include in their prices a charge for the fact that there is a limited supply of gasoline and redwood. Instead, we are asking future generations to bear the costs of not having supplies of these materials. We complain that Lake Erie is dying because society over the last 150 years did not accept the costs of keeping it clean. Our forefathers treated these as externality costs and passed them on to us. What will our great-grandchildren say about us when redwood is as scarce as ivory?

Weighing the Costs and Benefits

If a firm is forced to pay all costs, external and internal, we may have no pollution, but we may also have no jobs and no income. For a city like Gary, Indiana, which is heavily polluted by a few steel mills but has no other major economic base, would you prefer pollution or jobs? The usual economic answer is to force all firms to take on externality costs. That is, by general law, they must all stop doing something simultaneously. In this way, all incur the same costs and are therefore in the same relative position as before the law went into effect.

Or are they? Suppose that steel mills in the United States were forced to accept various externality pollution costs, and steel production costs became relatively higher than in countries where citizens are not so concerned about pollution. Not only would it be easier for foreign steel firms to sell in the American market, but also they would win in third-country markets as well. After a time, unemployment would probably rise in Gary and other U.S. steel centers, because the industry seemingly could not compete. Consequently, tax revenues from Gary would lag, Indiana colleges would not get funds, and some young people in Indiana could not go to college. This is an over-simplified, but not incorrect, view of what can happen when one part of a worldwide industry is saddled with costs other parts do not have.

Another aspect of the problem of distributing the costs of our increasing activities is whether Americans will be able to afford in the future the material standard of living they have enjoyed until now. If we are really serious about forcing firms to accept the externality costs that they never have accepted before, then someone will pay the bill and conceivably money incomes could decline. Since not all cleanup costs can be paid out of profits, workers, customers, stockholders, and the general public would have to share with companies the burden of paying externality costs.

Degrees of Pollution. Total and absolute abatement of pollution could reduce the American living standard twenty times over, bringing it down to about the level of India's. Instead of making $1000 to $1200 a month on graduation, a U.S. college graduate would have purchasing power equal to $50 to $60 a month at current prices. Pollution would be negligible, because very few people could afford to buy things that pollute.

Total pollution abatement may be unrealistic in itself. If a law were passed that only pure water could be discharged, then even distilling the discharge would be unsatisfactory, since distilled water contains a few parts per million of impurities. Certainly we will settle for less than absolute purity, but how much less?

We must realize also that cleaning up pollution may sometimes create pollution. A paper company that dumps its wastes into a river is forced by law to clean up. To do this, it needs certain chemicals whose production creates pollution some place else. It needs electricity, and generating this is potentially polluting. It has to hire new employees to handle the problem; these men and women are likely to buy more things and use more electricity than before. Because of the potential new pollution that could be created to correct the old problem, we may even be adding to total pollution. The way to stop the pollution absolutely is to shut down the plant—a solution that would also result in the elimination of income.

Partial pollution abatement would cost much less. How much of his standard of living will the average American want to trade for how much pollution abatement?

One Alternative: Passing the Buck. Americans may decide that they do not care that much about some aspects of social responsibility. By accepting further deterioration of Lake Erie, for example, the problem and the costs of correcting it are passed on to the next generation. This is not a totally unlikely outcome. Our parents and grandparents, who knew a lot about water pollution, made this decision, and we are stuck with the problem they passed on.

We may decide to do nothing also—except shift to someone else responsibility for solving the problem.

Another Alternative: Productivity Gains. Major breakthroughs in many fields may enable us to have our cake and eat it too. If national productivity were to rise at 5 percent a year (historically, it has gone up at about 3 percent) and if gradual acceptance of externality costs added 3 percent a year to costs, then we could both get a bit richer and have less pollution. As yet, however, no one knows how to assure gains in productivity of as much as 5 percent annually, or what levels of pollution will be acceptable to most citizens, or how much of the increases society will be willing to spend on pollution abatement and other socially desirable actions.

It is possible that the gains some firms make from being ecologically sound would affect their losses: recovery of valuable materials that previously went up the smokestack may offset the costs of smoke abatement; engineers, forced to develop new ways of avoiding water pollution, may come up with new processes that not only use less water, but also are cheaper. Occasionally, such things happen. When they do, firms are glad to comply with new requirements.

Already some corporations are undertaking research and development into new fields, such as cleaning the air. Firms specializing in cleaning up for other firms may also develop and even show considerable profit. As yet, no one can say how the new methods might work out in terms of income gains or losses. There would in any case be winners and losers. The worker in an old, dirty plant that is closed down would be bitter and demand certain rights, while more pollution-control engineers and technicians would be hired. As is typical of situations where social priorities are shifted, some citizens gain and feel that the change is obviously beneficial, while others lose and become upset. Corporations are caught in the middle—praised by some, criticized by others.

Corporate Legitimacy

All societies assign roles to different kinds of organizations. Police and armies keep the peace; lawyers and judges settle disputes; teachers educate; ministers deal with spiritual needs; government workers provide sewers, roads, bridges, and other public works; doctors and nurses heal the sick; and morticians bury the dead. In these ways society as a whole, in all times and places, creates and supports institutions to fill certain needs.

Roles can be and are redefined from time to time. Even though we have had large corporations for our entire lives, we need not assume that they cannot be replaced or must continue in their present forms. This is why large corporations are so sensitive to corporate social responsibility problems. If an organization does not meet real social needs or if it does so with undesirable side effects, the organization can become illegitimate and disappear. For example, from 1921 through 1933 alcoholic beverages could not be legally manufactured and sold in the United States. Wineries and distilleries that were legitimate in 1920 (and again in 1934) were forced to change businesses or go out of business altogether, even though some customers wanted their products. Similarly, if people were to consider the present General Motors Corporation too large for the general good, antitrust laws would break it up: the corporation would be declared illegitimate. At the present time it is illegitimate for a company to process and sell marijuana or other narcotics to the general public, even though many customers would happily buy the product if available. Private firms cannot run casinos in California or horseracing tracks in Indiana. Through laws, these states have declared such activities illegitimate, even though other states, such as Nevada, approve.

If society decides to make some activities illegal, it can do so and often has. Hence, the question of corporate social responsibility becomes critical for any large firm. What the managers think is important for the firm to do may be widely judged as disruptive, antisocial, or unethical; if so, society will probably destroy the firm.

Conclusion

Large firms have historically played a relatively simple role in society—namely, to produce goods and services efficiently. As firms grew larger and more complex and as American society satisfied its more basic demands for goods and services, companies have been pressured to do much more than produce. In effect, they have been directed—through laws, social pressures, and other means—to be more responsive to other perceived needs of society.

In this chapter we have considered the problems of defining corporate social responsibility, setting corporate goals, and distributing the costs of corporate actions. Since survival is perhaps the most important corporate goal of all, managers must determine what is essential to assure survival—that is, what the really critical intermediate goals are and how they can be achieved. Just because something is desirable does not necessarily mean that it can be done. Corporate legitimacy ultimately depends on how society evaluates the total impact of the firm, not just its economic impact.

2
A Manager's Approach to Corporate Social Responsibility

Often it is useful to structure a problem in a systematic way in order to get at what is involved. To sort out the various clienteles firms must work with and the groups that try to force firms to change, we will use the taxonomy shown in figure 2–1: managers, employees, stockholders, creditors, the trade, consumers, governments, suppliers, and the public. At points called interfaces these groups have direct contact with a firm and can apply pressure for change in the company's actions.

A pressure situation of consequences is also a bargaining situation. A group that tries to persuade a firm to change usually has some bargaining power with the firm: the union can call a strike; the stockholders can vote their stock against present management. Neither group has absolute power: the strike may fail or accomplish less than expected; the dissident stockholders may own only a small percentage of the shares voted. In working out the proper response to group pressure, the corporation has to compare its bargaining strength with that of its opponent. In this chapter we will discuss various bargaining stances.

First, however, we must clarify the role of the corporate manager in these issues lest we confuse his personal ethics with the social responsibility of the firm. Although corporate decisions are made and priorities set not by impersonal corporations but by people, these people act both individually and in groups on behalf of the corporation. They are corporate managers as well as citizens with their own lives and ethical standards. A person cannot separate completely one part of his life from the other parts, but he does behave differently in a managerial role than in his other roles.

Personal Social Responsibility

Although our views on how to behave may differ considerably, few of us would condone defecating on a public street, murdering for money, or beating children. We all realize that there are some things we must never do (or

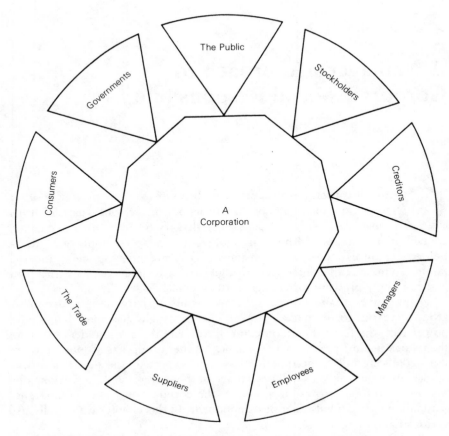

Figure 2–1. Pressure Groups Affecting the Corporation

face arrest and punishment if we do), some things we rarely do, and many things that are debatable. Among the last might be whether to march in a peace demonstration. Societies generally regard as taboo any personal activity that damages others. Most societies also have various formal and informal ways of controlling personal activities that may harm only the individual concerned, if anyone. The man who regularly plays the horses and is known to chase blondes is not likely to be a bank teller; the political radical will not normally reach the higher levels of the civil service; the person with the "wrong" religious values will not be given an executive position. One can be upset by such informal controls, but they are found everywhere in human society.

Each individual has a number of roles to play in society, and some of them are personal roles—member of a family, driver on the highway, consumer, adviser on a friend's problems, member of a club. Such roles are more or less separate from each other, but there is one common denominator: the individual has personal responsibility for his actions and is taking personal risks. If you take a risk in a personal role and win, the gain is yours; if you lose, the loss is yours. Since no man is an island, others are affected by your actions—spouse, friends, children, parents—but basically you are acting in each of your personal roles in your name and at your own risk.

Representing Someone Else's Interests

When you accept a position where your role is to act in the best interests of other people, you take an oath, formally or informally, to do your best for the people you represent, whether as a lawyer, treasurer of your church, ambassador of your country, leader of a Boy Scout troop, or manager in a firm. You consciously agree that in this role your own interests must take second place.

For the corporation, as for the individual, there are many forbidden things, many gray-area activities, and many permissible behavioral and ethical patterns. A corporation's decisions, however, are made by its managers for many people. A manager might easily decide to take a risk for himself, but it is different for him to decide to force that risk on others who not only might be quite unwilling to take it but also have not and could not be consulted. Long after the individual manager is gone, the corporation will still be around, and people yet unborn may be affected by some minor ethical point on which a manager has had to decide.

Managers and Personal Conflicts

Like the military commander who consciously sacrifices forty lives going up hill A to avoid sacrificing 200 lives going up hill B, the manager has to make a cost-benefit analysis in regard to *his own* ethics. People who cannot distinguish their own values from the corporation's values find it very difficult to function as managers in large corporations or other large institutions such as government agencies or universities. However, this is not a slave society. If a manager finds it very difficult to function, he can always quit.

A manager can (and many often do) take personal positions that are different from his firm's position. He or she should not do so, however, in the performance of his or her managerial duties. A manager of a steel mill that is polluting the countryside might resist public pressures to install multi-million dollar smoke-abatement equipment on the logical grounds that the cost disadvantage of installing the equipment might make the firm's competitive position untenable. The same man, as an individual, might feel that contributing to an antipollution campaign was the proper thing to do. He might even, as an individual, join a group or make speeches to promote antipollution causes.

A manager may also do many things to persuade the corporation to act more in line with his personal ethics. He might fight for what he thinks is correct within the company, mashaling arguments in favor of what he perceives to be a more responsible corporate position. While this dissension might appear to be disastrous for a manager's career, it usually is not, as both authors can testify from personal experience. A manager who dispassionately argues for what he feels would be a more ethical corporate position will be listened to. He may sometimes even win his point, particularly if he argues soundly that the action he recommends is for the long-term good of the corporation as a whole.

Only when a manager feels that the decision he must make cannot be reconciled with his personal ethics does he resign and leave the company. Normally, if he has worked his way up through the managerial hierarchy for many years, this will not occur for trivial reasons. Those who find corporate ethics intolerable would have left long before they moved very far up in the corporate management hierarchy.

Multiplicity of Roles

To those who perceive situations in all-or-nothing terms, it seems absurdly paradoxical that a manager might make corporate decisions that go against his personal ethics: a moral man acts morally in everything he does. It would be comforting if such a straightforward rule were workable in real life, as it may be for a saintly hermit in the desert. In ordinary life, the simple rule of acting morally in everything becomes difficult to follow as soon as you accept responsibility for someone else's interests.

Even more difficult is the situation where you are responsible for protecting, to some extent, the interests of many different groups of people. Is it moral for you to disregard your responsibility when it conflicts with your personal morality? What would you do in a situation where you must decide between two alternatives, neither of which suits your personal morality? You must decide, say, whether to fire an alcoholic who has a family to support but consistently falls asleep on his job as nightwatchman in spite of repeated warnings. What does a moral and compassionate person do?

Most of us perceive a problem from a personal viewpoint, since few of us have institutional roles requiring us to make ethical decisions on behalf of an entire organization. As a result, it is easy for us to frame cases in business ethics that are un-problems: it does not matter what the manager in question decides to do. In reality, he would either be wrong or be fired if he always took the personal view and failed to consider people who might be harmed by his decisions.

An Example of a Problem in Corporate Social Responsibility. A corporation operates a plant in a corruption-ridden foreign country where customs guards and officials, police, and union leaders must be bribed or paid off to prevent violence and strikes. Such deals are personally abhorrent to the manager in charge. Should he stop them? What would be the consequences?

As one consequence, the plant would probably close. If it did, employees in New Jersey who make parts for this plant may be out of jobs. These people were not asked about the problem, and yet the major cost may fall on them. In addition, stockholders may lose income. Maybe the plant is an important source of income for the citizens of the corruption-ridden country. Maybe its operations there have been slowly helping to reduce the amount of corruption in the country. Furthermore, there may be pressure from the U.S. government because the State Department wants good American firms to maintain contacts and activity in this country. The problem definitely involves more than one person's ethics. The manager who might decide to condone bribes in this situation may in his personal life be a very upright man who would never give money of his own to anyone illegally. If the general goal statement "The greatest good for the greatest number" is applied here, it still may be extremely difficult to decide just what decision should be made to lead to that goal.

Temptations and Retribution

It sometimes happens that corporate managers knowingly and willfully violate either the law (as in the case of price-fixing conspiracy) or some basic, generally held ethical position (as when a manager knowingly allows defective products to be shipped). No organization can teach ethics. If a man is willing to cut corners, and his corporation ignores his ethics, then it pays the price. One author once witnessed a fairly large corporation rot away under the control of some unethical managers who took the position (and encouraged it tacitly) that anything anyone could get away with was fine. This strategy worked until the managers began to steal from the corporation itself. Before long the company was in deep financial trouble. It recovered only after a complete change of management at the top, rapid removal of the rotten apples at all managerial levels, and radical changes in ethical postures.

Companies tend to hire and promote responsibly ethical people. It is just too dangerous to do otherwise. If someone will steal from and cheat outsiders, he or she might do it to the company. No company, however, can always hire only totally ethical people or avoid coming up against unethical attitudes. Companies themselves sometimes provide the stimulus for dishonest behavior by placing on their managers what are perceived to be intolerable pressures. If the shipment must go out or else the foreman will be fired, then maybe the shipment goes out even though the foreman knows that the product is defective.

The Superior Manager: A Modifying Influence

In theory, a large, successful company with profit maximization as its goal—a point I company—should be a cold, ruthless monster. Who would want to work for such a company? How can society let it prey on people? In reality, a profit-maximizing company need not be cold and ruthless in its dealings with its employees and the public, and few are. What makes the difference? We have already mentioned two major factors that curb the possibly ruthless tendencies of a profit-maximizing company: laws and its public image. The latter is effective if only because of the threat of additional punitive laws, reprisal from competitors and suppliers, and reduced sales to customers.

Another important factor that makes large, successful profit-maximizing companies act as reasonably decent and likable members of society is their absolute need to hire and retain a group of superior managers. The most important asset a successful company has is its present and potential superior managers. A company whose managers are better decision-makers by an average of even only 1 percent has an enormous advantage over its competitors. These managers demonstrate a tiny but definite, consistent superiority of judgment and performance. Vice-versa, a managerial group 1 percent poorer than competition means sure disaster in the long run unless the situation is corrected. A large, successful company in a competitive industry knows that achieving profit maximization means first of all finding, hiring, and keeping a group of managers who are, on the average, superior. The profits a company might gain by some kinds and extents of ruthlessness are far exceeded by the losses they would incur through the loss of many of their best managers.

Superior managers are by definition reasonably ethical. If they were not reasonably ethical in addition to being able in other ways, they would not be trusted by their superiors, peers, and subordinates and therefore could not manage well. Superior managers can and will quit rather than participate in some action they personally cannot tolerate.

Not too much should be made of this influence superior managers exert on the actions of their companies. Most ethical people with broad management experience come to have a fairly high tolerance level. Nevertheless, the possibility of losing an excessive number of superior managers does act as a real limiting influence on how ruthless a company might be.

Because superior managers are human beings, they have human weaknesses. To a certain extent they deceive themselves and rationalize their actions. While these weaknesses often harm the people or the companies they work for, sometimes the weaknesses lead to actions that social activists applaud. Many fine and able managers personally yearn to see additional profits for their company. Such managers want to think that in all their actions on behalf of the company they are guided only by the desire to maximize profits. Occasionally, though, they are guilty of self-deception and rationalization in deciding that a company gift to their old university or hiring students for summer jobs or sponsorship of a chamber music festival will pay off for the company in the long run.

In such real-life circumstances, theory has been violated, and the actions of an impersonal immortal corporation have been determined by the personal preferences of employees. That is not as it should theoretically be, and it is not at all clear that the net results are "good," however well intentioned the actions were. However, the situation is not likely to change as long as organizations are run by human beings.

Bargaining, Pressure Groups, and the Firm

Group A wants group B to change in some way; group B must figure out how to handle group A and its demands. This type of bargaining situation involves two considerations: first, how much bargaining power one group has relative to the other group and, second, what kinds of bargaining stances will be taken. The two considerations are interrelated. If I feel I have a great deal of power while you have very little, I will probably take a bargaining stance quite different from the one I would take if I felt your bargaining power was much greater than mine.

Any source of pressure on a firm can be categorized into one of the groups noted in figure 2–1. Each group applies pressure in a different way. A customer may refuse to buy from a firm—a nonviolent, socially acceptable method of pressuring a firm. If large numbers of customers refuse to buy, a firm is likely to respond quickly. A union might strike for better pay or work conditions—a direct and active method but not an option open to customers. A government may indict a firm for an alleged crime—an action other pressure groups cannot take. By categorizing these groups, we begin to see that there are not only many sources but also many types of pressure that can be brought to bear on firms.

Ordinarily, such pressures are incompatible, in that it is impossible for the firm to meet all demands. The union wants higher wages, the stockholders want higher dividends, and customers want lower prices. There is, however, only a certain amount of money. If the workers get much more, the stockholders or the customers get less, and vice-versa. How can such contradictory pressure be evaluated and reacted to?

Bargaining Strength

A manager (or group) usually has to rely on intuition to determine his (or their) strength. Often it is very difficult for him to evaluate his position at any one time or whether the firm is gaining or losing bargaining power through time. Being wrong here can result in being outbargained. A manager may lose more than he need have if he overestimates or underestimates his strength compared to that of his opponent.

A group's bargaining strength depends in part on how many persons in the group are interested in the question and how committed they are. If a pressure group has very little bargaining strength, there may be no need for a firm to bargain with it. A few stockholders owning ten shares each may want to bargain but cannot since their power is too little. Disadvantaged agricultural workers are also likely not to have enough power to get employers to the bargaining table, let alone to make any gains. Sometimes, however, the bargaining strengths are reversed, as when a powerful union in a key spot is able to dictate terms to a smaller company.

In addition to considering the total size and importance of a bargaining group, a manager must judge as accurately as possible the distribution of feelings within the group concerning the question raised. Figure 2–2 suggests what is involved. The vertical axis measures the percentage of the group involved; the horizontal axis measures a continuum of feeling about the problem. Some people might care very little about a problem; others may be willing to die for—or against—a cause.

A manager representing a corporation faced with the demands of a certain large group might not be too concerned if he perceived that the majority of the group did not care much (the light solid line in figure 2–2). This might be a common position for small shareholders. They all say they would like bigger dividends, but very few of them do more than talk about it. If, however, the group contained a few highly committed people willing to die for the cause (the light dotted line in figure 2–2), he might consider his response very carefully. University presidents have been placed in this position by student extremists who threaten to use force to gain their objectives.

In another pressure group, such as a trade union, the majority may be reasonably committed to what they think is correct (the heavy line in figure 2–2). It might happen that a manager would have to weigh the bargaining strength of this group against that of a largely indifferent group or against that of other constituencies such as governments, the public, and creditors. Using some judgmental calculus as yet undescribed in any rulebook, the manager must decide how far the firm should go in satisfying each group,

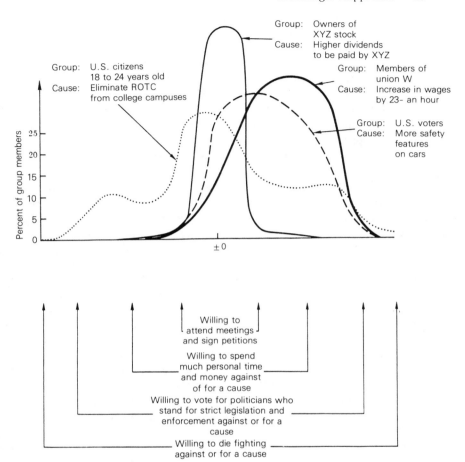

Figure 2–2. Pressure Group Opinions

while not alienating other groups. Even before he begins to bargain, he must determine the total importance of the group to the firm, calculate the weighted average opinion of the group on the subject under contention, and note any significant amount of extremely strong opinion. In order to survive, every large firm needs to satisfy at least minimally the desires of each of its constituencies. If the firm is able not only to survive but also to balance the amount of satisfaction it gives each of its constituencies with the importance of each constituency to the firm's profits, then it can achieve a major goal of corporate activity—maximization of profit.

Foreseeing Trends in Public Opinion

Those who are greatly concerned about a cause tend to be propagandists for it. They try to get others to share the intense concern they feel. If the committed persons are able to convert many others to strong commitment to their point of view, that viewpoint will be much more influential in the future. They may perform very violent or apparently irrational acts in the hope of attracting more people. (They must choose their acts very carefully since some acts will lose supporters.) With more believers, more deeply committed, the ability to apply effective pressure grows: the bargaining strength of the group increases.

One really tough task for any manager facing pressure is to forecast a group's future bargaining strength. This year it may appear that just some crackpot is making a wild and unrealistic demand; next year a million people might be demanding the same thing. One seeming crackpot can be ignored, but a million serious citizens cannot. What is the probability that next year there will in fact be a million concerned citizens? Judging such group feeling situations and trends is an art. No text or rulebook can tell managers how to handle the problem; no statistical tables can forecast the odds; no behavioral theory can give him good evidence for his forecast. Nevertheless, it must be done.

If a manager misjudges the probability, his firm may be put in a very difficult and costly position. A firm might quickly make an expensive reform and thus alienate some of the groups that it must at least minimally satisfy. If reform is overdue and the firm fails to act, however, it may be faced with punitive legislation or worse, with disastrous results for the firm's profits.

Most outsiders who have never managed or administered an organization fail to realize how difficult it is to get a large organization moving in any direction. The amount of inertia is enormous. Often, if a top manager wants a result five years from now, he has to begin today to set in motion the forces that eventually accomplish the task. Since most people do not perceive very clearly long-term risks and threats, they frequently choose to ignore them. Therefore, great amounts of managerial time and energy must go into implementing any significant change in policy.

This inertia makes it all the more necessary that a firm make reasonable forecasts about future public demands. In the 1950s, most people favored auto safety, but only a few cared very much; public opinion on this issue then could be graphed as the light solid line in figure 2–2. By the mid-1960s public concern for auto safety had changed rapidly and assumed a shape like the heavy broken line on figure 2–2: auto firms had to act. By the time the firms recognized the problem and began to consider options, it was too late to get their organizations moving in the right directions fast enough to avoid costly, punitive legislation. If they had correctly forecasted the popular appeal of auto safety features and begun to react accordingly in 1955, they might have responded to pressure much better than they did.

It would have been very difficult, however, to make this forecast. Expensive large-scale experiments in selling auto safety in the mid-1950s (mainly by Ford) did not work well. Ford emphasized the safety of its cars and lost market share to auto companies that emphasized styling and power. Executives throughout the auto industry naturally concluded that safety did not matter very much to the public. But by 1965, safety mattered a great deal, and the public's representatives voted that all U.S. auto consumers (and to a certain extent auto manufacturers) should carry extra financial costs in order to eliminate or reduce costs previously carried only by some victims in auto accidents.

We do not live in a perfect world, and there are more evils out there than anyone can handle. Some issues (e.g., in 1984 U.S. involvement in Central America) arouse general concern. Other issues perhaps even more significant in terms of human costs (e.g., the 1980–1984 famine in several African countries, which have killed millions of people) are not perceived by most people in the United States as really important problems. One could easily list several hundred real or imagined ills that should be corrected; in the next decade, possibly ten or twenty of these will become major issues. Which will these be? The firm that picks the wrong ten might be a noble organization, but it will still be raked over the coals for failing to do the "right" things. For this reason, too, the long-term forecasting of a pressure group's bargaining strength is critical to the problem of proper response by a firm to pressure for better corporate social responsibility.

Bargaining Stances

Often, who wins or loses how much, as the result of a bargain finally agreed on, depends on their initial bargaining stance. Figure 2–3 suggests a continuum of attitudes, or stances, either party might bring to the bargaining table. The continuum extends from agreement on basic issues to total disagreement. If there are several matters to be settled, each party might have a different attitude on each one. It is useful for a manager to decide before a bargaining session where his opponent's attitude on a given point is likely to fit on this continuum and what his own attitude is. It does not make much sense, for example, to consider cooperation if the other group is basically

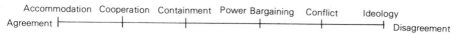

Figure 2–3. Bargaining Attitudes

at the conflict level. One's bargaining strategy may well be a function of where the potential bargaining attitudes fit on this continuum.

Accomodation. At this level a bargainer is willing to agree to the other party's goals and to work with him to get the best solution. One example might be a bargaining session between a civil rights group and a firm. The firm may accept from the start the group's goal of less discrimination in hiring. The problem is simply to work out precise details of the agreement. In this situation it is likely that a mutually acceptable change can be agreed on rather quickly.

Cooperation. Here the bargainers recognize that their major goals and interests are broadly the same, although they may differ on lesser matters such as the method of reaching a goal. The bargain again consists of working out details. A bargain between a good supplier and a firm, or between a stockholder group and managers, could be of this type. Note that there may be plenty of argument about the details, but the bargainers at least are able to agree on general principles and to accept each other's goals.

Containment. One group may try to extend its area of influence, while the other group tries to resist. These bargaining stances might be taken by a union trying to organize previously unorganized salesmen and a firm trying to resist the union's extension of its power. The firm is likely to take a traditional, formal, legalistic position in an attempt to contain the union.

Power Bargaining. The party with power tries to push the other party around. An example would be the way a firm is likely to treat a small, dissident group of stockholders. Since the stockholders have little power, their desires are pushed aside in favor of the desires of other groups. It is common in such situations for the group pushed aside to become extremely annoyed. If they are sufficiently committed, they may try to organize to get more power and come back to the bargaining table. If they do increase their strength, results of the next bargaining round may be different.

Conflict. The conflict situation is one where the bargainers cannot agree on any key points. Neither side accepts the other's major goals as valid, and each tries in every possible way for total victory. One example might be a group of dedicated conservationists trying to liquidate a stubborn strip-mining firm. If the conservationists win, the firm goes bankrupt. If the firm wins, the landscape is despoiled. Such a fight can be long and difficult, since neither party is willing to compromise.

Ideology. Parties take purely ideological positions and fight for them. This type of fight is likely to be the bloodiest of all because great moral principles are involved and individuals may be willing to die for them. Unfortunately, in ideological bargaining the participants cannot agree on a solution. Each side's moral values demand something the other side's moral values do not permit. There is no way to judge moral values objectively, and so discussion is not helpful. Each side feels that God, Right, and Truth are completely on its side: the other side is Evil. Examples of ideological conflicts are fortunately relatively rare in the United States, although the position of some radical groups who are prepared to assassinate their opponents, kidnap them, and blow up or burn down buildings is probably ideological.

A Suggested Approach to the Incidents

The incidents in chapters 5 through 13 are grouped according to the categories of pressure groups noted in figure 2–1. You will have to deal with the variety of pressures that these groups can apply. As you work through the incidents, you will see that there are some common themes running through them. Something is being done wrong by a firm or is not being done at all. A firm is being pressured to redefine its role and must weigh the costs of such redefinition. Groups or individuals and managers carry on some degree of implicit or explicit bargaining. In determining what Servex and its subsidiaries should do to be socially responsible, you will be discussing how priorities could be better assigned, evaluating the relative strengths of the various bargainers, sensing what tomorrow's demands will be, suggesting steps to meet them, and deciding who shall bear what costs. In the end, almost all social responsibility questions involve costs that someone must bear.

Here is one way to work out answers for each incident:

1. Identify the total costs and total benefits to the firm and to each of its constituencies.
2. Decide on your goals and on how you would like to reallocate costs. Remember that these costs include human as well as money costs and that it is possible to shift some of them to a future generation.
3. Evaluate and forecast the bargaining strength of each of the parties involved in an incident, and classify the bargaining stance each is likely to take on a particular issue.
4. Decide what would be the probable outcome in real life: who will probably bear what costs in the immediate future.
5. Decide what changes in the circumstances of the incident would make the probable outcome more (or less) desirable to you.

There are no right answers. No one has the correct answers for all of society, and few people feel that they have them even for themselves alone. Nevertheless, you must assume the role of a corporate manager: at stake is the social responsibility of the firm, not your personal ethics or individual responsibility. Be sure to keep in mind that socially responsible actions by a corporation are actions that, when judged by society in the future, are seen to have been of maximum help in providing necessary amounts of desired goods and services at minimum financial and social costs, distributed as equitably as possible.

3
The Servex Annual Report

This chapter presents in its entirety the 1983 Servex annual report. Such a report is routinely sent by a company to its stockholders, and anyone can obtain one by requesting it. The report presents financial results of the company for the preceding twelve-month period.

Since the incidents in chapters 5 through 13 are based on Servex and its subsidiaries, you should read this report carefully before working on the incidents. The financial resources of the firm are discussed in detail, and financial results for the various Servex operating divisions are given. You may discover in this information some clues to possible approaches to problems that come up in the incidents.

When reading the report, remember that the corporate officers are interested in looking as good as possible, consistent with legal requirements for truthfulness. Remember also that in its annual report a company is likely to suggest, through either specific mention or significant omission, what its officers consider to be important.

Servex
Consolidated Industries

Incorporated in Delaware in 1947

Annual Report
1983

Board of Directors
Chairman
   William T. Wilson
   Michael Allmer
   J. Baxter Bagby
   Peter W. Hayes
   John H. Johnson
   Oris Moot
   James Ott
   J. Samson Sagmire
   Wallace Taft
   Peter Wellman, II

Corporate Officers
President and Chief Executive Officer
   J. Baxter Bagby

Vice Presidents
   Alexander P. Botts
   John Gatsby
   Peter C. McMann
   John H. Smith
   Richard W. Warren
   Wilson W. Warren
   William W. Westwood

Controller
   Peter W. Abelgard

Treasurer
   Loran M. Roberts

Secretary
   George M. Cantrell

General Offices
   27421 Fifth Avenue
   New York, New York

Independent Accountants
   Pickwick, Pickwick, and Radebaugh
   1117 First Street
   New York, New York

General Counsel
   Watts, Watts, Watts, and Smith
   25 A Street, New York, New York

Stock Transfer Agent
   Wallward Trust Company
   8 B Street
   New York, New York

Registrar
   Eastland Bank
   1897 A Street
   New York, New York

38

Contents

Highlights

	1983	1982
Net sales (thousands)	$735,376	$592,894
Earnings before extraordinary items (thousands)	$ 28,782	$ 12,461
Per share	$ 2.87	$ 1.24
Net earnings (thousands)	$ 27,319	$ 12,461
Per share	$ 2.72	$ 1.24
Earnings per common share assuming full dilution		
Before extraordinary items	$ 2.61	$ 1.13
Net earnings	$ 2.48	$ 1.13
Dividends per share of common stock	$ .60	$ .40
Stockholders' equity (thousands)	$228,168	$207,560
Number of employees	30,800	21,900
Number of stockholders of record		
Preferred	8,200	7,300
Common	32,400	29,600

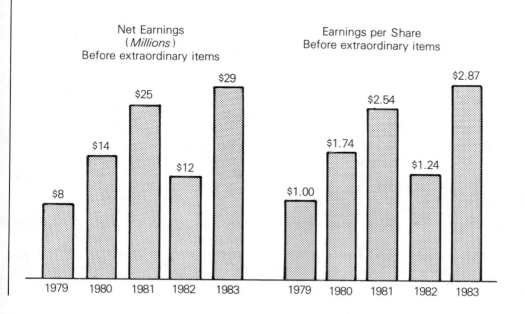

Net Earnings
(*Millions*)
Before extraordinary items

Earnings per Share
Before extraordinary items

Message to the Stockholders:

In 1983 Servex's worldwide sales and earnings were the highest in its history. Despite the severely depressed year of 1982, sales reached $735,376,000—a 24 percent increase—and earnings rose to $28,782,000—an increase of 119 percent.

We believe these results prove that Servex is basically strong and has achieved a healthy diversification. The improvement in sales and earnings came partly from continued growth in existing business, based on the gradual improvement in the economy at large. Since we are in eight basic markets—plastics and petrochemicals, retailing, transportation, machine tools, basic metals production, services, building materials, and household furnishings—your management has been able to take advantage of broad gains on many fronts. The gains stemmed also from the acquisition of Letson & Baker Chemical Company, which was fully integrated into our Plastics and Petrochemicals Group early in 1983. This acquisition added almost $100 million in sales and $16 million in profits to our operations.

Plans for Future Growth

Your corporation now ranks among the top 200 in the United States. Long-term plans for expansion in present markets and acquisitions should put us among the top 100 within a few years. While our sales are fast approaching the billion dollar mark, the potential in our eight basic markets is sufficiently large to make your management highly optimistic about future growth in our current products. Your corporation should continue to grow, particularly if the general economic advance is sustained.

By keeping management decentralized and yet tightly controlled in regard to both finances and planning, we have achieved maximum flexibility consistent with best profit results. Groups presidents are given maximum central headquarter staff support and expertise, but each of them is free to manage his group with imagination, flexibility, and aggressive action to capture markets.

Because of our decentralized structure, we can move quickly to take advantage of opportunities. Our group management teams are highly motivated by the freedom and responsibility they have, and they are amply rewarded for success through bonus and managerial stock option plans. Our group presidents have been responsible for many of our most profitable acquisitions. We expect this trend to continue.

Servex Consolidated Objectives

Our corporate objectives will be the same as they have been: (1) to achieve superior gains in earnings per share, (2) to earn a superior return on stockholders' investments, and (3) to behave responsibly as a corporate citizen. We are proud to have substantially achieved all of these objectives in recent years. We expect that we shall continue to achieve them.

We believe that, in regard to earnings per share, gains of 15 percent a year over the next five years are well within our reach. Over half of our sales are now in consumer-related activities. In accord with many economic forecasts, we expect that these areas will offer superior opportunities for growth in the next decade.

We have also expanded our international activities significantly in the past few years. Acquisition of Letson & Baker, whose sales abroad have made up as much as 40 percent of their total sales, is one example of this trend. We now have twelve plants overseas (including four Letson & Baker plants), most of which are relatively small operations located in western European countries. No one country has more than two plants (there are two each in West Germany and the

United Kingdom). Sales abroad totaled $116 million in 1983, compared to $71 million in 1982. We feel that the international potential for your corporation is excellent, and we plan to take full advantage of this potential in the coming years.

Outlook for 1984

As the economic advance continues and possibly even gathers momentum, we anticipate another good year for your company. We are relying on the presidents of our divisions in the United States to achieve still greater market shares and sales increases than in the recent past. We also expect strong expansion in our major markets in the developed economies abroad.

Cost inflation and high interest rates pose major problems, and great care will be necessary to avoid any upset of our plans and their implementation. Best economic forecasts still suggest relatively high interest rates and inflation levels for 1984, along with continued high unemployment, particularly among younger people. If these basic economic problems can be resolved or minimized, we can look forward to still greater gains in 1984, and beyond.

We feel that your corporation will continue to expand and grow and that Servex can look forward confidently to still further gains in profits and sales in 1984.

William T. Wilson
Chairman of the Board

J. Baxter Bagby
*President and Chief
Executive Officer*

The Year in Review

Sales. Sales for your company in 1983 reached an all-time high of over $735 million. This total represents an increase of 24 percent over 1982. We experienced sales growth in all our major markets except Machine Tools, where a weakness in capital investments in plant and equipment continued to create some difficulties. The largest gain in sales came in our Plastics and Petrochemicals Group as a result of the acquisition of Letson & Baker.

Profits. Operating profits showed sharp gains in all groups except Machine Tools, where a small loss was recorded. Forecasts for 1984 suggest that difficulties in the machine tool market are now largely overcome and that a sound and profitable operation in this group is foreseeable in coming years. Total profits of almost $29 million (before extraordinary items) were 119 percent above the $12 million profit in 1982. We are now back on our planned profit growth curve after experiencing considerable difficulties in the recession year of 1982, and we expect this trend to continue.

As a result of past projects and investments, very substantial profit gains were made in retailing, transportation equipment, basic metals production, and services. Given expected economic conditions and our continuous development of new markets in these areas, your management expects these trends to continue. We expect margins to improve in household furnishings and building materials as conditions in these markets improve.

Net Earnings. Net earnings were $27,319,000, or $2.72 per common share ($2.48, assuming full dilution).

Financial Position. Our major acquisition in 1983 was made without issuing additional shares. The purchase of Letson & Baker was financed mostly through retained earnings but also through long-term loans. We expect that our working capital position will improve rapidly during the coming year. The increasing average age of our receivables has caused some concern in the past year, and steps are being taken to correct this problem. The widely publicized shortages of money and tight secondary markets have made it difficult for some of our customers to pay as promptly as we would like.

Total assets reached an all-time high of $543,787,000. Stockholders' equity also reached an all time high of $228,168,000. Long-term debt totaled $152,463,000, approximately 40 percent of total capitalization.

In 1983 Servex spent a total of $47,451,000 on new plant and equipment, in addition to the Letson & Baker plant and equipment acquired. It is anticipated that approximately the same amount will be spent in 1984.

We believe that Servex's strong financial position will be important in helping achieve the steady long-term growth planned for your company.

Eight Markets

Group	Sales (millions of dollars)				Profits (Before Income Taxes and Extraordinary Items) (millions of dollars)			
	1983		1982		1983		1982	
	$	% of Total	$	% of Total	$	% of Total	$	% of Total
Plastics and petrochemicals	121.3	16.5	17.8	3.0	15.0	27.6	1.8	7.7
Retailing	310.4	42.2	300.0	50.6	5.6	10.3	2.1	9.1
Transportation	85.3	11.6	66.9	11.3	15.1	27.7	6.5	28.1
Machine tools	71.3	9.7	87.7	14.8	(1.2)		5.8	25.0
Basic metals production	56.6	7.7	48.0	8.1	5.6	10.3	5.4	23.4
Services	22.8	3.1	12.5	2.1	7.5	13.8		
Building materials	41.2	5.6	33.8	5.7	3.8	6.9	.8	3.5
Household furnishings	26.5	3.6	26.1	4.4	3.4	3.4	.7	3.2
Total	735.4	100.0	529.9	100.0	53.3	100.0	23.1	100.0

Plastics and Petrochemicals Group

Year	Sales (millions)	Net Profits (millions)
1983	$121.3	$15.0
1982	17.8	1.8
1981	21.4	2.1
1980	19.3	2.3
1979	12.2	0.7

The acquisition of the Letson & Baker Chemical Company early in the year pushed sales sharply upward in this group. Your company expects that in the future years this group will be one of the fastest growing in Servex.

Major products in the group include plastic extrusions, urea fertilizers, specialty high temperature paints, and high quality polyethylene plastics for extremely high and low temperature uses. The Letson & Baker acquisition has enabled Servex to enter urea fertilizer markets in a major way, and projections for growth in this area, particularly in foreign markets, are excellent.

Results in the group were extremely good in 1983, as paint and polyethylene also showed good sales gains. Major customers in these areas include truck and heavy equipment manufacturers, local and state governments, the federal government, and many foreign governments. Federal government sales, which were once dominant in this market, have been declining in recent years even though defense expenditures for new military systems have increased. However, excellent sales gains have been made in northern countries for military aircraft application, along with extended usage in northern states where equipment is exposed to severe winter weather. High temperature paints have found rapidly increasing applications in jet aircraft, both civilian and military, and Servex's patent-protected products—particularly in the HiFahr line—have no equal in many markets. This division also benefited from increased sales of turbo engines and other jet equipment during the year.

The Outlook. Prospects for sales in the group appear excellent. The "green revolution" in poorer countries suggests rising demand for fertilizers; developed countries are also rapidly increasing their use of fertilizers. The recent overcapacity that upset worldwide prices is disappearing because of this increasing demand. We are developing several revolutionary new products in associated market areas and plan to introduce them during the next few years. Foreign markets in particular appear very promising, and Servex expects to expand production overseas rapidly to serve these markets. A new paint plant is under construction in Belgium, with another planned for construction in Hong Kong during early 1984. This will mark the first expansion of your company into promising Asian markets.

Progress in plastics extrusion markets has been hampered by industry-wide excess capacity and excessive price cutting. We expect that these difficulties will be largely overcome in 1984 and this product line will move up to profitable status shortly.

Plastic Extrusions
    Almont & Sons
        John Maxwell, President

Fertilizers
    Letson & Baker, Inc.
        W. John Letson, II, President

Paints
    Sinbad Paint Company
        Perry M. Baxter, President
    SPECwerke, Hamburg, West Germany
        Dr. Otto Holshen, General Manager

Low Temperature Plastics
    EPIC Corporation
        Jackson Carr, President

Retailing Group

Year	Sales *(millions)*	Net Profits *(millions)*
1983	$310.4	$5.6
1982	300.1	2.1
1981	305.6	2.8
1980	281.7	1.3
1979	162.5	1.1

Your company's retailing operations had an outstanding year, almost tripling profits, because of careful cost controls. Sales, following national trends, rose only 3.4 percent, but in spite of relative sales stagnation, Servex's Retailing Group was able to improve profit performance by systematic planned improvement in all phases of distribution, purchasing, and systems analysis.

The largest operation in the group is the Lucky Jim discount chain which operates forty-seven major stores in Illinois, Indiana, Ohio, Michigan, and Wisconsin. A significant development in Servex retailing operations is the establishment in 1983 of three new discount stores in northern Mexico, operating under the Suerte Y Suerte name. Along with planned expansion of the XEX chain in Great Britain, the new Mexican development foreshadows still further foreign expansion planned for this group.

The Outlook. Consumer spending in the United States continues to rise sluggishly, but more rapid improvement is expected in 1984. Intense price cutting and competition have kept margins lower than usual during the past decade, but there are signs that this destructive practice is decreasing somewhat as the economy returns to normal. The Retailing Group plans construction of four more Lucky Jim discount stores in key Midwestern cities during 1984, along with four foreign stores (two each in Mexico and Great Britain). All the new stores will be 40,000 to 50,000 square feet in size, which has proved to be the most profitable size for Lucky Jim stores in the United States. Your management now has the most advanced physical distribution and inventory controls in the entire retailing industry, and further cost reduction programs are planned to improve margins.

While the Servex Retailing Groups is very interested in further expansion in the retail area in the United States and is studying the most attractive possibilities, prospects at present suggest caution. Consumer spending in the United States has not risen in the past two years as quickly or as much as initially forecast, and the current extreme competition and price cutting make retailing a difficult field for rapid expansion.

Foreign prospects continue to appear very good, and your company is planning expansion in several new markets in affluent countries. The discounting revolution is not as far along abroad as in the United States, and where legal and economic conditions are good, expansion prospects appear excellent.

Discount Operations
   Lucky Jim Discount Stores, Inc.
      Alexander P. Spencegood,
      President
   Suerte y Suerte de Mexico, S.A.
      Sr. Julio Gomez y Silva, President
   XEX, Ltd., London
      John P. Fitzhugh, O.B.E.
      Managing Director

Transportation Equipment Group

Year	Sales (millions)	Net Profits (millions)
1983	$85.3	$15.1
1982	66.9	6.5
1981	72.3	8.2
1980	70.1	4.5
1979	63.5	2.1

Accounting for 28 percent of Servex's total net profits for the year, the Transportation Equipment Group had another record-breaking year. Both sales and profits reached new highs. Servex is heavily involved in transportation equipment through three major companies. Allied Gear Cutting is a major supplier of gears for transmissions and differentials for many heavy-duty truck and tractor applications. It also manufactures axles and drive shafts for heavy equipment, along with springs and related steel parts. Astro Aeronautics is a major subcontractor for landing gear, tail surfaces, and other aircraft components for several major jet transports and military aircraft. Vepcoland Mobile manufactures large trailers for heavy truck hauling.

All companies in the Transportation Equipment Group performed exceptionally well in 1983, in spite of the general recession in the aerospace industry. Much of the progress can be attributed to new products and processes developed over the last few years by the group's research and development division. Contracts already signed enable the group to look forward to another record-breaking year in 1984.

The Outlook. Economic forecasts suggest that capital expenditures in transportation markets will reach a new high in 1984 and continue upwards thereafter. Based on patent-protected new products and tight cost controls, the operating divisions in the group look forward to further good results.

Foreign markets, particularly for Allied Gear Cutting and Vepcoland, appear to be growing at a rapid rate. During 1983, the new Allied plant in Manchester, England, was established to serve the British market; Allied also operates a plant in Baarn, the Netherlands. Vepcoland opened its first overseas manufacturing plant in Milan, Italy, late in 1983. It is anticipated that this plant will contribute substantially to net profits in 1984.

Road Transportation Equipment
Vepcoland Mobile, Inc.
Marvin J. Thomas, President

Aircraft Components
Astro Aeronautics
John H. Hambling, President

Automotive and Truck Components
Allied Gear Cutting, Inc.
Bart W. Adams, President

Machine Tools Group

Year	Sales (millions)	Net Profits (millions)
1983	$71.3	$(1.2)
1982	87.7	5.8
1981	81.5	3.5
1980	77.2	3.1
1979	83.7	3.9

Our machine tool operation, Westport Brass and Milling, had a difficult year in 1983. The very sluggish recovery in capital expenditures has had a major effect on all machine tool manufacturers. Current market recovery in this sector suggests that by the end of 1984, the demand problem will largely be resolved. Westport Brass and Milling is a leader in an important and growing segment of the machine tool field, and your management anticipates a return to growth and profits for Westport in the near future.

Start-up costs for a new line of advanced numeric-controlled large milling machines and shapers contributed to the small loss incurred in this division in 1983. These costs are nonrecurring, and management anticipates that sales and earnings of these extremely advanced and large machine tools will contribute significantly to the improved results expected in 1984.

The Outlook. Westport plans to introduce several revolutionary new machine tools of the most advanced design during 1984. These tools, which utilize the latest cybernetic principles and interlock with conventional computer systems, should prove to be a major part of Westport's business in coming years.

Most economic forecasts suggest that capital equipment spending will continue to advance rapidly through 1985. Your company is confident that its advanced technology will permit it to take full advantage of this growing market. Foreign sales have also increased significantly, particularly for the more advanced machines, which are not produced anywhere else in the world. Because of the advanced-technology design concepts involved in these models, they are produced in the United States and exported. Market forecasts suggest that European and Japanese markets for these advanced-technology tools will expand very rapidly. Several potential contracts now in negotiation with European buyers could more than double sales in 1985.

Machine Tools
Westport Brass and Milling, Inc.
Jason X. Lopata, President

48

Basic Metals Production Group

Year	Sales (millions)	Net Profits (millions)
1983	$56.6	$5.6
1982	48.0	5.4
1981	53.2	3.7
1980	51.7	3.5
1979	40.0	1.1

This group consists of two companies: the Petersford Mining Company and the Luckless Lake Uranium Mining Company of Canada, Ltd. Both companies posted record sales in 1983; but inflated costs, particularly wages, limited growth in profits. Copper production, which accounts for over 90 percent of the group's sales, reached new highs in spite of the stike that sharply affected the third quarter of 1983. Uranium sales held steady, since most output is sold under long-term contract to the Atomic Energy Commission.

Arizona has enacted further strict antipollution laws that require copper smelters, by the end of 1985, to eliminate their plant emissions all but 10 percent of the sulphur contained in the materials they treat. We anticipate that compliance with this law will require a capital investment by Petersford of about $18 million in 1984 and 1985.

The Outlook. In spite of a world surplus of copper, your company faces the future with confidence. In recent years, world production of copper has expanded faster than has the demand for it, resulting in considerable price weakness. All of our copper production is domestic, however; and events in Chile and other copper-producing foreign nations suggest the wisdom of this limited location. Supplies from several countries will probably be seriously interrupted during the next few years. Although these interruptions will not affect your company's production in any way, they may have major effects on our sales. We now have the production capacity to expand output sufficiently to meet any rapid expansion of demand. Our Arizona mine is one of the most modern, advanced facilities in the world. Furthermore, our production costs are below any anticipated low price that may be caused by overproduction.

Long-term consumption trends suggest that this group of your company will continue to do well. At present production rates, copper ore reserves will last for about forty-five years, and we have recently acquired rights to still more copper reserves in the United States. Proven uranium reserves of twenty-two years' supply, plus exploration rights to 245,000 acres in the Luckless Lake area, enable us to face the future with confidence in this sector of our business.

Basic Metals Production
Luckless Lake Uranium Mining Company of Canada, Ltd.
Mr. Basil B. M. Williams, President
Petersford Mining Company
Geoffrey G. Lorbell, President

Services Group

Year	Sales (millions)	Net Profits (millions)
1983	$22.8	$7.5
1982	12.5	0.02
1981	14.3	1.6
1980	10.1	0.4
1979	1.2	0.1

Your company's Services Group achieved all-time highs in both revenues and profits in 1983. All companies in this group shared in these increases. Merriweather Transport is in an excellent position, thanks to its efficient fleet of tankers. The Northeastern Insurance and Auto Claimants Group performed extremely well, in part because of unexpectedly low accident claims. The Oregon Finance Company prospered as consumer lending again began to advance and the cost of money eased somewhat from 1982 levels. Cybernetics School Systems obtained several key contracts for educational experiments in inner-city schools. A.P. Beams, Consultants, expanded by over 300 percent, largely in Western Europe. Our newly formed Computer Science Educational Services and Leasing Group performed far above expectations.

The Outlook. Your company intends to continue its rapid expansion in the service area. All economic forecasts suggest great growth possibilities, particularly in education and consulting; Servex intends to take full advantage of opportunities here. Merriweather Transport's program of modernization of the present tanker fleet will require substantial capital and the program will demand careful capital planning. It is also possible that new vessels in the program may be required to have extensive antipollution dumping gear, which would increase costs very substantially.

All indications are that the Services Group faces a profitable and expansive decade. Your management is confident that the operating companies can take full advantage of their opportunities.

Transportation
    Merriweather Transport
        Melvin M.P.C. Merriweather, IV, President

Insurance
    Northeastern Insurance and Auto Claimants Group
        Richard S. Richards, President

Education
    Cybernetics School Systems
        Dr. Peter P. Bedford, President

Finance
    Oregon Finance Company
        William W. Williams, President

Consulting
    A.P. Beams Consultants
        Daniel F. Faber, President
    Computer Science Educational Services and Leasing Group
        John Z. Smith, President

Building Materials Group

Year	Sales (millions)	Net Profits (millions)
1983	$41.2	$3.8
1982	33.8	0.8
1981	38.2	2.9
1980	32.1	1.8
1979	—	—

Servex's Building Materials Group reached a new high in sales in 1983. Profits were also the highest in history and would have been still better had it not been for severe inflation in wages and materials costs. The renewed expansion of home construction led several of our companies to new sales highs. Improvements in lumber prices also helped raise sales.

Masonry block operations were down because of intense competition and an unfavorable pricing structure. The steel fabricating group, however, showed all-time highs in both sales and profits, and government and commercial construction contracts increased.

The Outlook. Continued expansion of residential housing, commercial, and government construction should provide a solid base for expansion in the next few years. Single-family housing projects are particularly favorable because of the great increase in families with children as the "baby boom" children born in the 1950s reach their thirties. Economic forecasts suggest major increases in demand for new construction and Servex is well placed to take full advantage of them. We expect to reach new highs in sales and profits within the next few years.

Lumber
　　Wallace Lumber Company
　　　Alex M. Perlman, President

Steel Fabricating
　　West Coast Steel Company, Inc.
　　　Manfield B. Foster, President
　　Southwestern Construction Company
　　　Donald M. Martin, President

Building Materials
　　Union Concrete Fabricators, Inc.
　　　Jacob Epstein, President
　　Alpine Fiberboard
　　　Jack P. Jackson, President

Household Furnishings Group

Year	Sales (millions)	Net Profits (millions)
1983	$26.5	$1.9
1982	26.1	0.7
1981	4.3	0.6
1980	4.1	0.5
1979	1.0	0.2

Sales and profits increases were achieved in 1983 by this group in spite of continued sluggishness in the home market in the United States. Consumers still proved somewhat resistant to expanding their consumption, and this wariness limited sales and profit results to a considerable extent. Profits in our infant furniture group turned up slightly, as the total number of U.S. births increased (although birth rates per 1000 continued their downward trend).

The institutional market for furniture recovered somewhat from disappointing lows recorded in 1982. Wadman & Wadman and Union Pressed Metal manufacture a wide range of furniture for schools, hospitals, and offices, and increased spending in this sector led to considerable gains.

The Outlook. Further consolidation of the many small companies in the furniture manufacturing business appears inevitable, and Servex plans to be in a strong position to capture a leading market position in this rapidly evolving industry. Short-run forecasts of institutional spending for furniture are not particularly encouraging, but we expect to increase our sales significantly in both the institutional and home markets in the coming decade. Diversified product lines, which include a wide variety of institutional furniture, and volume sufficiently large to permit highly efficient production should enable your company to meet all foreseeable competition.

Home Furnishings
  Apex Home Company
    Watson P. Johns, President
  Lask Furniture Company
    P. George Gempler, President
  Maxim & Maxim, Inc.
    John H. Jackson, President
  Waywide, Inc.
    Peter P. McCarthy, President

Office and Industrial Furniture
  Wadman & Wadman
    Nicolas N. Adams, President
  Michel and Carson, Inc.
    Lars L. Larson, President
  Union Pressed Metal, Inc.
    Adam M. Zerring, President

Opinion of Independent Accountants

To the Stockholders and Directors of Servex Consolidated Industries:

In our opinion, the accompanying consolidated balance sheet, consolidated income statement, and consolidated statement of source and applications of funds present fairly the financial position of Servex Consolidated Industries for the year ended December 31, 1983. Our examination of these statements was made in accordance with generally accepted accounting standards, and accordingly included such tests of the accounting records as we considered necessary in such circumstances.

Pickwick, Pickwick, and Radebaugh

New York, New York
February 18, 1984

Notice to Stockholders

The annual meeting of stockholders will be held at 11:00 A.M., May 4, 1984, at Wilmington, Delaware. A notice of the meeting, proxy statement and proxy voting card will be sent closer to the time of the meeting.

Five-Year Summary

	1983	1982	1981	1980	1979
Net sales (thousands)	$735.376	$592.894	$590.8	$546.3	$364.1
Net profits (thousands)	$ 28.782	$ 12.461	$ 25.4	$ 13.9	$ 7.8
Earnings per share	$ 2.87*	$ 1.24	$ 2.54	$ 1.74*	$ 1.00
Year-end position (as reported)					
Working capital (millions)	$154.1	$133.0	$139.4	$119.5	$ 86.6
Plant, property, and equipment (millions)	$226.1	$168.9	$159.5	$151.7	$110.8
Total assets (millions)	$540.2	$441.7	$461.7	$448.5	$311.7
Long-term debt (millions)	$152.5	$101.3	$ 98.2	$100.7	$ 22.3
Stockholders' equity (millions)	$228.2	$207.6	$198.4	$130.4	$101.9
Number of common shares outstanding (millions)	10,041	10,028	9,983	8,010	7,754
Stockholders' equity per outstanding common share	$ 22.72	$ 20.69	$ 19.87	$ 16.28	$ 13.14

*Before extraordinary items.

Consolidated Balance Sheet

December 31, 1983 and 1982

Assets	1983 (thousands)	1982 (thousands)
Current assets		
Cash	$ 9,483	$ 11,285
Marketable securities, at cost		
(Market values: 1983, $1,294,000; 1982, $32,804,000)	1,216	31,022
Accounts receivable, less allowances		
(1983, $5,206,000; 1982, $1,099,000)	128,030	84,668
Inventories, at lower of cost or market	$153,254	124,779
Prepaid expenses and other current assets	6,787	6,204
Total current assets	$298,770	$257,958
Property, plant and equipment		
Land and improvements, at cost	25,478	8,841
Buildings and equipment, at cost	94,730	48,389
Machinery and equipment, at cost	234,121	209,402
	354,329	266,632
Less accumulated depreciation	128,193	97,744
Net total property, plant, and equipment	226,136	168,888
Other assets		
Prepayments and deferred charges	2,853	2,421
Intangibles (goodwill, patents, trademarks)	12,419	12,394
Total other assets	15,272	14,815
Total assets	$540,178	$441,661

Liabilities and Stockholders Equity	1983 (thousands)	1982 (thousands)
Current Liabilities		
Accounts payable	$ 78,820	$ 43,126
Notes payable	26,137	33,965
Long-term debt payable within one year	11,478	12,234
Accrued expenses payable	21,904	24,825
Federal and foreign income taxes payable	6,375	8,588
Vessel construcion fund to be deposited	—	2,191
Total current liabilities	$144,714	$124,929
Long-term liabilities		
Long-term debt	167,296	109,172
Total liabilities	312,010	234,101
Stockholders' equity		
Preferred stock, $1.40 cumulative, $5 par value each; authorized 1,000,000 shares, issued and outstanding 986,400 shares	4,932	4,932
Common stock, $1 par value each; authorized 15,000,000 shares; issued and outstanding 10,041,257 and 10,028,112 shares	10,041	10,028
Capital surplus	144,652	144,361
Accumulated retained earnings	73,464	53,547
	233,089	212,868
Less cost of common stock in treasury	4,921	5,308
Total stockholders' equity	228,168	207,560
Total liabilities	$540,178	$441,661

Consolidated Statement of Income and Retained Earnings

Years ended December 31, 1983 and 1982

	1983 (thousands)	1982 (thousands)
Revenues		
Net sales	$735,376	$592,894
Other income (including gains on sales of assets; 1983, $4,804,000; 1982, $643,000)	6,282	2,231
Total revenues	741,658	595,125
Expenses		
Cost of goods and services sold	536,795	456,545
Selling and administrative expenses	112,393	89,722
Depreciation	26,037	16,535
Interest expense	13,146	9,225
Total expenses	688,371	572,027
Profits		
Profit before income taxes and extraordinary item	53,287	23,098
Provision for federal and foreign income taxes	24,505	10,637
Profit before extraordinary item	28,782	12,461
Extraordinary item (provision for foreign exchange fluctuation, net of income tax effect of $448,000)	1,463	—
Net profit	27,319	12,461
Retained earnings		
At beginning of year	53,547	46,476
Dividends paid		
Preferred	(1,381)	(1,381)
Common (1983, $.60 per share; 1982, $.40 per share)	(6,021)	(4,009)
At end of year	$ 73,464	$ 53,547
Earnings per share		
Net earnings per share, before extraordinary item	2.87	$1.24
Net earnings per share, after extraordinary item	$2.72	$1.24
Net earnings per share, assuming full dilution	$2.48	$1.13

Consolidated Statement of Source and Application of Funds

	1983 (thousands)	1982 (thousands)
Source of funds		
Net profit	$ 27,319	$ 12,461
Depreciation	26,037	16,535
	53,356	28,996
Additional long-term debt, including refunding	70,374	12,054
Exercise of stock options	335	—
	124,065	41,050
Application of funds		
Net noncurrent assets of business (Letson & Baker) purchased	66,283	—
Additions to property, plant and equipment (net)	9,717	25,211
Dividends paid	7,402	5,390
Debt retirement, including amounts refunded	12,250	16,352
Vessel construction funds	2,191	—
Increase in other assets (net)	1,586	7,284
	99,429	54,237
Working capital		
Beginning of year	133,029	146,216
End of year	154,056	133,029
Increase (decrease) in working capital	21,027	(13,187)

4
Articles on Servex

The following three articles are fictitious, but they are similar to many articles that appear in business publications. They all concern Servex problems along with discussions of some of the officers of the company. As with the annual report, such reporting suggests what people consider to be important about a company. There are many clues as to what might be done in given incidents, along with useful background material about the company, its attitudes, and its managers. You should read the articles carefully before tackling the incidents.

CONGLOMERATES

Is SERVEX for real?

Can Servex maintain its 1983 earnings? Can it get back on its pre-1982 growth track and stay there? These are the key questions we recently asked the dynamic Mr. J. Baxter Bagby, Servex's Chief Executive Officer. He says yes, but financial analysts are less certain.

In 1981–82 Servex took a financial bath, as did most other conglomerates. The company had a common problem: after rapid expansion in the mid-1970s management seemed to lose control. In addition, there were sharp declines in demand for machine tools, petrochemicals, and other major items. Earnings per share slid 56 percent from the 1981 peak of $2.54 to $1.11 in 1982. In 1981, Servex common peaked at around

$57 per share; by mid-1982 it was selling in the $11 to $14 range. Many supposedly smart investors were badly burned.

According to Mr. Bagby, the collapse in the price of Servex's common was unjustified. "We still have the basic earning power," he told our reporter, "and profit results for 1983 demonstrate it." Servex is now selling in the $27 to $32 range, largely because of the rapid comeback in 1983 earnings to $2.61 per share.

A familiar story. Mr. Bagby feels that Servex is clearly back on its historic earnings curve and that 1982 was just one peculiarly bad year out of many good ones. "Everything that could go wrong," he claims, "went wrong in a single twelve-month period." The 52-year-old executive is emphatic as he points to Servex's strengths for the 1980s: "We're heavy now in advanced petrochemicals, which should show major earning gains for the next five years, as the economy develops strengths. We are strong both in consumer retailing and producer goods, a balance that will give us a real hedge against minor economic fluctuations. Also, we have a good mix between domestic and foreign sales, both by product line and country. Our household furnishings group, along with our housing materials operations, will grow rapidly as demographic factors favor us in the 1980s. And don't rule out the possibility of expansion by acquisition either."

The Realities. Still, analysts wonder whether Servex really can fulfill all these expectations. New family formations are lagging, and the birth rate is still dropping. Housing starts set a record in 1983, but no one can say with confidence that this market will continue to boom. Metals markets do not look to many experts as buoyant as Mr. Bagby's statements would suggest, nor does the outlook for foreign operations seem as favorable as it was five years ago. The West European slowdowns can only hurt the companies heavily involved there, as Servex is, and no one can say how long these slowdowns—especially Italy's—will last. Servex's machine tool division still is wallowing in the doldrums, like others in this dismal field. Maybe things will change for the better—and maybe not.

Analysts predict that Servex's 1984 earnings will be around $2.75 per share, and so to date Mr. Bagby is on target. The growth is still there, but not as rapid as in the 1970s. The big price/earnings multiples of 1979–1981 seem to be gone for good.

Potential liabilities. Still another factor to be considered is that Servex may incur major costs because of consumer pressures and anti-pollution drives. Its consumer divisions are under the same heavy pressure as are other retailers to give consumers a better deal in many ways that will reduce profitability. Several of Servex's mining and refining operations may face major cleanup costs. Local pressure in some communities has already forced the company to take expensive measures to reduce smoke emissions, and more such pressure may be on the way.

Pulling through. Servex survived the conglomerate shakeout in much better shape than most of its rivals. The company had a bad 1982, but prospects for the rest of the decade are good. The 1983 results prove that in recessions Servex can move quickly to locate and correct weak spots. In the late 1970s, the record would have been good enough to warrant a twenty or even thirty times price/earnings ratio. Nowadays, the market views such a conglomerate quite differently. But if J. Baxter Bagby proves to be right, Servex could be a real winner in the market.

SERVEX CONSOLIDATED INDUSTRIES

NYSE—Ticker symbol—SEC
Current common range: $27–$32
1983 earnings per share: $2.61
1984 forecast earnings per share: $2.65–$2.85
P/E on 1983 earnings: 10.3–12.3
P/E on 1984 forecast: 9.5–12.1

SERVEX Is Just Beginning to Roll

Conglomerates may be out of style, but J.B. Bagby,
Servex's Southern aristocrat C.E.O., hasn't heard
about it yet. He's still wheeling and dealing in the
pre-1981 manner — with more than a little success.
So far, the stockholders love it.

by *Arthur Reed*

When Servex common bottomed at $11 per share in early 1982,
J. (for nothing) Baxter Bagby was on a beach in Jamaica, talking
deals with W. John Letson, the major stockholder in Letson &
Baker. Servex was on its usual expansion path, which is to say that
old J.B. was wheeling and dealing again. A messenger rushed up to
the two men with the latest stock quotation.

"Do you want to call it off, J.B.?" Letson asked.

"Hell, no! I've just got to figure out how to buy you without giving away the rest of my company," J.B. snorted.

J.B. did. He even managed to finance the acquisition of Letson &
Baker, which had some serious profitability and estate tax problems, with a long-term loan from Amalgamated Insurance rather
than dilute his stockholders' equity with a new issue. He got his
prize: Letson & Baker fitted neatly into his plans for expansion of
Servex's chemical division, both now and in the long run.

Recently Servex sold at over $31 per share, and those who were
wise enough to bet on Servex' ability to come back were rewarded.
Those who got in during the palmy pre-1981 days still are licking
their wounds, since Servex common then was as high as $57 per
share. But J.B. intends to get it back up there "within a few years."

"The price/earnings ratios we saw in the late 1970s will probably not come again for any kind of company, certainly not for
conglomerates," he recently stated. "But Servex will be up there
because earnings are going up and up. Watch us go!"

And go Servex did. Earnings have jumped from $1 a share in
1979 to $2.61 in 1983, with the 1984 forecast around $2.75. Old
J.B. just might get back to his $60 per share yet, the hard way. No
huge multiples, just earnings in hand. And J.B. likes it that way.

Portrait of a gentleman

J. Baxter Bagby is an unlikely candidate for a wheeling and dealing conglomerator. He was born in Savannah, Georgia, in 1910, the only son of a prominent, landed Southern family. Any reasonable forecast for his career would have included sipping mint juleps while occasionally looking over the family plantations. The South he grew up in did not seem the place to develop hard-nosed entrepreneurs of the old breed. He had all the advantages, including exclusive prep schools and a sound technical education at Western Tech (1932). When he returned to the family estates in 1935, he took over from his father, then seriously ill. The pattern was being formed in the genteel, traditional Southern way.

But the war came along, and J.B. got involved early. He joined the Air Force in 1941, spent two years as a B-17 pilot over Europe, got shot up over Hamburg and staggered on to crash land in Sweden, where he was interned for the duration. It was there he met his first wife, Helga. They were married in Sweden in 1945 and, as J.B. puts it, "Somehow, settling down to be a 1945 version of a *Gone With the Wind* plantation aristocrat didn't seem too exciting after my particular war."

Returning to the United States, J.B. was offered by his family a chance to take over Almont & Sons, a new and struggling manufacturing firm in the then new plastics extrusions field. This company had been established in Atlanta before the war by J.B.'s uncle, Peter Almont, and Almont's sons were not interested in running the business. Peter was semi-retired (he died in 1959), and someone in the family was badly needed to take over. J.B. turned over his family estate, mainly plantation, to a professional administrator and took charge of Almont. It was a significant decision. J.B. has been manufacturing ever since, though he occasionally visits his farms.

Within four years, he had tripled Almont's sales—mainly in that old standby, the garden hose. Lots of suburbs were being built, and everyone needed a hose. J.B. made sure most of that hose was made by Almont.

It was at Almont that J.B. put together his basic concepts of control—letting others do the job while he got rewarded for it. J.B. gives his wife Helga much of the credit. "She gave me a very pragmatic, Swedish view of things I never could have learned in Savannah," he commented. Helga was killed in an auto accident in 1963, an event that nearly finished J.B.'s business career. "For five years, I just didn't give a damn," he says. "I let Almont cycle, missing all kinds of opportunities, but somehow it didn't seem to matter very much. After a while, I realized you can't turn back the clock. Besides, I kept running into deals with fantastic potentials—and no one else seemed to see them. You forget now that in the 1960s, Atlanta was a pretty conservative, old-fashioned kind of town. Why, there were companies lying around where even a mediocre manager could double net in two years."

So in 1968, J.B. began to move again. Perhaps a large part of his renewed interest in business came from his second wife, Pat, whom he married in 1967. Pat was a visiting New Yorker who met J.B. at an Atlanta party in late 1966. J.B. rarely talks about his wife publicly, but close friends say that she is almost as good an entrepreneur as he is and some less friendly acquaintances feel the real brains behind the fantastic Servex success have been hers. Pat ran her own chain of successful dress shops in New York before they were married, and she undoubtedly knows her way around a balance sheet as few women—or men—do.

By 1971, J.B. had acquired three other divisions, each larger than the original Almont. He first acquired Sinbad Paints, which deals in specialty high temperature coatings, then added Vepcoland Mobile, a manufacturer of semitrailers, which was having serious management problems. Last came Lucky Jim Discount Stores. By 1975, Servex sales were over $200 million a year. The Servex name itself came in 1974.

A winning strategy

J.B. has followed a simple, yet effective basic strategy in all his acquisitions. He looks for family-owned firms, typically those with fading management, estate tax problems, and too much family influence. Before 1975, he made most of his acquisitions with convertible preferred stock, but with recent lower market prices for Servex common he has shifted to obtaining long-term loans to obtain cash for acquisitions. Several major insurance companies have gone along with him since the mid-1970s and—unusual for a conglomerate—Servex has never come close to a real financial squeeze. Cash flow has been over three times interest charges ever since Servex began its real growth.

Where possible, J.B.'s philosophy is to leave existing management in charge. He pays well, and there are stock options and bonuses for performance. But the real key to Servex's success is its control system. "Most conglomerates can go out of control very easily," J.B. says. "Top management has no idea of what to control in a business strange to them. Hell, B-schools say that a good manager can manage anything. This is hogwash. To manage a complex business successfully, you have to know an awful lot about it. Few managers could handle specialty paints, for example. You just have to know a lot about the business—what the technology is, what marketing channels there are, how customers finance inventories, and all the rest. But we can, with our techniques, take a good manager who has specialized experience, give him full authority, and yet control him. We know what his basic goals and standards should be. These basics are pretty much the same for every business and we can work them out in a hand-tailored way so that they apply to any specialized business. Then we set targets with the managers, hold fat money carrots in front of them, sit back, and watch them produce. A really good company manager can make more money than I do—*if* he produces."

One proof of the effectiveness of J.B.'s plan and major key to Servex's success is the way its highly motivated managers work. Stock options are important here, and Servex got the Big Board in 1974, when it purchased Lucky Jim Discount Stores. Since then, managers get stock options, and they can make big money. (Of Servex's top twenty managers, at least fourteen have become millionaires in the last six years.) Because Servex managers know what they are supposed to do, and because most of them can do it, the company moves along through thick and thin. Even in 1982, when many conglomerates fell apart and Servex did have a sharp earnings decline, Servex still had respectable earnings and a sizable cash flow.

Associates say that J.B seems to be around all the time and always knows exactly what is going on, even in remove divisions. J.B. does travel heavily (each of Servex's two jets logs about 325,000 miles a year, carrying J.B. and other Servex executives) around his far-flung empire. His ability to pinpoint even minute problems sometimes amazes local managers. On a recent visit to Astro Aeronautics, Servex's aircraft subsidiary, J.B. walked through the plant, stopped, and asked, "Why did you change the rivet size?" Sure enough, a contract change called for different rivets. No one in the plant even knew that J.B. had ever seen the old size, but this attention to detail is typical of the way he operates.

Collecting autos—and subsidiaries?

Actually, J.B. spends relatively little time with his company or his managers. He claims that his control system is such that he can look at monthly or weekly control reports and see what is going on within a few minutes. Maybe he is right, since he appears to spend an increasing amount of time with his outside interests. He is one of the principal patrons of Atlanta's Symphony Orchestra and owns the most important collection of French Impressionist paintings in the South. He also has one of the best-known collections of antique autos anywhere in the world and at one time was a frequent visitor to Reno, where his late friend Bill Harrah, another famous collector of vintage cars, was headquartered.

Some of J.B.'s closest associates claim seriously that the main reason Servex is moving rapidly abroad (Servex's European sales have tripled in the last four years) is to enable J.B. to nose around the European countryside looking for both forgotten art and forgotten old cars. J.B. feels that this is a bad joke and says simply, "There's money in going abroad. We go where profits are. In lots of lines, having overseas subsidiaries is the only way to fly." In any case Servex, which began foreign expansion later than most major firms, is now moving at full speed into uncharted foreign waters. J.B. is particularly enthusiastic about foreign prospects for Servex's petrochemicals and retailing activities. "We go abroad because we can do something better than the foreigners can do it," he says. "And what we can do very well is high technology production in certain specialized fields, and consumer marketing. You know, what Servex *really* sells is knowledge—specialized technology, specialized marketing know-how. The products we sell are just vehicles for collecting money payments for our knowledge."

Certainly Servex's moves into foreign operations have paid off handsomely so far, but associates still note that J.B.'s great enthusiasm for foreign operations began at the time he went to England and bought a Duke's 1909 Rolls Royce Silver Ghost. J.B. had to stay a few extra days in London to complete the transaction, and before he left he also had arranged to buy the London based XEX chain of variety stores. So far, this chain has been a gold mine for Servex, yielding, by best outside estimates, over 30 percent on equity; but J.B. merely says that the acquisition happened along at exactly the right time.

Maybe so—but a close associate also notes wryly that Servex obtained its first turnkey project behind the Iron Curtain in 1983 in Poland, when J.B. went there to chase down an original Bugatti sports roadster (circa 1928). He bought the car (for about $18,000—it's one of four known to exist), got it out of Poland legally, and apparently just in passing set up the relationships that eventually led to a $4 million turnkey project for Sinbad Paints.

As one close friend and business colleague noted, "If a country just happens to have some old classic autos around, and if it just happens to have some good business available, Servex will be there on both counts. And who's to say that there's any better way to get to golden opportunities abroad?"

J.B. freely acknowledges that he chases around the world to add to his collections, but he insists that if business gets done also, it's purely coincidental. As he says, "My division managers make all the key overseas investment decisions. All I do is point out from time to time something that might be worth looking into." Since no Servex overseas investment has yet turned sour, perhaps he's right.

Looking out for the future

J.B. realizes that some of his strategies won't necessarily work in the future. This is one major reason why he is turning overseas. As a minor conglomerate, Servex had no antitrust problems, but the Letson & Baker acquisition was looked at very carefully by the Justice Department, and it is probable that there will be no more major acquisitions domestically for Servex without strong objections from Justice. The possibilities of antitrust action if Servex acquires another firm worth more than $100 million are so high that Servex may not take the chance. J.B. merely smiles and says that he is considering several bigger deals than Letson & Baker, but *foreign* deals. These could lead to a much bigger and very much more internationally oriented Servex. Meanwhile, there are a few small U.S. companies that look appealing to J.B., and it is likely that Servex will continue to expand in this way for the short term. But if Servex is to get earnings up much over $3 per share soon, another major acquisition will probably be needed.

Most conglomerates have faced the awkward problem of what to do with loss-producing oddball divisions, but Servex has not. Each one of J.B.'s acquisitions (so far) has been able to show at least modest profits. Servex, as most shareholders know, is one of the few conglomerates that publicly shows profits by divisions—a practice that would be rather embarrassing for many conglomerates. Only the Machine Tool division in recent years has failed to show a profit. Since machine tools have been a recent disaster area for everyone, this result is not too surprising—and J.B. insists that a major turnaround is coming soon. Not only is the total U.S. economy beginning to pick up, accompanied by an even faster pickup in corporate investment, but also in the numeric control field Servex has several innovations that could be major winners. With labor costs going steadily up, and with key patents protecting these innovations, J.B. feels "the Machine Tool division will be the most profitable one in the company within a few years."

J.B. has always had as his basic policy that the owners of Servex come first—his major goal is to maximize long-term return on capital. Investors who got in early in 1970, when Servex first went public, have had no reason to be disappointed in their stock—$10,000 invested then is worth well over $70,000 now, allowing for stock splits. Wherever the profits are, Servex will be.

The new entente with communist countries shows Servex's prime interest in pursuing the profit dollar. J.B. himself is politically conservative. He has been a major Reagan supporter and personally contributes to many moderate-to-right wing candidates. But politics takes second place to profits. Servex already is negotiating several major deals with Eastern countries for machine tools—and at fat markups. "No one ever had to love his customers to sell them good materials," J.B. says. "We stand to gain a lot more than they do by making money on good sales and service. And we just might get a chance to widen the East-West political dialogue, if we have an opportunity to service lots of our machinery behind the Iron Curtain."

Servex, with J.B. at the helm, has rolled merrily along, avoiding in large part the usual pitfalls of the typical conglomerate, but the future may be very different. Up to now, Servex has had little antitrust trouble, but it has become so large that any major U.S. acquisition will surely be looked at very closely indeed. Also, J.B. is an energetic 74, but analysts wonder whether he can successfully take on even one more major division, given his tight personal control system and also wonder whether his successor will be as dynamic. The overseas expansion path looks very good—but only on paper, since Servex has not yet really gone into foreign markets in a major way. In addition, some observers feel that Servex may be a few years too late in moving abroad. New currency uncertainties, both at home and abroad, new taxes and regulations, and general political uncertainties in the Third World countries may make Servex's expansion abroad difficult. Some wonder, in short, if Servex may be all dressed up with no place to go. J.B. smiles at these doubts and says, "Just watch us go—we know exactly where the profits are, we plan to get them, and we think we know how to get them."

Another winning strategy?

While some successful conglomerates, most notably STT, regularly lose top executives to other companies, Servex rarely does. J.B. says this is because he keeps his managers "lean with work and happy with fat bonuses and stock options"; others wonder if the low turnover shows some weakness in Servex top ranks. So far, no obvious successor to J.B. has appeared. Lesser executives give the impression of competence and dedication, but the type of manager Servex evidently seeks does not seem to be much in demand by others, at least not at Servex-size compensation. Most present Servex management came to the company through acquisitions and stayed; several very capable people originally owned the companies Servex bought. Rarely has Servex gone outside to obtain a key person. (One notable exception is Loran Roberts, the Treasurer, who came over from Amalgamated Brass in 1977 and is widely regarded as one of the best financial planners in U.S. industry.) Servex is not a major talent recruiter in B-schools, nor does it plan to be so. "Those schools may train great theorists," J.B. says, "but we need line managers who can manage. And we can find them right within our own divisions."

Maybe so—but once again Servex is relying on following its own strategy, this time in the vital area of management personnel. The strategy has not been tested fully enough for success to be guaranteed.

Coming of age

Servex also faces considerable cleanup and ecological costs in the next decade. Its mining operations in particular may turn out to have major, multimillion dollar cleanup costs hanging over it. So far, the whole pollution problem has been a minor one for Servex. Like other firms, Servex has no real idea how large cleanup costs will be, except that they clearly will be larger than they were in the past.

Servex is getting big enough to be noticed and criticized. Until 1982, few reformers even knew the company existed. Now, feminist groups, minority groups and various government agencies have discovered Servex. To date, Servex has avoided many of the emotion-packed ideas that have caused trouble for other large firms. Only 0.8 percent of Servex's employees are black, with none anywhere near top management levels. No women have any key positions in the firm. J.B. says "Servex always obeys the law" (e.g., the Fair Employment Act of 1964), but so far there is little sign Servex has done much to follow the spirit of antidiscrimination or other social legislation. Future pressure seems certain, particularly since J.B. himself comes from a background some might call feudal. J.B.'s reaction? "Send me top people of any height, weight, shape, nationality, religion, color, race or sex, and I'll put them all to work. It's hard enough to find able, motivated people. We'd hire polka-dotted green Martians if they were good managers!"

So far the strategy has worked, but Servex may have to change in the future. Servex in many ways is a classic company, straight out of the nineteenth century. It did its job well, grew rapidly, and made money. Perhaps more than profit growth is needed in the 1980s, as social responsibility concepts keep expanding. In the end, Servex may have to shift its philosophy considerably, as consumers, minority groups, governments, and labor apply new kinds of pressure. And perhaps, the scion of an old Southern family will find that for the next twenty years the old way is not exactly the right way. Up to here, however, J. Baxter Bagby has conclusively demonstrated that the old way works just fine for Servex. And his stockholders enthusiastically agree.

Mint Juleps
and
Discrimination

Can an old line southern
president satisfy Women's Lib,
the Blacks, and Chicanos?

Servex moves into the new world

By DAVID BARCLEY
Staff writer of BUSINESS TIMES

PHILADELPHIA, Pa. Every morning at 7:00, three pickets gather at the plant gate of Vepcoland Mobile, a major manufacturer of those huge truck semitrailers you see on the interstates and a subsidiary of that almost invisible conglomerate, Servex. Rose McAllister carries a picket sign denouncing Servex for failing to employ more women in responsible positions. Jose Gomez carries a sign denouncing the company for failing to hire more Chicanos. And Pete Washington wears a sandwich board demanding that Servex hire more blacks.

Mike Posencowich, one of Vepcoland's most senior workers, mutters profanities as he crosses the picket line. A trade unionist since 1945 and a shop steward since 1964, he is not disturbed by this demonstration. "If those s——would leave us alone, everybody'd be a lot better off," he says, "We've got enough troubles as it is."

More Basic Problems

Vepcoland's inner Philadelphia Plant No. 4 certainly has an ample share of problems without worrying about minority hiring rights. For three years, it has been rumored that the plant will shut down. Vepcoland's president, Mr. Marvin J. Thomas, refuses to confirm or deny these reports. Located in a grimy, cramped, warehouse section of the inner city, Plant No. 4 surely does not present an image of the dynamic, growing company that Servex's operating record shows it is. Sales have quadrupled since the early 1970s and, unlike many conglomerates, Servex weathered the recession very well.

Since Servex acquired Vepcoland Mobile, it has built a new, highly automated plant in suburban Oakford, twenty miles from downtown Philadelphia. Most Oakford workers drive to their jobs. There is no parking around old Plant No. 4. Most of the work force (now cut to only 55) have commuted there by streetcar or bus for as long as anyone can remember. The average age of the workers matches that of the antiquated factory. Plant No. 4 last hired a blue-collar worker in 1975.

Discrimination

So why do the pickets march? "It's here," says Mr. Washington. "And it's lily white—there never has been a black man working there." He gestures at the tall wire fence. "There never will be either, unless we apply some pressure."

"Servex is a very hard company to locate," says Mrs. McAllister. "We've found out that Servex has $800 million in sales, but no big plants. Instead it has small plants with kooky names all over the place. Every time we nail Servex down, it turns out that they have some other factory we never heard of, in another city." Mrs. McAllister, a handsome, vigorous woman in her forties, points to her sign. "These creeps never hire women for anything but secretaries, typists, and cleaning women. And they never will, unless we hit them where it hurts."

"These guys think they have problems," Mr. Gomez says. "Hell, Servex has no Chicanos or Puerto Ricans at all in any of their plants—not even as janitors. They hired one once in L.A., but he quit after two days. The Anglo guys rode him so hard he had to. Actually threatened to kill him. What do you expect, with that old southern gentleman as president. Hell, he never sees anybody but WASPs, and he never will. Until we figure out how to get him better, this is the best we can do." And he picks up his sign and marches past the plant gate once more.

Sometimes the three pickets are joined by students (male and female, black and white) from two nearby colleges. The blue-collar, middle-aged work force trades insults with them at lunch and quitting time, but so far there has been no violence. Indeed, on a fine spring day, everyone seems to enjoy the ritual.

"Pigs!" the students shout.

"Go to Russia, you commies!" the workers shout back.

On the Job

Mr. Posencowich is typical of the remaining workers at Plant No. 4. He began at Vepcoland as a riveter in 1944. Now in his late fifties, he is worried about losing his job. "What can a man like me do, if he's laid off?" he asks. "I lose my pension, I can't find another job at my age, and I got a kid in college." He sighs. "Believe me, after seeing these kids yell at us, I don't know why—but what's a man to do? Anything is better than this mess we got here."

According to Mr. Samuel Johnson, Servex's PR representative, all of the Plant No. 4 workers been offered transfers to the new Oakford plant, but all have refused. "Apparently they prefer to remain where they are," Mr. Johnson commented. "And we have no intention of abandoning high-seniority workers and laying them off after years of loyal service."

Mr. Posencowich's union, the Amalgamated International Welders, thinks differently. "Those guys would steal their grandmother's false teeth and sell them for a buck," the local's president, Sam Bronski, commented to this reporter. "Hell, have you read what old J.B. Bagby, the president, said recently in *Business Today*? Profits come first—and he means it. To deal with these guys, you have to count your gold fillings after you leave the bargaining table. They give away nothing."

Mr. Johnson also commented on Servex's recent efforts to recruit minorities for many highly skilled and managerial jobs in the company. "We are an equal opportunity employer," he stated. "We will hire any qualified person who applies, for any vacancy we have. If anyone thinks differently, they should apply at our employment offices."

Mr. Washington has quite different views. "Sure, if you're qualified, you can get hired. A black friend of mine did apply. At least they were polite. He's got a college degree, and they told him he was unqualified to work as an accountant. What the hell do they want—God?"

Mrs. McAllister is equally vehement about Servex. "They've lost five or six really top women managers to other companies. They just don't pay you much or promote you if you're a woman. And if you think they are trying to hire qualified women, you're nuts. They carefully recruit their top managers at business schools like Harvard and Indiana, where there are almost no women—and they they complain that they can't get qualified people!"

J.B. Bagby a Problem

All the pickets seem to agree that J. Baxter Bagby himself is the key to the problem. Mr. Bagby, one of this generation's very successful entrepreneurs, has in the past fifteen years put Servex together from virtually nothing. But he is the son of a Southern aristocrat, from whom he inherited over 20,000 acres of prime agricultural land in Georgia (he still owns that land), and he was raised in the Southern tradition. The pickets claim he simply cannot understand what is going on in the modern world. "He's still living in the nineteenth century," Mr. Gomez says. "We've got to wake him up before it's too late!"

Mr. Johnson points out that Servex now has 26 women in middle or upper management throughout the company, as compared to only one in 1981. The company now employs over 2400 blacks, as compared to 325 in 1981, including seven in middle management, plus eleven in highly skilled technical white-collar jobs, and eight foremen. And Mr. Johnson disagrees flatly with Mr. Gomez—Servex now has over 800 Latin surnamed employees, as compared to 35 in 1980.

"We are not hiring anyone at Vepcoland Plant No. 4," Mr. Johnson commented, "and it is not likely that we will be in the near future. I suggest that these people come to our employment office. They might find that their stereotyped ideas would change a great deal."

Still, Mrs. McAllister, Mr. Gomez, and Mr. Washington show up daily at 7:00 A.M. to picket. Mr. Posencowich still mumbles unprintable things at them, as do the other 54 workers. Rain or shine, cold or hot, the pickets plod with their signs, joined from time to time by some young students.

By now, the pickets know each other well. "Got a cigarette, Jose?" Mr. Washington asks.

"No—ask Rose," he replies.

And in Atlanta, J. Baxter Bagby keeps on making money for Servex, expanding his firm, hiring thousands more workers every year, including many women and blacks and even a few Chicanos. But somehow, in the far-flung Servex empire, this message never gets down to the placarded sidewalks around the grimy brick walls and wire fences of Plant No. 4.

5
The Managers

Superior managers are the most important asset a successful company can have. Usually such a company can survive and recover if its factory and machinery happen to blow up or burn down: it builds a factory that is better than the old one and equips it with more modern and efficient machinery. Similarly, a successful company can withstand the loss of its famous brand names; it introduces new ones and makes them even more famous than the old. The loss a company cannot stand is the loss of the majority of its superior managers, especially the few who are at the very top and are responsible for the company's total activities.

Why Are Managers Important to a Company?

Although individual superior employees of lower ranks are important to a company, they are less important than individual higher-ranking superior managers. At each successively higher level the managers have more influence over more of the company's business. The top individual managers help establish the basic company policies that determine in what directions and with what success the entire company moves.

A superior manager combines exceptional intelligence, energy, and self-confidence with superior insight into what is profitable for his company. He is also very highly motivated to obtain psychological and financial rewards for himself through finding ways to make his company more profitable. Because of these attributes, superior managers are hard to find. No wonder they are considered by their companies to be extraordinarily valuable.

What Bargaining Strengths Do Superior Managers Have?

The work each individual superior manager does for the company leads to profit many times greater than his cost. This is the greatest bargaining strength: the company's potential profit would decrease if he were to leave.

In addition, an individual superior manager usually has some influence on other superior managers, both inside and outside the company where he works. His acquaintances listen carefully and respectfully to his opinions on matters in which he has demonstrated good judgment. If he were to leave the company, other managers, bankers, suppliers, and possibly even the business news media would be very interested to learn why he left. His explanations might convince either other superior managers inside the company to leave or superior managers outside the company not to join or bankers to tighten up on credit to the company. He would again cause the company's potential profitability to decrease.

Finally, a superior manager could leave and join a competitive company. There are laws limiting the information a manager can give his new employer in such cases; and sometimes competitive companies make informal, tacit agreements not to hire each other's managers. Nevertheless, such hiring happens often and represents a real threat to the profitability of the manager's previous company. Even if the manager does not reveal any of his previous company's specific plans or formulae, he inevitably reveals a great deal about its general situation and attitudes, its young managers, (perhaps which ones are strong and a little underpaid), and many other matters. Knowledge of this kind can be used by a competitive company to gain position in the market, with resultant harm to the previous company's profit.

Conflicts of Interest

Philosophically, the relationship of high-ranking superior managers to their successful companies is a fascinating subject. On the one hand, a company's high-ranking managers, as a group, determine what actions are in the company's best interests on all matters, including how they themselves should be treated by the company. On the other hand, as individuals they may have personal interests, needs, and desires that conflict with maximization of the profits of the companies whose actions they determine.

There are laws forbidding certain types of conflict of interest. It is, for example, illegal for a high-ranking manager to sell land to his company, at a sizable personal profit, without revealing the facts about his ownership to all the other managers and directors and to the stockholders. Every large company has many rules and internal policies designed to prevent conflicts of interest. A typical company has rules that prohibit nepotism, limit the size of gift a manager can accept from a supplier, prohibit managers from owning any sizable investment in a company supplier or competitor, prohibit all employees from benefiting personally from kickbacks from customers or suppliers or transportation companies, and so on.

In fact, in any well-managed company a manager's only question in making a decision should be: "What action will be in the company's best interests?" His personal interests should have no influence whatsoever on his decisions. Where possible, the company tries to keep a manager from getting into a position where he might be influenced by his personal interests. Because all managers are human and fallible and a few managers even in the best-run companies are dishonest, the rule is not always followed closely. Employees loyal to a particular manager may, for example, be promoted ahead of employees who are slightly less loyal. He may favor this loyalty consciously or subconsciously, and his promotion decisions may even be in the company's best interests. It is extremely difficult both to follow and to enforce the rule that the company's best interests should be the only criterion in decision-making, no matter how clear and important the rule is.

What happens when it is in a manager's personal interest for the company to act in a "more socially responsible" way than the company feels is in its best interests? A manager might feel, for example, that his company should at least triple its customary contribution to the university from which he graduated. We discussed such situations in chapter 1, and in the following incidents you will have opportunities to decide for yourself what the company's action should be. These incidents deal with various dimensions of managerial activities. Everyone is watching—banks, stockholders, workers, relatives, suppliers, unions, financial advisors, major customers, governmental units, and many others. Even minor items can become major issues if the manager misjudges or misbehaves and is observed in the act of misjudging or misbehaving.

The United Fund Chairman

"Why, hello, Miss Pickwick," John James said over the phone, "I'm delighted to hear from you again. How can I help you?" John groaned inwardly. What did she want now?

"John, you know that the United Fund is about to get under way this year," Miss Pickwick said. "Of course, I'm on the executive board again, and we absolutely must find a really capable chairman this year. You remember that last year Mr. Fostman did the job, and although he may be a great attorney, he surely is not a very good organizer or fund raiser. I admit that the big case he got into right in the middle of the campaign didn't help, but even so, you would think that a man in his position—"

"Yes, yes, I remember that," John interrupted.

"Well, in any case, we went over all the possible candidates, and your name kept coming out at the head of the list."

Oh, boy, John thought. "Why, that's very flattering, Miss Pickwick."

"Of course, I was the one who helped push," Miss Pickwick said. "After all, I've been following your company for years. You remember that my father helped found the original firm, and while I must say that I was a bit shocked when Servex took over our old company, and when you first came as plant manager, I can say I have been most impressed with you, John—most impressed. You're exactly the kind of dynamic leader the Fund needs."

"It's very nice of you to say that, Miss Pickwick," John replied, "but you know that I'm really very busy at this time."

"Bosh! If you weren't busy, I'd never have suggested your name. Only busy men can get a job like this done right."

"Well, I hope that you'll let me think it over for a day or so, Miss Pickwick."

Of course, John. And when you've thought it over, let me know. I'd like to announce your acceptance at the next executive meeting on Friday."

John mumbled his thanks and good-bys and hung up. How did I get into this, he thought. He had been on the plant committee last year, and Fostman really had loused up the campaign something awful. Why, for years the Fund had been barely functioning in the city—he could probably double pledges if he could sell the executive committee on a few key changes. John had helped raise money for his church some years back, and enjoyed both the skill and art it took to make people give more generously than they thought they would. It was a lot like marketing, his pet subject, except that you sold ideals instead of roofing materials.

He shuddered. But where would he find the time? The new plant expansion was coming up, and the United Fund chairmanship would take all his evenings, to say nothing of what was left of his days, for at least six months. He knew from experience that fund-raising was one of the biggest time-eaters there ever was—all the phone calls, lunches, and evening meetings to recruit canvassers, organize committees, stir up enthusiasm. How could he squeeze it all in! He was already spending much less time with his family. Also, this plant expansion was complex and important. When he recommended it, he knew that it would mean a lot of extra work; but if it went well, he was one big jump ahead of his competitors in the race to be president of Servex. Equally, if he bobbled the plant expansion even a little, his standing with the company would drop—maybe good-by presidency.

Miss Pickwick was quite a character. She owned maybe 2 percent of total Servex stock, most of which she picked up when Servex bought out her father's firm five years back. And she was a really influential person in the city. When she said jump, people jumped. No wonder they put her on the selection committee! She could get anyone in town!

John thought a bit about his own pet charity, the Boy's Club. They were having a hard time financially, mainly because the United Fund fell short last year. Expenditures had to be cut. But where would he find the time?

He made a note to call Miss Pickwick in the morning, and turned to the new plant electrical contracting bids. They seemed a bit high, and he would have to dig through the four bids to find out why. Darn it, with Joe sick, he could wind up doing his work too! But it was fun to go back and pick up this work he had not done for five years or more. He buzzed his secretary. "Anne, ask Pete Miller to come up. We'll be going over the electrical bids for the rest of the afternoon. And please call my wife and tell her I'll probably be late tonight. I think this will take quite a bit of time."

Questions

1. Should John accept the chairmanship of the fund drive? Why or why not?
2. Suppose that if John accepts, his managerial work will suffer considerably; as a result, he will not be as effective for Servex as he could have been, and he may not be promoted next year. Is your answer the same?
3. Should John discuss Miss Pickwick's offer of the chairmanship of the fund drive with the manager to whom he reports in Servex? What specific points is John's superior likely to raise if there is a discussion? What should be John's reaction to these points?
4. Advise John *exactly* what to tell Miss Pickwick when he calls her tomorrow.

Nepotism and Romance

"So Sam finally got married, huh?" John James said to Pete Bowers, his administrative assistant. "Boy, he's thirty-five . . . I thought he'd stay a confirmed bachelor forever!"

Pete grinned. "So did he. But Lila Martin finally convinced him. Sam's really shy, John. He almost never got around to where the women are. But now that lots of women are managers, well, he met Lila on business."

"What does she do, Pete?"

"She has an M.B.A. from Indiana University. She's a technical sales rep for Gladstone & Sells. We buy a lot from them, and he met her that way." Pete looked thoughtful. "Hey, John, what kind of policy do we have on such things? I mean, Gladstone sells us over a million dollars worth of components every year, and Sam's our buyer. Lila's their seller. We could have a real conflict of interest here."

John shrugged his shoulders. "How many of our managers have ever married another manager? For a competitor, supplier, or anything?"

"None, I guess, John. So we have no policy, right?"

"Right. It just never came up before."

"It could be sticky, John. I mean, suppose you were a buyer, and your wife were trying to sell you some very competitive products. Boy, I'm glad my wife isn't in that position! I'd buy everything from her for sure! Will Sam?"

"Sam's one of our best people, Pete. He's got his head on right. And yet . . . yeah, it could be rough. But I hate to mess with our employees' private lives. What do you think we should do?"

Questions

1. Should Servex have a policy covering this situation? If not, why not? If so, what?
2. What should Sam do, if anything? Why?
3. What should Lila do, if anything? Why?
4. What should Gladstone & Sells do, if anything? Why?

Do Nice Guys Finish Last?

"John, I've got a problem," Miles Baker said. "You know that we have to replace Nick Adams, president of Wadman & Wadman. He's retiring early next year."

"Sure, Miles. But what's the problem? Jack Armstrong is your obvious candidate. He's bright, knows the job well, and when Nick was sick last year, he did a super job. Better than old Nick, in fact. He's your obvious replacement."

Miles sighed. "In the old days, you'd be right. But you know how much equal rights pressure we've been getting recently. Servex is alleged to be a WASP company, with all our top people being from the white male establishment."

John grinned at Miles. "Right . . . we are. How many women of minorities are among our top managers? Only Maxine Beams, who's a vice-president of A.P. Beams, and she's the ex-owner's daughter. We *are* a WASP male company, Miles."

"I know. But darn it, John, we ought to change! We've been recruiting minorities and women for ten years now, but either they're really not quite top management caliber, or they're still too young for top management. And yet, the board, and I myself, really want to show that we're giving everyone a chance."

"So who have we got besides Jack?"

"Well, Mildred Markham looks real good. She's young yet, and she's just not as good as Jack. Still, maybe we should take a chance on her."

"Jack is a real loser, Miles. Not only is he a WASP, but he's from an old New England family . . . came over on the *Mayflower,* I believe. He inherited lots of money, and he went to Harvard. He's Episcopalian, his wife went to

Vassar, and his family is in the society 400. Poor guy . . . he doesn't stand a chance!"

Miles smiled sheepishly. "He also happens to be a superior manager, John. He's really good. If we pass him over, he'll probably leave. His uncle has been after him to take over one of the family companies that's stagnating. But if I skip Mildred, she may leave, and darn it, she does have potential! Five more years of experience, and . . . who knows? She could be great. But I hate to pick a person who, in my best judgment, just isn't quite good enough and isn't the best available."

"I agree, Miles. We just have to go with the best. Still . . . "

Miles nodded. "You see what I mean. We announce that Jack is the new president, and we get more heat. Worse, we may have some trouble recruiting some truly superior females from good M.B.A. programs. Already our recruiters get sticky questions. Sure, we can always hire women, but we have to get the very best. Jack's thirty-eight years old. If I appoint him, that top slot is closed off for a long time. We just stay WASPish for that many more years."

"So what are you going to do, Miles?"

Questions

1. What should Miles do? Be specific.
2. When, if ever, should a firm promote the person who is just not quite as good as another candidate? Why?
3. Suppose that Servex appoints Mildred, and Jack leaves the company. What has Servex lost here?

The Impatient Alumni

"So Western Tech's in trouble again," Sam Jones said, tossing the letter on Loran Roberts' desk.

Mr. Roberts leaned back. "You know it is. All the private schools are in a real cost crunch, and Tech's probably in worse trouble than most. They really don't have the endowment they should."

"J.B. went there, didn't he?"

"Of course. Why else would they send us the letter? Yes, our dear chief executive officer learned all he knows at dear old Tech. It is a darned fine school."

Sam looked at the letter again. "Let's see, they want Servex to match the gifts of all the Western Tech alumni working for us, for their hundredth anniversary fund drive. How many Tech alumni have we got, anyhow?"

"Oh, fifteen or twenty—maybe fifty, if you count the younger men. We recruit a lot of engineers there." Mr. Roberts sighed. "But the real problem is J.B. He's just likely to give them a personal million or so—he has it, you know, and since he doesn't have any children, well, why not? He's always been a very loyal alumnus." Mr. Roberts looked up at the ceiling. "Of course, he may not—I understand his wife is very interested in the new hospital in New Haven, and I know it has cost problems too."

"How come the Tech letter winds up on your desk, Mr. Roberts?"

"Well, I'm not only Servex's treasurer, but also the president of Servex's charitable foundation. Every year Servex gives a very large lump sum to the foundation to distribute. When sticky requests come in that are irreproachable, from excellent charitable causes or institutions, and so on, they come to me. It takes the heat off the company. Then the trustees of the foundation can decide to give or not to give. Very convenient."

"We give over a million a year to the foundation, don't we?"

"One point eight, to be exact. It seems a lot to some of the shareholders— they questioned it at the last shareholders' meeting. But it doesn't go very far these days. Lots of good causes desperately need lots of money."

"Does J.B. get in on the act?"

"Directly, no. Of course, he is one of the foundation's trustees, although he rarely attends a meeting, and he does indicate from time to time particular gifts that might be useful. Actually, he has excellent taste and judgment most of the time. We usually go along with what he says."

"How about this one?"

Mr. Roberts sighed. "I don't know. He sent the letter down to me without comment. I think he's a little hesitant to say anything on this one. Yet just the other day at lunch, he was commenting at length about what a great job Tech was doing with their new programs. He felt that we should do more recruiting there—said we probably could get even more really superior people from now on."

"Sounds like he wants to have us go along."

"Perhaps," Mr. Roberts agreed. "But it's the open-endedness as well as the size of this one that worries me. If we match ordinary gifts, we might end up giving, perhaps, a hundred thousand or less. But if one of our top men digs down and gives a lot, we could really be stuck. And there's something else that bothers me." Roberts dug around and came up with a file of letters. "Here are requests from eight other colleges. They alone want something like nine million dollars from us this year! They're all in genuine money trouble too, and we have alumni from all of them in our top management. Not to mention the colleges that haven't written—yet."

Sam stood up. "Well, I'm glad it's your problem, Mr. Roberts. One question: why did you show all this stuff to me? I haven't got much good advice to give."

"Well, Sam, you know Allmer is retiring this month, and he's been one of our trustees for the foundation. The foundation trustees think you would make an excellent replacement. If you accept, you'll be at next month's meeting, when Western Tech's request is taken up."

Questions

1. If you were in Mr. Roberts's position, what would you think should be the foundation's reply to Western Tech? Why?
2. If you were J.B. Bagby, what action, if any, would you take concerning Western Tech's request?
3. Suppose you are a Servex manager who is an alumnus of another engineering school. What would you think the foundation should do about Western Tech's request? What do you think of the foundation as an idea and of the size of Servex's current annual contribution to the foundation?
4. If you were Sam Jones, would you be eager to be a trustee of the foundation?

The Gift

"J.B. did *what?*" Maxwell asked.

"He gave $25,000 to the local Republicans to help Pellham in the senatorial race," Bill Hatcher said again to his boss in the Servex public relations office.

"Who knows about it?" Maxwell asked.

"Gee, I don't know—I heard about it from Jack Applegate at lunch. Jack's really active in the Republican Party, you know. I think he's a precinct worker or something. He was pleased as could be. Felt that at last Servex is getting on the right track."

"Who's Applegate?" Maxwell asked.

"Oh, he works down in accounting. I'm not really sure what he does."

"Was it a personal gift, or did the company do it?"

"Oh, it was personal. J.B.'s a very wealthy man. I hear that he's pretty conservative, too."

"Does J.B. understand the law about political gifts, Bill?"

"How should I know? Hey, this was just a rumor I picked up. I thought you might be interested, since you're a pretty good Republican, too." Bill was flustered. He had not expected the reaction he was getting from Mr. Maxwell. "Are we going to have a release on this, Mr. Maxwell?"

"Oh, boy, I can see the headlines now in that scummy radical sheet downstate: Servex Tries to Buy Election—President Makes Huge Gift. And us with a union contract coming up for negotiation. To say nothing of the fact that Pellham doesn't have a chance. Our reelected Democratic senator will have more seniority and end up on more key committees. Did you see what he said at the Democratic rally last week over at Millsburgh, about our pollution there?"

"He sounded pretty angry, Mr Maxwell."

"He wasn't only angry. He's got an antipollution bill in the works that could kill us. If that thing gets through, it could cost us four or five million just on the Millsburgh operation alone."

"Well, Mr. Maxwell, I should think that J.B. has a right to give his money to anyone he wants."

"Personally, I couldn't care less what he does with it, except that I wish he'd give some to me. But don't you see? He's not just J.B. Bagby, private citizen, but J.B. Bagby, chief executive officer of Servex. When this news gets out, everybody out there will think that the company gave it, not J.B. They're the same, as far as most people are concerned."

"Well, he must believe strongly in his convictions."

"I can tell you that he sure does. But I hope he gives away his cash very quietly."

"Jack Applegate is spreading the word as fast as he can," Bill said. "Should we do something?"

Questions

1. What should Mr. Maxwell do?
2. If you feel that Mr. Maxwell should issue a press release, write it up the way you think it should be done.
3. If Mr. Maxwell does nothing, what, if anything, do you think will happen?
4. What other options are open to Mr. Maxwell?

The Maharaja Manager

"How was the trip, J.B.?" Loran Roberts asked, as they settled back in the car coming back from the airport.

"Fine, Loran, fine—the overseas branches are doing very well. Oh, there are a few problems, but generally they look very good." J.B. lit his cigar. "You know, Loran, it still seems strange, having all that stuff overseas. When I first went into business, going abroad was something you did after you made a million. You made the Grand Tour. Later, you went as a GI. Now fifteen plants in ten countries, and sales there rising twice as fast as at home. It seems strange."

"We go where the profit opportunities are, J.B. You said that yourself over ten years ago."

"Yes, I suppose we have to. Say, Loran, how much do we pay that fellow Winslow—you know, the Indian manager?"

"Why, I'd have to look it up, J.B. Perhaps $58,000, plus our standard overseas allowances."

"That stop in India bothered me, Loran."

"Why?"

"Well, Winslow's a good man—you know that. The plant there is doing well. And you remember how dubious we all were when it was proposed. But he's got everything going pretty well, and 30 percent return on equity isn't anything to laugh at."

"It's one of our most profitable operations, J.B."

"Winslow, of course, had me out to his house, near Bombay. They have suburbs there too, you know. I must say I was a bit shocked."

"Why? Winslow's very sound."

"Oh, he's a delightful host. But good Lord, Loran, you should see his establishment! I counted eleven servants before I got confused. The house is twice the size of mine—and mine's not so small, you know. I have only one servant, and my wife thinks she's lucky. Why, Winslow lives like a maharaja!"

"I suppose $58,000 goes a long way in India, J.B."

"I guess it does. We had a feast the likes of which I've never seen before. Twenty courses at least. But that's not really what bothered me. During the visit, several Indian officials politely indicated that while we were most welcome in India, and while we were contributing to the economic development of the country, it might be better for foreigners not to display so much wealth. By that I'm inclined to think they meant our manager's living style."

"We never have tried to tell any manager how he should spend his money."

J.B. sighed. "I know—and Winslow's wife obviously loved it all. She's a nice midwestern woman, and I think that all those servants are going to her head. It'll be tougher to get Winslow back next year than it was to persuade him to go to India—and you remember how tough that was. But I saw some local newspaper clippings—most papers are in English, you know—commenting at length about wealthy Americans exploiting India while the country starves. And Lord knows, the country is poor enough—you could see it everywhere. Stinking poverty—and Winslow living it up like an old English aristocrat. It doesn't make us look very good."

"I suppose we could talk to Winslow."

"It was quite a difference in Turkey, where Alinson is. He's exactly the opposite—has a small house in town, his wife speaks the native language well and is teaching in a well-baby clinic, and Alinson rarely entertains. Everyone I spoke to in Turkey was very high on him. He seems to be locked into the local culture well—maybe too well. I think he might be making some decisions too much for the benefit of the Turks, and not enough for us. Already his wage rates are twice the local standard."

"His profits are way up too, J.B."

"I know, and I really can't complain. He obviously knows what he's doing. But perhaps we should get him back for a while, too—I sense that he is getting too locked in. His wife is more Turkish than American now, and after only four years."

Loran smiled. "It seems that you can't have it both ways, J.B. Here you are, worried because in Turkey Alinson is maybe becoming local, while in India Winslow is spending too much living it up like a foreigner."

J.B. laughed. "You're right, Loran. But darn it, you know as well as I that we have to watch our image, particularly in those poorer countries. The local citizens are sensitive and becoming more so—the left wing can always make political hay by accusing us of exploiting them, taking the life blood out of the country, and all that. Winslow may be putting us in a vulnerable position. One of the officials I talked to suggested that we might expect serious labor trouble if the unrest goes on much longer the way it has been. I visited his house, too—he's a very important man, and he lives about one-tenth as well as Winslow. It seemed obvious to me that this irritated him."

"Well, what do you suggest we do?"

J.B. sighed and leaned forward. "Darned if I know. I hate to get into the business of dictating the life style of any manager—they're spending their own money, which they work hard to earn. Also, they frequently have to put up with problems they would not have here in the states—poor medical facilities, great distances from relatives and friends, shortages of quality consumer goods. . . . I suppose they have to make up for such disadvantages somehow. But we wouldn't hesitate here if a manager came in with a beard and sandals, or if he got on dope or drank too much or did something else that might interfere with Servex's business. Maybe the overseas people should have similar constraints."

"I don't know, J.B. The overseas stuff seems different."

"Well, we should do something."

Questions

1. What, if anything, should Servex do? Why?
2. Is there any difference in life styles and impacts of American managers abroad as compared to within the United States? Why or why not?
3. When, if ever, should a corporation tell its managers how they should live off the job? Is this ethical?

The Investment

John McPeirson, the sales manager for Servex's Plastics and Petrochemicals Group, has not been very successful in his personal investments. The money he inherited in 1968 he invested in long-term 4 percent corporate bonds; by the 1970s interest rates were around 8 percent, and the capital values of the bonds went down accordingly. His 1981 bonus he sank into the market as the Dow Jones Industrial Average reached 980; and the DJIA promptly sank to about 870. This year, John's division has been doing extremely well, and he anticipates receiving a bonus of approximately $20,000 in cash.

The Clean Air Corporation recently came to John with an investment proposal. It is a small but rapidly growing, ecologically oriented firm that performs factory emission analyses and then recommends and applies remedies if the air is found to be polluted by the emissions. The company's strong point is its highly skilled technical staff of twelve, most of whom John knows personally because Clean Air has been a growing customer for some of the chemicals his division sells. Servex's sales to Clean Air for last year were about $840,000, and they will be higher this year. John worked closely with several of his key salesmen in helping Clean Air get the best possible chemicals for any given job and at the lowest prices. He became quite interested in Clean Air's ideas and management at that time. As a result of John's interest and the high quality and competitive prices of Servex's products, Servex now supplies the majority of Clean Air's chemical needs.

Mr. Bibsby, Clean Air's owner and president, is considering obtaining more outside capital, perhaps by selling common stock to the public for the first time. Knowing John's interest in Clean Air, he approached John and offered him some of the Bibsby family's stock. If John invests $50,000, he will get about 4 percent of Clean Air stock (the rest to be held by Mr. Bibsby and family), plus an offer of a seat on the board of directors. Within two years, Clean Air will probably go public and have its stock listed on the American Stock Exchange. If sales and profits continue to rise as fast as they have been, it is likely that John will make a handsome capital gain on his shares.

One major reason Mr. Bibsby approached John is that he was very impressed with John's marketing abilities. He would like to get John on the board because he feels he could make valuable contributions to the company in the marketing area. Since Mr. Bibsby is basically a technically oriented manager, he recognizes that Clean Air needs this type of expertise.

In considering this offer, John was troubled by the sales of his group to Clean Air. If Clean Air moved ahead as fast as he felt it could, he would be making rapidly increasing sales to Clean Air. He believed (based on some sales analysis provided him by his staff) that potential sales of Servex chemicals to Clean Air and similar firms could reach $20 million annually within five years. (Current total Servex sales in this market, including those to Clean Air, come to about $2.6 million.) As a board member of Clean Air, he would, of course, insist that key purchases be made at the lowest possible prices and for the best terms. As sales manager for the Plastics and Petrochemicals Group of Servex, he was sure that his company could be very competitive. Why not? He would know all about Clean Air, and he would have the inside track on what would be happening.

John felt that there might be a conflict of interest here, but the Clean Air proposition seemed to be an extremely good way to recoup his investment losses. Still, it was a risky proposition, and he enjoyed his work at Servex. He decided to talk to his boss, Mr. Botts, about the offer before making a decision.

Questions

1. What advice would you suggest that Mr. Botts give John McPeirson? Why?
2. Is there a conflict of interest here?
3. Suppose John did make the investment and became a member of Clean Air's board. How should he handle any discussion of purchases of items that might be supplied by Servex?
4. What should John do? Why?

6
The Employees

To employers, wages are a cost—a high one. From 10 to 85 percent of a firm's operating costs are labor costs, and any manager interested in improving performance takes a close look at payrolls first of all. Historically, labor costs have been reduced through layoffs, wage decreases, and the like, since few managers knew other ways to reduce labor costs or other areas in which to reduce costs. Such tactics are still used, but they are being increasingly replaced by more humane treatment. Managers find it very difficult to order a person to do a creative (i.e., a highly skilled) job task. Putting the squeeze on labor these days is at least as likely to be counterproductive as to cut costs.

To workers, the employer is the person who generates their incomes and locks them into a job for eight hours a day, five days a week. He is often seen as the manager of a dark satanic mill. Each employee knows that he is worth more than the boss pays and that many working procedures are badly thought out and often counterproductive. He suspects many people of trying to make a buck at his expense. Hence, he must always be on the alert to safeguard his own welfare in terms of better working conditions and higher pay. Various professional associations and trade unions have developed over the years to demand these improvements and to protect workers from their bosses.

Although a certain amount of antagonism between workers and employers is inevitable, in the past forty years the conflict has been complicated by two factors: increases in the productive output of each worker and involvement of government in labor disputes. Both the worker and the firm can benefit from increased productivity. Indeed, this is how any country becomes rich. If we still plowed with horses and lifted bales onto ships by hand, we all would be a lot poorer. Productivity increases, however, can be harrowing and upsetting for many managers as well as other employees. Managers and senior technicians have to learn new routines, and often entire job categories are eliminated. A worker may recognize that a new system of containerization will generally lower costs and allow real wages to rise; but if he loses his job because of the change, he will probably fight containerization.

We are all familiar with governmental attempts to protect the right to strike, but now government has also begun to concern itself with hiring practices, safety conditions, pension protection, and many other work areas. An abuse such as discrimination is perceived, a new state or federal law is passed, and government becomes directly involved. When this happens, reasonable people are likely to take opposite stands, especially if a worker's income or perquisite becomes an employer's cost.

As individuals, employees are much less important to a company than are individual managers. An individual employee's performance affects a smaller fraction of the company's business than does a manager's; an employee who leaves is a great deal easier to replace, at much lower cost, than is a manager. As a group, however, a company's employees are indispensable. If the employees all strike togethr, ordinarily the company's business stops.

The chief bargaining strength of employees in dealing with a company lies in their potential group action. Unlike managers, who tend to bargain individually, employees try hard to persuade all members of their group to commit themselves as strongly as possible to their demands. In addition, they try to persuade third parties such as employees of other companies, governments, company customers, and the public in general to be at least neutral and at best strongly committed to the employee side of the dispute, thus increasing the total group pressure.

A company tries to avoid a situation where all its employees are totally committed to certain demands and other groups tend to favor the demands as well. If a company provides—perhaps by choice—better working conditions, better pay, better promotion opportunities, and generally fairer treatment of employees than do other companies in the community, smaller percentages of its employees may be committed to further demands—and those smaller percentages may be less committed.

Interestingly, there appear to be limits on how much better than normal a company should treat its employees to obtain their optimum cooperation. If a company vastly exceeds the accepted norms for employees in a given community, its employees may become even more demanding of benefits than are less well off employees of other companies. For example, in poorer foreign countries where lower-rank employees have traditionally been treated very badly (by the standards of industrialized countries), an overly enlightened employer who treats his employees extremely well (pays them, say, 40¢ an hour instead of the customary 20¢) may find himself in trouble not only with local employers and with the government but also with his employees, who condemn him as a blood-sucking capitalist leech or worse. Apparently the employees interpret the higher wages as a bribe not to interfere with the company's profit flow, which they think must be very high. Some variation of this reaction has happened fairly frequently to American subsidiaries in underdeveloped countries. It can also happen to foreign-educated natives of poor countries who return home to manage a family business according to the humanitarian principles taught in foreign universities.

The following incidents illustrate some of the common problems firms and their employees have. In a complex real United States with 100 million employees, 10 million firms, and thousands of governmental units, these are only a sampling of what might be expected, even for Servex. You will be wrestling with such issues in one form or another all your business life.

The Old Cost More

Servex prides itself on its very liberal pension plan for its employees in the United States. On reaching age sixty-five, a Servex employee with twenty years of service has a right to receive 40 percent of his final salary until he dies. If he has worked for Servex over forty years, he is eligible to receive the maximum pension—80 percent of his final salary. The portion of his final salary that an employee may receive gradually increases from 40 to 80 percent as his length of service increases from twenty to forty years.

Like most other firms (and like the U.S. government with its Social Security plan), Servex has not fully funded its pension plan. Insurance experts would say that Servex's pension plan is not actuarially sound. That is, Servex has not put in sufficient capital so that the pension fund, together with future earnings on the fund's capital and future contributions by Servex at the customary rate, can provide all the pension payments promised to past and present employees. Table 6–1 suggests the current pattern: about 25 percent of the foreseeable pension liability is funded, while the rest must come out of profits. Servex's pension system is noncontributory. In other words, employees do not have to make payments into the fund from their salaries or wages.

Recently a number of individuals and organizations have asked for clarification of Servex's policy toward hiring older workers. A group called "We Over 40" has alleged that the company rarely hires anyone over age thirty-five. It has asked that this practice be stopped, since men and women over forty find it difficult to get good jobs. The group also argues that Servex owes it to the country to employ older workers who are able, experienced, and willing to work. Moreover, discriminating against older workers is illegal, and this organization stated that it would not hesitate to bring legal action against any company it felt was practicing such discrimination. Several government departments, responding to various pressures from around the country, have asked for more information about the hiring of older workers.

Table 6–1
Pension Fund Coverage and Payments

Year	Pension Fund Capital (millions)	Percentage (of Total Needed to Make Fund Actuarially Sound[a])	Payments to Pensioners (millions)
1977	$204.5	20	$28.4
1984	251.3	25	41.5
1992	325.5[b]	10[b]	133.6

[a]Actuarially sound based on certain assumptions about age composition of work force, average life expectancy of pensioners, future interest rates, increases in average final salaries of workers due to inflation and productivity increases, average turnover rate of work force, and the like.
[b]These estimates are based on the assumption that Servex contributions will continue to be made at the same rate as in the past.

The government questionnaires on this subject filtered up through the organization to Mr. Loran Roberts, the treasurer. Since the pension problem is, among other factors, a major deterrent to hiring older workers, he assigned several members of his staff to study what would happen to the pension fund if older workers were hired. The staff report contained the following points.

1. When the fund was set up in 1962, worker turnover was projected to be about 15 percent a year. Since pension rights were not vested (that is, a worker who left lost all rights to his pension), 15 percent annual turnover meant that relatively few employees actually received a pension, compared to the tens of thousands who would have been eligible if they stayed with the company. From 1962 through 1967, this 15 percent predicted rate of turnover was accurate within half a percentage point; since that time, turnover has declined sharply. It was 4 percent in 1982. In short, the decline in employee turnover has led to the very sharp decline in the percentage of the total pensions funded forecast for 1992 (table 6–1). At that time, Servex will be facing a severe pension crunch.

2. If more older workers—aged forty to forty-five—are hired, they will become eligible for the minimum 40 percent pension payments in about twenty years. Furthermore, the turnover rate for older workers is lower than that for younger workers, and so a larger proportion of older workers would further reduce the average turnover rate. These factors could lead to very rapid increases in pension liabilities.

3. If only 10 percent of the people being hired were over forty, by 2002 the fund would probably be so "actuarially unsound" as to make the present system unviable. As a result, workers who stay on would probably get smaller pensions than now promised.

4. Under Servex's present pension plan, new workers over forty-five would receive no pension at all, since they would not be able to accumulate twenty years of service by the time they reached the compulsory retirement age of sixty-five. Any change in the minimum service or age of retirement would probably entail very difficult and expensive problems. In conclusion, the report emphasized that stopgap contributions to the fund are already a major drain on corporate profits; if more older workers were hired, this drain would be intensified.

Questions

1. What should Servex's policy be toward hiring older workers? Why?
2. Is it fair to present workers to risk their pensions so that others not now on the payroll can find work? Why or why not?
3. What rights should older unemployed people (e.g., over forty) have with respect to major corporations? Why?
5. Should there be a law requiring companies not to discriminate against older workers? Why or why not?

Reverse Discrimination

"Mike's going to sue us, Jason," Jean Farwell, Westport Brass and Milling's personnel director, said.

"Jean, I wish we never got into the computer programming business! All it seems to lead to is a lot of static from these computer jock primadonnas!"

"And big profits," Jean observed dryly.

Jason, the company president sighed. "I know. We started as a small milling machine company, and now we make robots. In the old days, the boys wore blue collars and were machinists. The personnel director was an old guy who liked people. Now I have a female director, and the guys . . . and girls . . . wear all sorts of clothes, sometimes even ties. They have beards and put pinups on their cubicle walls. Jean, I'm glad I'm retiring next year! This game is so different! OK, what's our troublemaking friend, Mike Wojinski, complaining about now?"

"He says we're discriminating against white males."

"At least that's a new one. Just how are we doing this?"

"The last six promotions out of the programming group have been Asians." Jean smiled. "At least two of them were women, so he can't accuse us of sex discrimination!"

"The facts, Jean, as usual." Jason nodded as she put the papers on his desk. Old Peterson was methodical, but he never got it all together. Jean was really efficient . . . thank heaven that at least this nondiscrimination business had led him to get a really top personnel director! He scanned the papers. "He's right; all of them were Asians. Five Americans and Kim, the Korean."

Jason looked up at Jean. "Why did we promote these geniuses, as if I didn't know?"

Jean smiled. "Because they're the best. Kim's got a Ph.D. in computer science from Stanford; Suzuki was a straight A student in MIT; Lee Kong was the top 1980 grad from Cal Tech . . . need I go on?"

"No. Jean, Westport has tried to promote the best people for over fifty years. In the old days, they were all white males. Then, fifteen or sixteen years ago, we finally discovered the Civil Rights Act of 1965, and we began to look at everyone. We also began to get into automated machine tools and robots. You got there; those Asians got here. We still try to hire the best and promote the best."

"Maybe that's why we make so much money, Jason, and stay ahead of the competition technically."

"What kind of case does Mike have, Jean?"

Jean frowned. "I don't know . . . there are very few legal precedents. He is pretty good, even though he complains a lot. He's got a good degree from Purdue. On paper, he looks good. But he just doesn't have that extra edge of brilliance, Jason, that Kim or Suzuki or Kong has. If he does sue, it will cost us plenty in legal fees, no matter who wins. He's got a lawyer who's willing to take the case on speculation, and she's really good."

"Suppose we promote him, that new slot is opening up. What will he do?"

"Drop the case. He's not interested in solving the world's problems, Jason, just in getting ahead himself. But Leong, the Vietnamese, is clearly better for the job. He has the extra edge, Jason. I was going to recommend him soon, and his boss, Suzuki, concurs."

You have no idea how tough it is to get good technical people in the computer field! Ten years ago, we hired our first Asian Americans, and I think the word got around. Westport is a good place to work, fair, and all that. And look at the results . . . we do lead our field."

"That last discrimination suit we fought cost over $850,000 in legal fees, Jean. Perhaps we should just promote Mike and forget it."

"Jason, those computer jocks know who's good. If you promote someone who they know isn't quite good enough, you'll really be in trouble. Mike has a big problem, actually, he knows, way down deep, that he really isn't the best. I think that's the reason he complains so much. It bothers him."

"It bothers me, too, Jean. OK, what do we do?"

Questions

1. What should Westport do about Mike? Why?
2. Does it ever make sense to promote the second- or third-best person? When?

3. How do coworkers and subordinates likely react when they also know that the company is promoting not quite qualified people? Is this a relevant issue here?

4. Should a company ever duck a lawsuit it feels is not right in order to avoid huge legal fees and much loss of time? When?

Exporting Jobs

For over twenty years, the Sinbad Paint Company, which is a highly profitable part of Servex's plastics and Petrochemicals Group, has been exporting special aircraft paints to South American markets. Although a relatively small percentage of the world market, these markets have grown steadily through the years.

In 1981, the Brazilian government asked Sinbad to consider building a plant in the country to supply most of South America. Sinbad would be the only producer of special aircraft paints in the Latin American Free Trade Association and would therefore have access to all the LAFTA countries from this plant. The LAFTA countries would have a uniformly high tariff on the paints to protect the plant from low-priced competition from imports. The Brazilian officials stated frankly that, if Sinbad did not wish to install a plant under these conditions, it would be necessary to invite a European firm to provide the plant. All of this discussion was tentative and quite general, but Sinbad's management felt that it was definitely an advance warning of what might happen.

Accordingly, a quick survey was made of Latin American markets for the special paints. Given reasonable expectations of growth, it seemed economically feasible that a plant could be built by 1985, and Sinbad began advance planning for it.

By 1984 work was well along on Sinbad's final construction plans. In March union officials in Sinbad's main plant in Los Angeles got wind of the Brazilian project. They visited Sinbad's management and asked for facts, which management provided as follows.

Selected Data from Sinbad
About the Proposed Brazilian Subsidiary

Present (July, 1984) sales in the LAFTA countries are $1.1 million. Sales are rising at about 10 percent annually. Sales for an economic-sized plant should be at least $1.5 million.

If the Brazilian plant is built, we expect to send seven U.S. technicians there to train a group of local technicians. The seven technical staff, plus two management personnel, will be recruited from our Los Angeles facility, where we now have 200 employees. (This facility produces $18.9 million worth of sales, including $8.5 million of special aircraft paints.) Since no one has produced these paints in Latin America to date, we can expect considerable troubles at the outset. For the foreseeable future, product costs will be somewhat higher than in the United States.

The Brazilian plant will require an estimated 225 people to produce $4.5 million in sales. Wage rates for unskilled laborers where the plant will be built average about $1.49 an hour, but skilled wage rates go as high as $4 an hour. Since most of the workers will be skilled, the total wage bill should be about $1,300,000 annually.

If we do not build this plant, it is quite likely that Yashimoto Paints will build it. Their aircraft paints are somewhat inferior to ours, but they are also somewhat cheaper and Yashimoto's share of exports to the world market has been growing. Moreover, if Yashimoto does build, Sinbad will lose practically the entire Latin American market, since the tariffs on the paints will very likely be set at high enough levels for all Latin American markets to make us uncompetitive with Yashimoto. A major German firm (G.U. Heit, G.M.B.H.) has been quietly exploring the market and may apply to build the plant. If so, they may approach us for licensing rights to our patents, since they do not appear to have the necessary technology to do the job right now.

If Sinbad goes ahead to build, principal money estimates are as follows:

Total capital cost land, buildings, machinery	$875,000
Initial working capital	625,000
Total capital investment	$1,500,000
Local cruzerio loans available (20% interest)	700,000
U.S. $ investment required	800,000
(of which, $630,000 in U.S.-built (Servex) machinery)	
Initial annual sales	1,500,000
Initial annual operating cost including interest	1,410,000
(of which, $340,000 for U.S.-made raw (Servex) and packing materials and U.S. technicians)	
1987 annual sales	2,900,000
1987 annual profit after local taxes	420,000
Payout period	6.7 years

Within two weeks after union officials learned these facts, the local union paper printed the following article.

Sinbad Gives More Jobs Away to Foreigners

Our Los Angeles Local Number 397 is about to lose over 225 jobs to foreigners, according to a March 16 report from the local. The Sinbad Paint Company, a division of the giant conglomerate Servex, has arranged to begin construction of a new plant in Sao Paulo, Brazil, which will employ 225 people. Up to now, the large quantities of Sinbad's special aircraft paints exported to Latin America have come from Sinbad's Los Angeles plant. Now the new Brazilian plant is expected to produce the paints to meet this demand.

How long will Washington allow such nonsense to continue? Your union's steady efforts to win U.S. paint workers a living wage have brought average pay at Sinbad to above $8.25 an hour. Now Sinbad is skipping out of the country to have their paints made by $1.40-an-hour, non-union, exploited labor in Brazil. And, of course, 225 of us will be over at the Los Angeles unemployment office, picking up our $100 a week. There ought to be a law!

Not long after this article appeared, three congressmen from Los Angeles districts wrote Servex's top management to ask why the company was exporting jobs at a time when unemployment was so high in Los Angeles.

Questions

1. Write a letter to the congressmen, giving them the company's side of this story.
2. How many jobs (if any) is Sinbad exporting because of the plant under construction? Why?
3. What should Sinbad do? Why?
4. What should the union in Los Angeles do? Why?

Job Seniority

1981 and 1982 were very good years for Westport Brass and Milling. The demand for machine tools was so great that the New Haven plant had to backlog many orders and hire sixty new employees. By the end of 1982, it had 240 employees.

In 1980, Westport's president Jason Lopata was under considerable pressure to hire black workers since there were only eight blacks among the 180 employees and they worked as unskilled laborers and sweepers. Mr. Lopata realized that he would have to hire more workers anyway; besides, he felt it his duty to increase the number of black employees. Therefore, he agreed with a local black coalition group to hire as many hard-core unemployed blacks as he could and to join a federally sponsored training program to try to upgrade these workers.

The training program had its ups and downs. The first group of ten black trainees proved to be very badly chosen: within the first few weeks nine of them either had been fired for cause or had quit. Mr. Lopata then got in touch with Wiley Jackston, an aggressive and very capable black minister in New Haven. Reverend Jackston was able to find hard-core unemployed men and women with more potential and motivation, and he also worked with them to help them adjust to plant discipline. Turnover dropped markedly, and some of the new black workers made excellent progress in training. One exceptional young man even became a foreman. By late 1982, forty-one new blacks were on the payroll.

The 1983 nationwide slump in capital expenditures hit Westport Brass very hard, and sales dipped badly. By mid-year, Mr. Lopata faced the difficult task of reducing the work force to the level in 1977—130. The future looked good because of the excellent potential of the new cybernetic line, but sales were still a year away. With 110 workers to be laid off, everyone concerned became very nervous.

Under union rules at the plant, seniority was clear-cut: the last hired should be the first laid off. These rules had been in existence since the big Westport strike in 1937, and a whole generation of workers had accepted them without question. This time the blacks objected. Reverend Jackston came by Mr. Lopata's office to point out that Westport had hired very few blacks before 1981; hence most of them had little seniority and would be laid off. Since they did not have a part in the original seniority agreement, they saw no need to observe it. At the time the seniority agreement was made, the union was lily-white too, and no blacks had ever had a chance to have their say on the subject. If the black workers were laid off, Westport could expect major racial trouble. Reverend Jackston noted that other major corporations had been boycotted for less—perhaps Servex would get the same treatment. The black communications grapevine was very good, and Mr. Lopata should remember that a number of Lucky Jim stores (also a Servex operation) in the Midwest were heavily patronized by black customers.

Soon after Reverend Jackston left, Peter Alonzio, the union shop steward, came in. He had heard that the company was thinking of keeping on the blacks, thereby violating the seniority agreement with the union. If the company did, it would face a strike. The union had fought hard for seniority, and it was not about to give up its contractual rights. Old-time (white) union members were already saying that the company was laying off more men than it had to—nearly half the work force—to increase profits and, maybe, to weaken the union. If the layoffs hit only the old-time union members, in violation of the seniority agreement, there would surely be a strike.

Realizing that his problem affected more of Servex than just his group, Mr. Lopata called headquarters to discuss the problem with vice president Smith.

Questions

1. Mr. Smith promised to write a memo instructing Mr. Lopata what he should do. Write that memo.
2. What rights do older (white) workers have at Westport, or should they have? Why?
3. What rights do blacks have at Westport, or should they have? Why?

The Marginal Facility

"Crazy as it sounds, I think they're going to strike," Marvin Thomas said.

"Even after you pointed out how high cost the plant is?" his boss, Pete McMann, asked. "Marv, that union is out of its mind!"

"You know the story, Pete. Vepcoland got that plant in the Allen deal. What a plant! Down in that dreary, World War I industrial section of Philadelphia, where our physical distribution costs are high, our insurance cost is out of this world, and we can't get people to come in at night. If that old plant were half as good as the plant we have just outside Philly now, that would be another story. But the guys are all old. They remember the stories about the union busting in 1937, the war years, and all that. They think we're bluffing."

"What *are* unit costs there, Marv?"

"Per trailer, about 30 percent over the suburban Philly plant, for just about every model. Everything costs more, including labor. Particularly labor, because an old work force means a lot more seniority payments."

"And they want 40 percent pay increases spread over the next three years," Pete mused. "What do you think we should do, Marv?"

"If they strike, we should just close it down. Hell, we can pick up all the production in the outer Philly plant, even more easily now that sales are off 20 percent from last year." Marv began to pace up and down. "Forty percent! That would run costs sky high. We just can't do it!"

"How do labor costs there compare to those at our other plants?"

"Really not too badly. In fact, they are just a bit on the high side compared to our national average. That suburban Philly plant is our lowest cost plant. But Pete, it's not just labor trouble that's making me say shut it down—you know that. It's a broken-down, 1906 building, no access for big trucks, a lousy and inefficient electrical system. It's everything! The plant is just a dinosaur—a high-cost, old operation!"

"Calm down, Marv," Pete said. "Suppose we do close it down. What about the men?"

"They all live around there. I doubt that we could pick up many in the suburban plant. It's almost fifty miles away, and across town at that."

"So, fifty-five men are out?"

"They'd be out. And they deserve it. Forty percent! The guys are nuts!"

"Most of them have worked for us, or for Allen before us, for twenty or thirty years, Marv."

"Sure, of the fifty-five about forty-five are over fifty years old, and most of them are real old timers. But they've pushed us just too far, Pete. They deserve what they get."

"Pay at the outer Philly plant is lower, isn't it?"

Marv nodded. "Sure, a little bit. We built that one just two years ago, and we built it right. Average base rate hourly pay is lower than at the old plant. However, in lots of categories the base rate at the new plant is higher because the guys are worth a lot more. They punch out more stuff per shift. That's one of the beefs at the old plant. They think they should have the same pay as the other fellows in all categories, plus seniority, even if they don't do as much work."

"And the union agrees?"

"The union agrees."

"Well, Marv, when is the strike supposed to happen, if it does happen?"

"Next week, starting Tuesday."

"OK, let's decide what to do."

Questions

1. What should Marv and Pete decide? Why?
2. Does Vepcoland owe its long-term employees anything in this situation? If so, what? If not, why not?
3. Why would a union get into this kind of spot? What is their image of this company?

Safety Costs

One of Servex's plants in Chicago has a very dangerous punch press. In the past four years, six men have been seriously disabled because of it. The only press of its kind, it produces a peculiar type of stamping done in only a few places in the world. The men who operate this press are carefully warned and trained as to the dangers but, sooner or later, there is an accident and someone loses a finger or even a hand. When a man is injured in this way, he is covered by Workmen's Compensation insurance. Payments cover disabilities, medical costs, and related costs. Servex pays, as do other companies, the state insurance premiums that cover this cost.

Servex's safety engineers have gone over this machine carefully several times. They figure that, for $800,000, in about fifteen months they can build a safe machine that will produce at the same cost per unit for materials and direct labor as the dangerous old machine. The new machine would, of course, be "safe" only in a relative sense, just as the old one was "very dangerous" only in a relative sense. In the Chicago plant, machinery is currently considered "safe" if, when operated by properly trained workers of average skill, it results in 2.2 to 2.5 (per million man-hours of operation) lost-time accidents of which not more than .2 cause permanent disability or death. The old machine was rated "very dangerous" because its lost-time accident rate was 329.3 per million man-hours (15 accidents, including the maimings, in about 45,000 man-hours) and its serious accident (the six maimings) rate was 133.0.

The new $800,000 machine would be designed to bring both the lost-time and the serious accident rates within the "safe" range. The safety engineers estimate, however, that to reduce lost-time accidents by an additional 10 percent (i.e., to a rate of between 2.0 and 2.2 per million man-hours) would mean an increase of about $175,000 in the cost of the new machine—a total cost of $975,000. No one knows how to design a machine that does the job at an estimated lost-time accident rate below 2.0. In gathering cost estimates, Servex found out also that a "dangerous" machine—one with a lost-time accident rate of 11.0 to 100.0—could be built for approximately $120,000; a "high-risk" machine—one with a lost-time accident rate of 2.6 to 10.0—would cost approximately $225,000.

If Servex decides to build a new, safer machine, it will have to do it itself, because no manufacturer makes such a machine. If the special parts it produces are not made, the whole plant will have to close down, since they are critical to the total product.

Workmen's Compensation insurance for this plant costs $35,000. Since the premium is based on actual accident experience, it would probably drop to $29,000 a year for the $800,000 machine.

Questions

1. What should Servex do? Why?
2. Accidents are inevitable, and no industrial job can be totally safe. How much money should a company spend to be as safe as it can? Why?
3. Is there really a choice of trade-offs that can be made here between misery and costs? Can you think of examples in civilian life where society through its governments chooses to accept citizens' injuries or deaths rather than spend money?

Gay Decisions

John Maxwell, president of Servex's Almont & Sons, is a born-again Christian. He believes firmly in following Christian precepts in business. John never pushes his beliefs on anyone, but he does try to live a Christian life, and one result is that his company never gets involved in dubious contracts, kickbacks, illegal dealings of any sort, or any shady activities. His customers appreciate the excellent and courteous services they receive, and reorder rates are high.

At the company picnic this year, Wallace Moore, Almont's new chief assistant accountant, showed up with his boyfriend. John had never met this young man before, and he really didn't quite know what was going on until someone made a comment about Wally's being gay. It turned out that everyone knew it but Maxwell. Since Wally was regarded as a star performer, his personal life obviously did not affect his professional life.

It did affect Mr. Maxwell, however. A few days after the picnic, Alton Commer, Almont's personnel director, received a handwritten memo from Maxwell instructing him to fire Moore immediately. Alton had been at the picnic, and he strongly suspected that Moore was being discharged just for being gay. If proved, this might be illegal, and Commer was a bit disturbed by the principle of the thing anyhow. Why fire anyone who was performing well, for something in his or her personal life?

Questions

1. What should Mr. Commer do? Be specific.
2. It is ever proper to fire someone for something involving one's personal life? If so, when?

7
The Stockholders

Maximum profitability for a company (and therefore for its stockholders) has been said to occur when its stock prices rise the most over long periods of time. Because of this chance for gain, many people, both inside and outside a company, pay very close attention to stock values.

Investors in General

People tend to judge overall managerial abilities in a large firm chiefly by how well the firm's stock behaves on the market in the long term. If the firm seems successful but the price of its stock does not rise, then something may be deeply wrong with its method of conducting business. If the price of its stock rises rapidly and stockholders are rewarded, then management must be doing the right things. The stock market is looked on as an external, impartial, and omniscient judge of internal managerial performance.

Investor interest in market performance is enhanced by the fact that buying shares at $5 each and selling them at $10 each creates not income but capital gains that are taxed at a much lower rate. Many stock owners, especially those in fairly high income tax brackets, look for stocks that offer capital gains through growth rather than income from dividends. The "good" stocks and companies are those whose stock prices keep rising.

Management and a Company's Stock

A company's management may well seek to picture its profits and growth in the best possible way, perhaps even at the expense of the actual facts. It may gloss over bad news or overinflate good news. If the buying public is convinced, many people associated with the company may gain large amounts of money. The stock buying public, however, is typically very sophisticated.

They know that a company may try to present a more favorable picture than is justified. As a result, large stockholders, bankers, stock market analysts, and many others tend to dig deep for evidence that what a company says to promote itself is true.

Stock Options

Many managers, especially those in key positions, are interested in stock prices because of their stock options. A newly hired vice-president, for example, might be given a ten-year option to buy (from stock held in the corporate treasury) 1000 shares at $45 per share, the average price at which the stock sold on the New York Stock Exchange on the day the option was granted. Such an option serves as a reward. If he does a job that is recognized as good by present and potential stockholders, public demand for the stock will probably cause its price to rise—perhaps to $200 within ten years. He can then buy the 1000 shares at $45 each and, to make a sizeable low-taxed capital gain, sell the shares at $200 after holding them at least six months. If, however, the stock price *fell* from what it was on the date of the grant, the option would be worthless—also a just reward, it is argued, for managers in a poorly managed firm.

Insider Gains

If you, as a highly placed Servex executive, buy in the market today because you know that tomorrow news of a major new discovery by the company will be made public, then you can watch your capital gains mount as the stock price soars. There are U.S. laws against such practices. Enforcement of these laws is becoming stricter, but borderline cases of misuse of inside information seem to be very common.

Insider use of unreleased information to make personal gains is very different from personal gains by executives through stock options. It can be argued that with stock options no one—except possibly the tax collector—loses. However, the stock the insider may buy on the strength of unreleased information is bought from someone who definitely loses as a result of not having access to the information. Anyone who sells stock in the company from the time the insider places his order to buy until the time the information is released has received less for his stock than he should have. Stock options may be of questionable social value in the judgment of some people, but misuse of insider information is actually a type of theft.

The Rights of Stockholders

Legally, the holders of stock in a firm own the firm. In practice, it often happens that no one holder of stock in a complex, large, publicly owned firm owns enough to control it. Indeed, few stockholders bother to vote their shares themselves; more commonly, stockholders give their proxies to management, and so in effect the firm controls itself. The stockholders are, however, the legal owners, and they have a right to the firm's net income.

Bargaining Strengths and Weaknesses

Stockholders have some measure of strength in dealing with a company because of (1) the right of a majority of the shares to control the company; (2) the legal right of a stockholder to sue the company, its directors, and its managers if he has evidence of actions taken against the interests of stockholders; and (3) the effect of stockholder attitudes on the price of the stock and thus on the reputations and personal finances of the company's managers. When top managers allow a firm's earnings to slump and stay slumped, stockholders sometimes band together to vote them out. Furthermore, is a firm pays little attention to the needs and demands of existing and potential stockholders, then it may have problems when it has to go to the money markets to raise cash by selling a new stock issue.

Despite these potential strengths, stockholders are usually in a weak bargaining position because, for a typical company, the stock is very widely held. Thousands or tens of thousands of investors might each hold a tiny fraction of 1 percent of the total shares. As a result, no individual stockholder feels confident of his ability to master a majority of the shares. If he is dissatisfied with the company's activities, he is likely to sell his shares rather than go to the trouble and expense of trying to form a majority.

Raising the Dividend

In July 1984 the president of Servex Consolidated Industries received the following letter from a woman in Kokomo, Indiana.

```
Dear President Bagby:

In 1982 I inherited 4000 shares of Servex stock from
my late husband.  He always told me to hold on to
your stock, and the dividends you send me are an
important part of my income.

I was, of course, glad that in 1983 you raised the
quarterly dividend from 10 cents to 15 cents.  I
really need this extra money.  But I saw in the 1983
annual report that net earnings were $2.40 per share.
```

This puzzles me, since I cannot understand why you do not send your stockholders the entire profit. I badly need additional money, because I will probably have to buy a new car soon and fix my porch roof.

Frankly, Mr. Bagby, it is quite irritating to me to think that for some reason you are withholding my money, particularly at a time when I need it. I would have had $7200 more share of the company's profit.

I have talked to the other ladies in the investment club I belong to here in Kokomo, and none of them understands either why you cannot pay a much bigger dividend now that the company's profits are going up so fast. We ladies have about 11,254 shares of Servex, and all of us would like to receive bigger dividends.

Please don't misunderstand. We are all very pleased with the progress of our company in 1983, but we would like to have a larger share in the profits. I could sell my stock, of course, but if I did, I would have no income from Servex at all.

I would appreciate your explaining this situation to me as soon as possible.

Very truly yours,

Gladys Burton

The president's secretary passed the letter on to the public relations division, with a note to answer this query politely.

Questions

1. You are the public relations assistant to whom this letter has been forwarded. Write an answer to Mrs. Burton explaining the company's dividend policy.
2. Is such a letter worth answering? Why or why not? What could an investment club in Kokomo possibly do to a huge firm like Servex?

Inside Dope

Seymour Welby is one of the great modern billionaires. The son of a British planter in Jamaica, he inherited about $5 million in 1939, dropped from sight during the war, and emerged in 1948 with a net worth of around $100 million. During the Korean War he got into the boom market in ocean shipping. Later he picked up a piece of a major foreign oil concession, which hit big, and bought a few charter airlines, which he sold within two years for a $136 million profit. In 1963 he invested heavily in both Chrysler Motors and American Motors stock in the 1970s and purchased controlling interests in several major machine tool companies in 1982. In 1983, he retired with an estimated net worth of $1.5 billion. Now in his early eighties; five times married, he lives on a yacht anchored in the Mediterranean just off his estate at Cap d'Antibes in the south of France.

Mr. Welby is noted for his quick temper; cutting wit, and split-second decisiveness. He can make mental calculations with lightning speed and yet appear very relaxed amidst his obvious wealth. Associates and partners speak of him in awe, and he is known to be rough on subordinates, "Being chewed out by S.W. is like being caught up in the funnel of a tornado," as one ex-aide put it.

Recently, Mr. Welby has been buying large blocks of Servex stock. He now owns over 1,500,000 shares, bought mainly during the sharp downturn in 1982, when the stock was selling for $11 to $15 per share. His holdings give him over 15 percent of the total stock outstanding. To date, Mr. Welby has not asked for a seat on the board of directors, although he is the single largest stockholder. Servex officials have become increasingly apprehensive as Mr. Welby has acquired more and more stock. They wonder if he is thinking of buying absolute control of the company. Every report on Mr. Welby's financial status suggests that he could do so. J. Baxter Bagby and his family own 12.1 percent of Servex's common stock; but other directors and managers as a group control only 5.6 percent and almost 28 percent is owned by various institutions and large investors who would doubtless be willing to sell if the price were right.

Yesterday a gentleman called on Mr. Abelgard, Servex's controller, and announced that he was acting as agent for Mr. Welby. Mr. Abelgard had met this man several times before, usually at meetings of security analysts, where Mr. Abelgard was asked various questions about Servex's financial position and projected results. Mr. Sweet, the agent, had asked quite perceptive questions and taken many notes on such occasions. Around New York's financial district, he was known as a schrewd investor of his own money, as well as a major source of Mr. Welby's financial information and advice. Apparently he was a trusted associate of the billionaire.

This time, Mr. Sweet asked a number of questions about Servex's Machine Tools Group. He wanted verification of a rumor that the group had developed a numerically controlled machine that promised to revolutionize the control system part of the industry. He also had heard that Servex was planning to close several marginal plants, an act that would significantly improve financial results for 1985. In addition, he asked Mr. Abelgard to give him some unit cost figures for three plants. He understood that Servex had the lowest costs in the industry, and if the new numerically controlled machines were produced, they could be priced to yield very high profit margins and still be well below current prices for competitive machines.

Mr. Abelgard, as comptroller, had at hand most of the information Mr. Sweet wanted. However, all of it was highly confidential. He was well aware that an outsider could use the information to gain a significant advantage in the market over the general public and even over serious stock market followers such as security analysts. Further, he was painfully aware that Mr. Sweet was in a position to advise Servex's largest stockholder. If he gave the wrong answers, it could be most unpleasant for both Servex and Mr. Abelgard.

Mr. Abelgard stalled a bit. "Mr. Sweet," he said, "while I am, of course, eager to give you any information I can, I should point out that the particular information you're requesting is highly confidential."

"Of course, it is!" replied Mr. Sweet. "I wouldn't want it if it weren't confidential. To Mr. Welby and to me, information everybody already has isn't worth having! Look, Mr. Abelgard, you must know that Mr. Welby has not been invited to join the Servex board of directors, and he hasn't embarrassed you by pressing to be on the board, as he surely could have. If he were on the board, you'd give him the information I'm requesting on his behalf, and give it with no question at all. Now, why not leave things as they are—quiet and peaceful? Give me the information without Mr. Welby's having to press for one or more seats on the board."

Mr. Abelgard asked Mr. Sweet for a few days to gather the information he had requested. As soon as Mr. Sweet left his office, Mr. Abelgard called Mr. Bagby, Servex's president, and Mr. Roberts, the treasurer, and arranged a quick luncheon meeting. He wanted to be very sure of his ground before he met Mr. Sweet again.

Questions

1. Should Mr. Abelgard give the information to Mr. Sweet? Why or why not?
2. Suppose that the information, when released publicly in a month, caused Servex stock to jump by ten points per share—from $28 to $38. Stockholders selling today and each day until the information is made public

(Servex stock is sold at an average rate of 8000 shares a day on the New York Stock Exchange) would lose this potential gain. What rights do they have here, if any? Why?

3. There is a federal law preventing insiders in corporations from taking advantage of inside information. Does this law have any bearing on this situation? Mr. Bagby, Mr. Abelgard, and Mr. Roberts all have significant holdings of Servex stock.

3. Advise Mr. Abelgard what to do, assuming that you are the president, Mr. Bagby.

Greenmail

As the largest single Servex stockholder, Mr. Seymour Welby owns about 15 percent of the total stock outstanding. Recently, he has been buying more stock at around $28 per share. Since owners of common shares are registered by the corporation and Mr. Welby has chosen to have at least some of his purchases registered in his name or in the names of corporations he controls, Servex's management knows that Mr. Welby is adding to his Servex holdings. Mr. Welby has already advised the Securities Exchange Commission (SEC), as he must legally do, that he controls over 5 percent of Servex's stock—15.4 percent, to be exact. Also, Servex management has nervously noticed that a number of rich individuals, who are well known as frequent co-investors with Mr. Welby, have also begun to buy Servex stock. Even now, Mr. Welby could easily place one or two directors on the Servex board, although he has not yet attempted to do so; with perhaps 20 percent of the stock, he could be a major factor in determining Servex's future. Worse yet, in the personal views of Servex's top managers, Mr. Welby might want to fire the present top management and put his own people in top positions.

Recently, Mr. Bagby heard some disturbing rumors. A major New York firm that handles proxy fights sent one of their key representatives to the Mediterranean, where Mr. Welby lives on his yacht. A friend of Mr. Babgy heard that this representative was to meet with Mr. Welby about Servex. Mr. Sweet, who is Mr. Welby's New York representative, has been pumping just about everyone in regard to Servex. Mr. Bagby feels that Mr. Welby may be planning a proxy fight to take over Servex.

This possibility was discussed at the last directors' meeting of Servex. Since an outside takeover would mean that not only management but also the whole board of directors might be removed, everyone was understandably concerned. Several board members had heard stories similar to those Mr. Bagby had heard. One member related that a broker friend of his commented that in one conversation he had been involved in, Servex's earnings record and growth performance were seen as dismal. Perhaps new blood in management could make a difference. Specific attention was directed to the Machine Tool Group, where recovery from the loss position seemed to be very slow and sluggish. With the recent revival of the economy, this division should have picked up sharply in profits by now, but so far had not. Management clearly was not too sharp in this situation.

In general discussion, the board agreed to strengthen its relations with all Servex stockholders and to consider a dividend increase at the next board meeting. In the meantime, Servex Public Relations Department would send an attractive brochure to stockholders explaining how well the Machine Tool Group was doing compared to competition and promising profit improvement 'soon. Servex directors who had excellent connections with the financial community were delegated to make personal calls on the twenty-two institutions (mutual funds, trust companies, pension funds) that owned large blocks of Servex stock.

While these defensive actions were being taken, Mr. Abelgard, Servex's controller, once again received a visit from Mr. Sweet, one of Mr. Welby's agents. After pleasantries, Mr. Sweet indicated that Mr. Welby might consider selling all of his Servex stock to Servex for $41 per share and arranging for his friends to do the same. This would net Mr. Welby and his friends a profit of about $26 million. If Servex bought back its own stock, fewer shares would be in public hands, so earnings per share would rise. Everyone would be better off, most notably Servex's officers and board members, who otherwise might be ousted.

Mr. Abelgard listened without comment and then noted to Mr. Wells that he would discuss the matter further with relevant Servex officials. Mr. Wells smiled and observed that Servex had better act rather quickly, given Mr. Welby's well-known impatience. He might change his mind.

Mr. Abelgard was aware that this practice of buying a large block of a company's stock and then reselling it to the company at a much higher price was known as greenmail. It was not illegal in 1984, although many business observers thought it somewhat unethical. In effect, Mr. Welby was threatening the jobs of Servex's key officials and demanding they spend many millions of dollars of the stockholder's money to buy back their own company . . . and their own jobs.

Questions

1. Is this type of greenmail ethical? Why or why not?
2. What other options do Servex top officials have in this case?
3. Many stock market and company observers think that greenmail is unethical, but few do anything to stop it. Should they? Why or why not?
4. Market followers can often deduce, from seeing large blocks of company stock being traded, which companies might be involved in a greenmail

situation. In such cases, it is common for the price of the stock to rise rapidly as speculators bet on the outcome of greenmail activities or hope for a bigger rival takeover bid. You are fairly sure that Servex is involved in a greenmail attempt. Would you buy Servex stock now at about $28 per share when you figure that the greenmail attempt might drive Servex's stock price up to about $39 or $40 within a month or so? Why or why not?

Corporate Disclosure

The Securities and Exchange Commission has been studying proposals to make conglomerate corporations disclose in their published reports more information about their activities than they already do. One item of information that keeps being mentioned as desirable is a complete breakdown of income and costs for all subsidiary companies. Instead of grouping income into one lump sum, with costs equally lumped, a firm such as Servex might be required to report in detail for each product group and major subdivision, including all foreign subsidiaries.

The SEC is going to take testimony from all interested parties at a hearing in Washington in early 1984. Servex has been invited to testify, and Servex's finance committee met recently to consider what the corporation's position on detailed disclosure should be.

Mr. Roberts began by stating his opinion that the firm should fight any additional disclosure. Servex already presented more data than the law required, as witnessed by the annual report showing costs and revenues in each of the groups. Few conglomerates went even that far. Of course, he would not object to rule changes that made others do what Servex already was doing. More detailed breakdowns, however, would only help competitors fight Servex more effectively. Already the disclosures in the annual report had proved awkward, as for example in the Machine Tools Group. The president, Mr. Bagby, had to answer many difficult questions at the annual meeting as a result. If every subsidiary's accounts were made public, too many awkward questions might be asked.

Bynam Watts, of Watts, Watts, Watts, and Smith, Servex's general counsel, reminded the meeting that stockholders often felt that they had a basic right to know exactly how their money was being used. Already Servex was in court on two stockholders' suits somewhat related to misinformation (it was alleged) about profits. One dealt with profits in the Retailing Group. A stockholder felt that he needed complete cost information to determine the facts.

Mr. Watts was particularly concerned about revealing information about foreign subsidiaries since, whether U.S.-owned or not, they are "corporate citizens of foreign countries." He felt that the U.S. government had no right to control the foreign activities of foreign citizens and certainly had no business requiring Servex to disclose publicly what it did abroad (except for tax purposes). Few, if any, foreign governments required public disclosure of as much information as the U.S. government already did. Moreover, some of the most profitable enterprises in Servex were abroad, and public disclosure of foreign operations would be a real asset to foreign competitors who did not have to disclose.

Others at the meeting also felt that further disclosure would be of enormous value to competitors. They would know the exact strengths and weaknesses of Servex. Knowing this, they could plot their own strategies. Mr. Watts then pointed out that the reverse would also be true: Servex could examine the disclosures of its U.S. competitors with great care and find out similar things. Further, Mr. Watts reminded them, a large part of the justification for disclosure rested on the stockholders' right to know. No one was claiming that competitors had a right to know. The question was: Would stockholders gain more through detailed disclosure than they stood to lose by, for example, giving additional information to competition?

Questions

1. What position should Servex take in presenting its testimony at the SEC hearing? Why?
2. What do stockholders have a right to know? Why?
3. Is Servex currently giving stockholders adequate information to allow them to make good investment decisions? Why or Why not?
4. Suppose that a given subsidiary abroad is making 50 percent on its net worth, and Servex must reveal this information. Who would care? Why?
5. Suppose that of Servex's total annual profit on the operations of a particular foreign subsidiary, 45 percent is taken in the country where the subsidiary is incorporated, 25 percent is taken in Servex's Swiss company (as license fees for the use of trademarks and patents), and 30 percent is taken in Servex's U.S. operations (as purchasing fees for raw and packing materials furnished the subsidiary). Should Servex have to reveal this breakdown publicly? Why or why not?

Who's on First?

Mr. J. Baxter Bagby, president of Servex Consolidated Industries, has argued for years that really good management is badly underpaid. He has stated that some of his best managers add tens of millions of dollars to profits and even more to the capital gains of the shareholders, and yet very few of them annually earn more than $200,000 before income taxes. Such people are certainly not very well paid, if their after-tax income is compared to that of some entrepreneurs who establish their own companies.

Mr. Bagby makes the point that Servex has often bought a company from an entrepreneur for $5 million or $6 million, which gives the owner-manager a capital gain of as much as $2 million to $3 million at capital gain tax rates rather than income tax rates. Often the Servex manager taking the purchased company into his division has doubled or tripled the company's profits within a short time, and yet there are few ways to reward such superlative performance.

Since he feels this way, Mr. Bagby is very much in favor of stock options. As used by Servex, the granting of stock option consists of giving a division or group manager a long-term option to buy a number of shares of Servex stock (owned by the Servex treasury) at the price prevailing in the market when the manager was granted the option—which is, ordinarily, during the year in which the manager took charge of his division or group. If Servex's profits and sales rise, it is likely that the stock price will rise in the market; before the end of a stated period, say, ten years, the manager is able to buy at the option price and sell in the market at the higher price. If Servex does not do well over the next ten years, its stock price will stay low, and the options will be worthless. These options give managers personal incentives to do the best they can for Servex and its stockholders.

In 1983, Servex stock was selling in the $30 to $35 range. In 1981, it sold for $60 to $75, while in 1982, a year of depressed earnings, it reached a low of $11 to $15. Managers with stock options granted in 1981 had worthless options in 1983, whereas those managers given options in 1982 had a valuable asset. Several group managers were given options in 1981, while several others received options in 1982. As a result, some managers were very happy and some were very disappointed. The options ranged widely, as table 7–1 shows. Under American law, firms who grant stock options to directors or top managers must make this information public.

Mr. Bagby has for some time been disturbed about Servex's apparently inequitable treatment of its group managers caused by the differences in the value of the options they hold. In 1981, Servex was seen as a high-flying conglomerate, whose earnings would rise forever, and its stock price reflected this feeling. By mid-1982, all conglomerates were seen as dubious ventures, and stock prices clearly were extremely depressed. Both the highs and lows in recent years appeared to be overreactions, fluctuating around a more consistent uptrend. Mr. Bagby feels that something should be done to correct the inequities in the value of stock options given to Servex's high-ranking executives.

Some of Servex's outside stockholders have complained both in letters to

Table 7–1
Stock Options for Key Servex Managers

Date Option Granted	Person	Title	Unexercised Options Outstanding (shares)
June, 1977	J.B. Bagby	President and Chief Executive Officer	80,000 ($18/share)
April, 1979	W.W. Westwood	Vice-President Manager, Plastics and Petrochemicals	2000 ($25/share)
January, 1981	P.C. Mc.Mann	Vice-President Manager, Retailing	15,000 ($60/share)
May, 1982	R.W. Warren	Vice-President	15,000 ($74/share)
May, 1982	A.P. Botts	Vice-President Manager, Basic Metals Production	2000 ($74/share)
December, 1976	J. Gatsby	Vice-President Manager, Household Furnishings	10,000 ($12/share)
August, 1978	W.W. Warren	Vice-President Manager, Services	16,000 ($21/share)
May, 1983	J.H. Smith	Vice-President Manager, Machine Tools	22,000 ($31/share)
May, 1983	P.W. Abelgard	Controller	5000 ($31/share)
May, 1982	L.M. Roberts	Treasurer	38,000 ($74/share)
December, 1976	G.M. Cantrell	Secretary	5000 ($12/share)

Note: Present market price for Servex stock is $34 per share.

Mr. Bargy and in stockholders' meetings that stock options take money from them. When treasury stock is sold to managers at lower than market prices, the stockholders lose. Since there appear to be plenty of competent managers available who will work very hard with extra bonuses, there really is no reason to give such options. If they are nevertheless given and then turn out badly, that is just tough for those who expected to make an unearned gain.

Various students of corporate accounting have pointed out that large stock options give managers an incentive to show apparently large profits, no matter their actual size. They cite some conglomerates who, on acquiring firms, engage in "creative" accounting—that is, altering depreciation rates and other itmes to show the maximum profit possible. A frequent side effect of such accounting is that the firm ends up paying more taxes than it is legally required to, as table 7–2 shows. In such cases, while stock's price may rise temporarily in the market, stockholders are hurt in the long run.

Table 7–2
Creative Accounting: Increasing Profits on Paper

Method of Calculating Depreciation	Assets (millions)	Annual Depreciation Expense (millions)	Depreciation Period (years)	Profits after Depreciation (millions)	Income Taxes (millions)	Net Profits (millions)
Declining balance	$50	$8	10	$10	$4 (40%)	$6
Straight line	$50	$5	10	$13	$5.2 (40%)	$7.8

Note: This is a highly simplified example, since there are many other expenses besides depreciation that can legally be accounted for in a variety of ways. Moreover, sales and costs change each year, usually making it more difficult to follow such changes than suggested here.

Many of Servex's stockholders bought their stock at prices higher than now prevailing. Already they are not too pleased with present management and tend to feel that somehow they were robbed. Yet Mr. Bagby still feels that his stock option program should be revised to give all his key managers a fairer share than they now get.

Questions

1. Do you agree with Mr. Bagby or with his stockholders? Why?
2. If you were revising the stock options for key managers noted in table 7–1, how would you do it? Why?
3. Do you think that stockholders are hurt by stock options? Why or why not?
4. Servex currently follows a conservative accounting policy. If stock options are very attractive, do you feel that key managers might be tempted by more liberal accounting? Why or why not? What controls might they face?
5. Is it reasonable for stockholders who bought Servex shares at high prices to feel robbed when prices go lower? Why or why not?

Foreign Stockholders

For many years there has been much agitation in Canada about the takeover of the Canadian economy by U.S. firms. Many newspapers and journals have discussed the problem, and it is widely feared in Canada that the Americans will end up owning everything important.

Servex has always followed a policy of owning all the stock of each of its foreign subsidiaries, including a small Canadian subsidiary that is part of the Household Furnishings Group. This subsidiary is owned by Wadman and Wadman and was formed in 1931, after sudden increases in Canadian customs duties on office furniture (following, it might be noted, equally sudden and sharp increases in American customs duties on Canadian products). Sales were about Can. $1.4 million in 1983, and profits were Can. $88,000. Since 1934, customs duties in both countries have gradually drifted lower. Wadman and Wadman's Canadian subsidiary has never flourished or expanded much, since headquarters has preferred to supply from the American plants most items sold in Canada. The subsidiary is profitable, though, and it has a net worth of Can. $750,000.

Recently Mr. E.U. Whelmer, a Canadian entrepreneur, has protested that Canadians cannot invest in good Canadian companies owned entirely by foreigners. His brother-in-law once worked for Wadman and Wadman, and so he knows something about this minor subsidiary, which he has chosen as a whipping boy for his arguments. He is a noisy person with a minor genius for striking photogenic poses and making quotable, provocative statements. His comments are frequently publicized by the Canadian press and television.

Servex's public relations department at first ignored Mr. Whelmer's statements, on the grounds that he had little influence and that trying to refute him would simply add to his publicity. However, Mr. Whelmer kept talking, and his quotable comments kept being quoted. Finally, Servex sent out a release emphasizing that any Canadian citizen who wanted to own part of Servex could buy stock in the parent corporation, just as could anyone in the United States. Mr. Whelmer flourished a copy of this statement during a party celebrating the opening of a new, American-owned supermarket in Ontario. He declared that Servex's statement was a classic example of America's neo-imperialistic attitude toward Canada. What he and numerous other Canadians wanted was a piece of the action in their own country, not a tiny slice of a huge conglomerate. If Canadians were allowed to buy stock in the relatively small Canadian subsidiaries of giant American firms, then perhaps Canadians could determine their own destiny.

His timing was extremely good: the Canadian prime minister happened to make a major speech on American ownership of Canadian industry the same weekend, and most Canadian and many American papers picked up the story. Servex then received a number of letters and cables from Canadians who held stock in the U.S. parent company, along with a discreet inquiry from the American State Department asking what was going on.

Questions

1. What, if anything, should Servex do about this problem? Why?
2. You work in Servex's public relations department. Prepare a statement

for urgent release tomorrow, defending the company's Canadian policies.

3. You are convinced that Mr. Whelmer is interested only in his own gain, and you have some evidence (though not enough to stand up in court) to prove it. Does this make your task in question 2 easier or more difficult? Why?
4. Do you feel that Servex's policy of 100 percent ownership of foreign subsidiaries is a good one? Why or why not?

Boycotts and Stockholders' Pressure

For many years, various American groups have been pressuring firms about their investments in South Africa. These groups contend that the overtly racist society should be totally boycotted, and one way to do this is for U.S. firms to withdraw all investments in the country.

Recently Mr. J.B. Bagby, CEO of Servex, received a letter from a group called Concerned Citizens against South Africa. The letter noted that its members held significant stock in Servex, and at the forthcoming stockholder's meeting, these stockholders would present a resolution demanding that Servex withdraw from South Africa. Mr. Bagby turned the letter over to Mr. Bornstein, his in-house legal counsel, for comment.

Mr. Bornstein investigated and discovered that Servex has only a small investment in South Africa, totaling a bit over $2.4 million, in a distribution company. This company, a part of the West Coast Steel Company, has about thirty-nine employees, of whom thirty are black and three are colored (Asian). It owns a warehouse that handles the distribution of a few specialty fabricated steel sections for the South African market. Since Bill Jefferson, an able young financial planner from corporate headquarters, was taking a trip in the general area, Mr. Bornstein asked him to visit South Africa and see what was happening. Mr. Jefferson is black.

In a month, Mr. Jefferson returned with his findings. He was surprised to find that the thirty black workers were anxious to have West Coast stay in South Africa. Although they earned (as is typical in South Africa) less than half the salary a white worker would earn doing similar work, they felt that jobs were hard to get, and they were doing extremely well by black African standards. It would be nice to earn more, but it was better to be working than not. The three colored workers felt the same. No Americans were employed in this facility; all of the white supervisors were South Africans.

Mr. Jefferson pointed out that this facility was marginal in terms of profitability, averaging less than 10 percent return on capital and 2 percent on sales in recent years. Historically, in the 1970s, it had been very profitable, but changing economic conditions in the steel fabrication industry had made it of dubious value. Indeed, a few years ago, Mr. M.B. Foster, West Coast's president, had seriously considered closing the South African operation, but it would have been difficult to sell, and since it was earning a little on capital, which could not easily be repatriated, he decided to continue operations. No new investment had been made since 1976.

Mr. Bornstein asked Bill Jefferson what he thought about the situation, as both a financial analyst and a black. "Mr. Bornstein, I just don't know. Financially, it's very marginal. If we close it down, we would lose next to nothing, perhaps a few hundred thousand dollars a year, and we could probably gain most of that back through export sales. If you want to make a grand gesture, Servex can announce at the stockholders' meeting that we are withdrawing from South Africa, and we support this stockholders' resolution. We might even make a few dollars when we sell the land; it's in a good location in Capetown. Perhaps doing this would make some American liberals feel good.

"But I was surprised to find that the blacks who work for us would like us to stay. We pay good wages by local standards; of course, the discrimination is terrible. Still, something is better than nothing. We have some very good people there, Mr. Bornstein, with families to support. If we close the facility and sell the land, they lose their jobs. And jobs for black workers in South Africa are hard to get, particularly fairly good ones of the sort we provide."

Mr. Jefferson shook his head. "Boy, I'm confused! I've never been to South Africa before; you can feel the hate and discrimination everywhere. It's like Mississippi must have been around 1900. It was very depressing, believe me. If we stay, we are tacitly supporting apartheid. But if we go, we not only cause employees to lose their jobs, but we lose any opportunity to influence for the better whatever goes on in South Africa in the future. I must say that I enjoyed, in a perverse way, the discomfort I caused a lot of whites while I was there. They had to treat me as an honorary white. Of course, the South African government is very anxious for us to stay. But to watch those characters trying to be polite to me was kind of fun. Mr. Bornstein, I just don't know!"

The annual meeting was coming up fast, and Mr. Bornstein had to make a recommendation to Mr. Bagby. He was aware that in these situations, the stockholdings of persons making such a resolution was typically perhaps 1 or 2 percent of shares outstanding, so the resolution could easily be voted down by management proxies. But he was also aware that such resolutions gained extensive publicity in many quarters, even though they were inevitably defeated. Moreover, when a company was targeted in this way, various persons and groups would put Servex stock on a boycott list, meaning that they would never buy it. Such groups included church and trade union pension funds, which had significant, though relatively small, buying power in the stock market.

Questions

1. What should Mr. Bornstein advise Mr. Bagby? Draft a copy of his letter to Mr. Bagby, giving his best advice.
2. What rights do West Coast's South African workers have in this situation? Why?
3. It is true that South African blacks earn less than a third as much on the average as South African whites. It is also true that South African blacks earn more than three times as much, on the average, as African blacks in general. West Coast pays more to its blacks than the South African average. Is West Coast doing these South African black workers a favor, or is it discriminating against them? Why or why not?

8
The Creditors

Modern firms have many creditors—persons or institutions to whom they owe money. Among a company's creditors may be bondholders, commercial banks, factors (discounters of accounts receivable), and insurance companies.

One of the most frequent causes of business bankruptcy in the United States is under-capitalization. A company must have a certain amount of capital to finance inventories, in-process goods, receivables, buildings, machinery, and other business necessities. Companies, especially those that are young and fast growing, frequently need more capital than they can retain from earnings, and they would like to get their capital cheap. Sometimes large companies have surprising difficulty getting the loans they need in order to grow or, perhaps, even to survive.

Lenders have money, but they want the highest return with minimum risk. A potential creditor has two major bargaining strengths in dealing with a company: it can grant or deny a loan request and quote a low or high interest rate. Once again there is potential conflict concerning issues on which reasonable people can take quite different positions. Negotiations for a big loan can become very complex and delicate, as each side maneuvers to obtain the best possible terms.

A firm's indebtedness affects other groups. The cost of capital may be passed on to consumers and other people or companies who depend on the company for certain products or services. Loans may have an adverse effect on stockholders' equity as well.

In the end all the factors affecting corporate social responsibility interrelate not only in theory but also at the level of solving problems. The following incidents may suggest why.

Without Bread You're Dead

During the first few months of 1984 Loran Roberts, corporate treasurer of Servex, was busy searching for the best way for Servex to obtain, by the middle of the year, $90 million to $100 million in additional cash for a period of not less than ten years. After careful study of the treasurer's memo concerning cash flow forecasts for 1984 (figure 8–1), Mr. J. Baxter Bagby, president and chief executive office of Servex, finally agreed with him that a minimum of $45 million to $50 million additional cash was needed and that $90 million to $100 million was desirable. Mr. Bagby and the whole board of directors of Servex had been reluctant to try to raise the money immediately, because interest rates in 1984 were high. However, as Mr. Roberts pointed out to Mr. William T. Wilson, chairman of the Board of Directors, even though 1984 interest rates were high there was a great deal of loan money available—much more than was available in 1982 and 1983 and more loan money than would probably be available in 1985, when the newly elected U.S. president would most likely have to tighten money to control inflation.

Figure 8–1. Excerpts from a Memo, Roberts to Bagby, January 5, 1984

Simplified Consolidated Cash Flow Forecasts for Calendar 1984

Non-Operating Items

Expected Cash Receipts	$000	
From depreciation and amortization	29,246	
From earnings before taxes	61,921	
	91,167	(rounded to $91,200,000)
Expected Cash Disbursements		
Federal, state, and foreign income taxes	28,492	
Interest expense	15,780	
Capital investments (replacements plus new)	30,175	
Dividends (on preferred stock)	1,381	
(on common stock)	6,025	(minimum)
Repayments (short-term borrowing)	26,137	
(long-term borrowing)	11,478	
	118,468	(rounded to $118,500,000)
Additional Cash Needed		
to meet minimum requirements	$27,300,000	
Less Cash Now Frozen		
as compensating balances for bank loans, which will be freed when loans repaid	5,000,000	
Net Additional Cash Needed		
to meet minimum requirements	$22,300,000	

Figure 8–1 (continued)

Notes on Operating Items Not Shown

Additional cash ($24,700,000) will be needed to finance the increase in inventories, plus the increase in the net of net receivables less payables, required to support Servex's expected 12 percent increase in sales volume in 1984.

	$000	Increase Over 12/31/83 $000
Inventories (Dec. 31, 1983 level + 12%)	171,644	18,390
Net Receivables (Dec. 31, 1983 level + 12%)	147,436	15,797
Payables (Dec. 31 1983 level + 12%)	(88,278)	(9,458)
Total net increase		24,729

Furthermore, it would be highly desirable, though not absolutely necessary, to increase the present ratios of inventories-to-sales, receivables-to-sales, and cash balances-to-sales, and to reduce the present ratio of payables-to-sales, each by 10 percent or more with a further addition of $43,000,000 cash as follows:

Increase in average inventories by about 10 percent $17,000,000

(To reduce production delays and machine changeovers because of materials being out of stock and to reduce costs of transshipment of materials and finished goods necessary to balance inventories between depots)

Increase in average receivables by about 10 percent $15,000,000

(To increase earnings through larger sales volume at higher average prices obtainable if more and longer credit can be extended to customers)

Reduction in average payables by about 10 percent $10,000,000

(To reduce production costs by permitting lower costs for supplies through prompter payment and taking advantage of cash discounts and the like)

Increase in average free (not needed as compensating balances under our bank loan agreements) cash balances by about 20 percent $1,000,000

(To reduce overhead costs by decreasing overtime work in treasurer's office, excess costs of procedures to transfer funds rapidly, and so on)

Total $43,000,000

The percentages for the changes desired are ball-park estimates. The managers who made these estimates feel that about 10 percent or 20 percent would be desirable but that only experience can show whether slightly more or less is needed to achieve the desired results.

Figure 8–1 (continued)

Summary

Additional Cash Needed	
For non-operating items	$22,300,000
For expanded sales volumes	24,700,000
Minimum total needed	$48,000,000
Further Additional Cash Desired to improve operating results	$43,000,000
Recommended Proceeds of Total Long-Term Financing to be sought	$91,000,000

Although Mr. Roberts was glad to have the board's approval, he shuddered at what he expected the attitude of underwriters and lenders to be. In his heart of hearts—something he would never have confessed even to his wife—Mr. Roberts believed that Servex was financially somewhat shaky. It had become shaky, he felt, because Mr. Bagby, hard-driving entrepreneur and salesman that he was, was not sufficiently respectful of and willing to follow the conservative opinions of money managers such as bankers, pension fund managers, trust officers—and Mr. Roberts himself. Mr. Roberts was afraid that, because of Servex's lack of conservative top management, other money managers would not be inclined to loan Servex the enormous amount it so badly needed.

And what, thought Mr. Roberts, if we can't get a loan at all, or have to pay 20 to 30 percent or more a year? Then all Servex can do is hold a fire sale—get rid of subsidiaries and divisions at distress prices, as so many sister conglomerates had to do in 1982 and 1983. If, however, Servex can get $100 million and if the risks of the business come out reasonably right and if, dear God, Bagby will slow down on expensive acquisitions and treat money respectfully, then Servex may do extremely well. Who knows? By 1985 all of Servex's top management may be hailed in the media as heroes of American enterprise.

Servex's basic difficulty was that $37,615,000 in short- and long-term borrowing was coming due in 1984, at a time when Servex's business was increasing and requiring still more capital. The repayments and the financing of increases in business were going to need over $60 million, of which only $12 million was available from net earnings and net depreciation, after taxes, interest, and a minimum dividend had been paid and obsolete capital items had been replaced.

Mr. Roberts had looked at various items on the December 30, 1983, balance sheet as possible sources for some of the necessary cash, but with discouraging results. For example, the "cash" item of $9 million to $10 million was no help. Almost $5 million had to stay on deposit in various banks as the compensating balances that were a condition of Servex's short-term bank borrowings. The remaining $4 million to $5 million was scattered among the 114 checking accounts that Servex and its subsidiaries maintained in the United States and abroad, not to mention several hundred petty-cash and postage accounts, expense advances to travelers, and similar incidentals. Split up that way, the working balances in the 114 checking accounts averaged only about $40,000 each, which was, in Mr. Roberts' opinion, very much too low on average. Payment of one good-sized invoice from a supplier or one good-sized payroll could almost wipe out an average account.

The money itemized on the balance sheet under "payables" (invoices to Servex), "receivables" (invoices from Servex), and "inventories" had already been squeezed as hard as feasible to turn up extra cash. Payables were paid as slowly as could be done while maintaining Servex's credit. Servex's purchasing department was instructed to push suppliers hard for longer credit—90 or 120 days to pay instead of 30 or 60—with the result that sometimes Servex paid higher prices for supplies in order to obtain longer credit. On receivables, Servex's current policy was to extend credit for the shortest possible periods (sometimes accepting a lower price than usual to speed up payment) and to press for prompt payment of any amount due. Inventories of raw and packing materials and of finished goods were currently being held to absolute minimums.

The policy of minimizing receivables and inventories and maximizing payables was designed to maximize Servex's cash, but it was hard on Servex's employees and reputation—and earnings. For that reason, Mr. Roberts pushed for board approval to raise an additional $43,000,000 to ease the operational squeeze.

When Mr. Roberts began a long series of meetings with various money managers, his fears was at once confirmed. Financial vice-presidents of insurance companies, heads of underwriting houses, bankers, stockbrokers, factors, individual wealthy lenders to whom he spoke were polite but pessimistic.

Every potential lender pointed out that the debt/equity ratio on Servex's December 31, 1983, balance sheet was about 45/55. "Add another $62 million in debt—past the $38 million debt you'll be paying off—and your debt/equity ratio will be something like 53/47," said one typical underwriter. "When over 50 percent of your capital is somebody else's money, the somebody else worries, which means any bonds you float will carry a below-par rating. My firm, frankly, doesn't like the idea of underwriting speculative bond issues. At the least, Mr. Roberts, our fee would be bigger than usual—and if that sounds like trading squeamishness for money, well, that's the way it is."

Several of the money men suggested that Servex consider raising cash by selling additional common stock, but J. Baxter Bagby emphatically vetoed that as a possibility. To sell $100 million worth of new Servex common stock would ruin the market price per share of the currently outstanding common stock, cut the earnings per current common share by at least 30 to 40 percent, and outrage every holder of Servex common—perhaps even get Mr. Bagby and the other directors fired. There were almost 5 million unissued shares of common stock in the Servex treasury, but they were intended to be used for acquisitions of new companies whose earnings would contribute to the Servex total.

In the end, Mr. Roberts put together two possible deals for bond issues and reported to the board of directors. The two deals were much alike in their provisions for maturity (July 1, 1997 in both cases), call (repurchase of the bonds at Servex's option), and sinking funds (amounts to be put aside by Servex annually and to be used exclusively for redemption or repurchase of the bonds). There were, however, some important differences, as outlined in table 8–1.

The bond indenture agreement proposed by Skinner Fleabody and Slalom Brothers would require two additional commitments on the part of Servex: (1) not to distribute in dividends on common and preferred stock any more than the cumulative total of two-thirds of all annual net earnings after payments for sinking funds, interest, debt repayment, taxes of all kinds, and any excess of capital investment over depreciation allowances; and (2) not to dispose of any capital assets unless the proceeds were added to the sinking fund or used to repay other debts. The second obligation was to be binding

Table 8–1
Two Possible Deals for Obtaining Additional Cash for Servex

Underwriter	Price of Bond Issue	Face Value of Bonds (millions)	Annual Interest on Bonds	Warrants (millions)	Conversion Option	Sale Procedure
Prudent Fireman's Life Insurance Co.	$100,000,000	$100	14.1%	None	Convertible to common at $20 per share at any time	Prudent Fireman's to buy whole issue for own portfolio
Skinner Fleabody and Slalom Bros.	$96,135,000	$100	13.8%	3	Each warrant convertible to one share of common with additional payment of $16.67 cash to Servex	Bonds to be sold in units of $1000 (30 warrants with each $1000 as a "sweetener")

on Servex's subsidiaries as well. Lastly, there was to be a gentlemen's agreement that the next issue of securities by Servex would be underwritten by Skinner Fleabody and Slalom Brothers.

Questions

1. What other groups would be affected and how by Servex's choice of one deal or the other?
2. Should the general public approve or disapprove of a lender's restricting a company's freedom of action in some ways, as in the deal proposed by Skinner Fleabody and Slalom Brothers?
3. From the point of view of Servex's management, what are the actual and potential disadvantages of each deal? Actual and potential advantages?

Bail-Out or Bankruptcy?

The Wallace Lumber Company was no prize when Servex acquired 86 percent of its stock in 1978, and its situation did not improve over the next few years. Although Mr. Alex Perlman, the president of Wallace, was hard working, enthusiastic, and likable, he had no previous business experience when his father-in-law, Mr. Wallace, made him president of the little company in 1977, and he was slow to acquire the necessary business acumen.

Mr. J. Baxter Bagby, president and chief executive officer of Servex, never visited this small Servex subsidiary, even though business trips took him several times a year to the large Pacific Coast city in which the Wallace lumberyard was located. As far as Mr. Bagby and the other top managers of Servex were concerned, acquisition of the Wallace Lumber Company and the granting of a five-year contract of employment (at an outrageously high salary) to Mr. Wallace's son-in-law were merely part of the price Servex had to pay for the Alpine Fiberboard Company, which Mr. Wallace also owned and Servex really wanted. Mr. Bagby had in mind to sell Servex's shares of Wallace stock whenever a reasonable opportunity came along. However, up to 1982 there were always higher-priority projects than selling off Wallace, and these prevented Servex's top managers from taking the time to search seriously for a buyer.

1982 was a bad year for most U.S. businesses. Money was extremely tight. Interest rates were the highest since the Civil War. Even at exorbitant interest rates lenders were reluctant to lend. Economic activity throughout the United States slowed sharply. The aerospace industry on the West Coast was particularly hard hit by cutbacks in production for the Air Force. Demand for housing and commercial building dropped to almost zero in the city where the Wallace lumberyard was located.

In these circumstances most U.S. businesses were preoccupied with pre-serving their cash and, if possible, increasing it. One basic formula widely used to try to build up cash positions was to collect from customers quickly and pay suppliers slowly. Turning excess inventories into cash was another. Firing employees who had been hired in more exuberant days was also popular.

The Wallace Lumber Company was, of course, in very deep trouble almost immediately following the first signs of recession. In years of generally good business, it had suffered because of Mr. Perlman's poor management. In as bad a year as 1982, Wallace's situation was hopeless.

The worst blow to Wallace came in August, 1982, when the Lavatt Home Company declared bankruptcy, after taking delivery in July of $68,000 worth of lumber from Wallace. In all, Wallace was stuck for $117,000 due from Lavatt. The talk at the creditors' meeting made it clear that there was little hope of collecting more than 10¢ on the dollar from the liquidation of Lavatt's assets.

Worse, in Mr. Perlman's eyes, was that the Lavatt bankruptcy caused the Bank of All the Americas to take a hard look at Wallace Lumber's total financial position at the end of August, 1982. The bank representatives who talked to Mr. Perlman about the results of the examination were polite but very firm. The Bank of All the Americas had for years financed Wallace's inventories and receivables. Over the last six months, Wallace's receivables had soared to $326,000—far past their previous level of about $150,000 to $160,000. "And remember, Alex," one of the representatives reminded Mr. Perlman, "I told you last December that we thought $160,000 in receivables was more than your sales volume warranted and more than the bank was willing to finance long term. Now, you've got over twice that in receivables. Your customers are into you for $326,000, of which the $117,000 from Lavatt is almost certainly a dead loss."

Wallace's inventories were in poor condition, too, the bank's examination found. Inventories were unbalanced, with up to eighteen months sales volume of some items in stock, but little or no stock in several faster-selling items. Besides, poor storage and handling damaged some of the inventory and made it unsalable. The bank had extended Wallace credit of $123,000 to finance these inventories but their real value seemed closer to $100,000. The difficulties cited by the bank officials went on and on, culminating in the sad facts that Wallace's net profit, after years of slow decline, had been only $5134 in 1981 and showed an operating loss of $12,867 for the first eight months of 1982.

"I'll put it briefly, Alex," said one official. "Obviously, the bank can't extend you any further credit, at least not until you reduce your loans from us to a total of $200,000 maximum. What you have to do is to arrange for Servex, your parent company, to put at least $442,000 additional capital into

Table 8–2
Approximate Wallace Position

	8/31/82	Add Capital from Servex	Desired
Assets			
Land, buildings, equipment	85		85
Inventories	100	+ 30	130
Receivables	326		326
Cash	7	+ 163	170
	518		711
Liabilities			
Payables	27		27
Bank loans	449	+ 249	200
Reserve for bad debts	120		120
	596		347
Net worth	(78)		364

Wallace. Look, I'll show you—"and the man pulled out a brief statement of the company's assets and liabilities (table 8–2).

"Face it. Your company is bankrupt for $78,000 and losing money every month on operations. Unless fresh capital is added, the bank is reluctantly going to have to blow the whistle on you—call your loans and put you in bankruptcy. We hate to do that to our customers if there's any alternative, but I can't see you working your way out of this situation. We have to protect the bank's money."

When Mr. Perlman telephoned Mr. Bagby in panic, it took some time to get the story straight. The following day, Mr. Bagby discussed the future of Wallace Lumber Company with his top managers.

"The way I see it, gentlemen," Mr. Bagby began, "is that, first and foremost, I surely hope we'll all learn from this mess that Servex shouldn't have any operation that isn't supervised regularly and closely by a proved excellent manager. If we weren't going to supervise Wallace properly, we should have gotten out of it—sold it for whatever it would bring or just closed it down if we had to. It's my own fault we didn't do that. I hope I've learned a lesson and that you have all learned by my mistake.

"The question now is what to do. Basically, we can take about a half-million dollars out of our other companies and bail the Wallace operation out—actually, dammit, bail the bank out, because the bank would surely lose a big chunk of its $449,000 if Wallace went bankrupt. We'd have to put in someone able to turn Wallace, of course. We're bound by contract to let Perlman stay on as president, but luckily the contract doesn't say he has to be the real boss—the chief executive officer.

"To my mind, a bail-out has a couple of advantages. Chiefly, it keeps Servex's credit clean with the Bank of All the Americas and the whole banking community. It's important to us to have the banks on our side, or we'll find that every one of Servex's operations will have constant trouble getting reasonably large bank loans at reasonable interest. Not to mention that bank-managed trust funds and pension funds are the main buyers of Servex stock these days. Second, I'd like to avoid the bad publicity the bankruptcy of a Servex subsidiary would get us in the business press. Just imagine how it would look—"Servex Subsidiary Goes Bankrupt for $78,000." Servex would look like a nickel-and-dime outfit in trouble over a lousy $78,000 and it would, I think, make a lot of our suppliers tighten up on credit to other Servex operations. Also, it surely wouldn't help the market price of Servex bonds or stock, or please our stockholders and bondholders.

"Still, let's look at the other side. What if we do let Wallace go bankrupt? It definitely would be cheaper. It would save us about a half-million dollars as well as the expensive fuss of trying to salvage a two-bit operation. I just can't picture ever making a profit of our half-million—even if we use, say, young Joe Vogel to run Wallace. What if he did turn Wallace around so it was making $20,000 to $25,000 a year? That might look like a profit, but the same half-million dollars and the same bright, young Joe would make us $100,000 a year or more on any one of the really attractive expansion projects in Europe or the United States.

'What do you gentlemen think? Bail-out or bankruptcy?"

Questions

1. Should Servex let Wallace go bankrupt or not? Why?
2. What groups will be affected by Servex's decision? What rights, if any, do they have in the matter?
3. Suppose that, if Wallace were to go bankrupt, its eigteen employees would lose not only their jobs (at a time and place where jobs are extremely hard to find) but also their accumulated pension rights. Does that supposition make a difference to your decision? Why or why not?

9
The Trade

A manufacturing company must have a method of selling and delivering its products to the people or companies who use them. Because a company making diesel locomotives has so few potential customers, it can simply send its own salesmen to sell to the railroads, its final consumers. When a manufacturer's products are less expensive and the number of potential consumers is larger, a manufacturer usually relies on a chain of independent middlemen—agents, distributors, wholesalers, and retailers—to sell to final consumers. These middlemen are called "the trade." In the United States some cosmetics and vacuum cleaners are still sold door-to-door by a manufacturer's own salespeople but, in general, consumer goods and inexpensive industrial products are bought from manufacturers by middlemen for eventual resale to consumers.

The manufacturer wants the trade to favor his products over those of competitors by working harder at selling his goods; by displaying, advertising, and promoting them more; and by selling them at lower prices (and lower dealer profits). He also wants the trade to buy maximum quantities at list prices; to maintain high inventories of all the manufacturer's products; to accept delivery in truckload or carload lots to a single destination; to handle and warehouse the products carefully; to service them (if necessary) to each consumer's complete satisfaction; and to pay for them as early as possible.

Satisfying any one of the manufacturer's desires costs the trade extra money. The trade naturally wants the manufacturer not only to bear these costs but also to accept some of the trade's costs. These include the cost of handling coupons (most manufacturers now pay a handling fee for coupons, which the trade feels is insufficient) and extra costs of display space (some manufacturers now "rent" retailers' display spaces for their product). Above all, a wholesaler or retailer wants a lower price from the manufacturer than he charges competitors. Although the Robinson-Patman Act forbids unjustified price differences, there are many legal ways in which a manufacturer can reduce his price to the trade. He can, for example, grant longer than usual credit.

As is usual when a corporation deals with any of its constituencies, there is potential conflict. The manufacturer can help or hurt a member of the trade (a wholesaler or retailer) who in turn can help or hurt the manufacturer. The exact bargaining strength of each side over a period of time determines which of them is helped or hurt in what ways when. Each absolutely needs the other: the manufacturer must have the trade to get his goods sold to consumers, and the trade must have plentiful supplies of attractive, reasonably priced goods that its customers want to buy. How much of what distribution costs is it "fair" for each party to pay? Neither side can always get the best deal.

Other parties are affected by what happens between manufacturers and the trade. A poor deal for a retailer can mean higher prices to people who buy from him; a poor deal for a manufacturer may force him to lay off workers or pay them less. Everything relates to everything else. The following incidents suggest only a few of the many problems involved in this complicated area of corporate social responsibility.

The Operator

The Sinbad Paint Company, a division of Servex's Plastic and Petrochemicals Group, has a fairly extensive export business. Its usual procedure for distributing its products in a foreign country is to have a local distributor sell them. The product with which it normally does very well abroad is a specially prepared, high-temperature aircraft paint. In most export countries special aircraft paint accounts for 75 to 80 percent of Sinbad's sales and over 90 percent of its profits. However, in a certain small Latin American country, its distributor has done very poorly with aircraft paint. Annual sales for all brands of such special paints in this country are small—only about $85,000 total—but Sinbad sells less than $2000 a year or less than 2 percent of the market. Curiously, the local distributor does well with some other Sinbad paints and chemicals, and the company has 20 to 30 percent of the market in a few very competitive types of standard product. In spite of Japanese, German, and other American competition in standard products, these Sinbad sales look pretty good. Sales volume in Sinbad's standard products in the country has risen steadily over the years, from $6000 in 1965 to $138,000 in 1983.

Mr. Baxter, the president of Sinbad, recently took a trip around Latin America to visit distributors, and he accidentally discovered why Sinbad's aircraft paints were doing so poorly in this one country. Sinbad's local distributor, Mr. Gomes, was a very able man and a real star as a salesman. After half a day with him visiting the trade, Mr. Baxter felt that Mr. Gomes could easily sell the legendary iceboxes to Eskimos. The trade on which they called, however, did not carry any special aircraft paint. In a casual dinner conversation with another American businessman, Mr. Baxter discovered that the country had only a very few privately owned aircraft that might use Sinbad's special paints. It did have a small air force and a state-owned airline. Selecting a supplier of paint for the government's needs was a simple procedure: the distributor with the most political pull got the orders. No one really knew what was good or bad in specialty paints—the important thing was who knew whom. Mr. Gomes, unfortunately, belonged to the Nacional party, which was "out" politically. The distributor for the Japanese competitive line, Mr. Jorges, was "in." In fact, Mr. Jorges was the son-in-law of the president of the country. Hence, the Japanese paint got the military and government orders, at very fat markups.

A few months later, Mr. Baxter received a letter from Mr. Jorges. Mr. Jorges' letter requested that Sinbad consider appointing him exclusive distributor in that country for Sinbad's aircraft specialty line of paints. Mr. Jorges felt that if he were distributor and proper distributor margins were established, he could increase sales to perhaps $200,000 a year.

Mr. Baxter had a distributor's contract with Mr. Gomes that permitted Sinbad to cancel all or any part of the agreement if the distributor were not performing reasonably well. "Reasonably" was not defined, but failure to obtain a decent market share could be seen as cause for partial or total cancellation.

While Mr. Baxter was thinking over how he should reply, he received word through the industry grapevine that Mr. Jorges had also requested the country-wide distributorships for one German and two other American specialty aircraft paint lines. Apparently Mr. Jorges was trying to set up a local monopoly in special aircraft paints. He clearly had the only market in the country locked in. If he were distributor for all the aircraft paint sold there, he could probably get the price up and profit heavily. One American competitor was said to be about to grant the request on the grounds that any sales were better than none. The intentions of the German firm were not known.

Questions

1. What should Mr. Baxter do about Mr. Jorges' request for exclusive distribution rights in this Latin American country? Why?
2. Does Mr. Gomes have any rights here? If so, what are they?
3. Suppose that in the past forty years the country has had thirty-three changes of the party in power, the most recent being eighteen months ago. Or suppose the same party has been in power for the last twenty-seven years. Would this make any difference in your answer? Why or why not?

4. Does it ever make good sense to rely on political connections in the sale of highly technical products? When?

Price Cutting

One of the Lask Furniture Company's major customers is the A-to-Z Home Furnishings Company, a regional chain of retail outlets, located mainly in the southern United States. This chain carries home furnishings of all sorts, offers easy credit, and advertises heavily on television. In 1981 Lask's sales to this company were $500,000 out of Lask's total sales of about $1.3 million.

In early 1982 the A-to-Z chain was in deep financial trouble, which led to its acquisition in mid-1970 by an eastern entrepreneur. He immediately began to switch the A-to-Z stores to discount operations, stressing very low prices but little or no credit. Up to this time, the usual retail gross profit margin on Lask products was 36 percent; with its new discount policy, A-to-Z's margins on Lask goods were as low as 12 percent because of sharp retail price reductions. Lask did not change its prices, although A-to-Z purchasing people indicated that A-to-Z's orders for 1983 might go as high as $900,000. The new discount-for-cash policy seemed to be working well for A-to-Z, and sales were rising rapidly.

At a December 1982 furniture buyers' convention, Mr. George Gempler, president of Lask, heard many complaints about A-to-Z from his other customers in the South. They were very disturbed by the price competition caused by A-to-Z's heavy discounting, and they were angry at Lask for allowing it. They felt that they were losing sales rapidly and demanded that Lask do something about disciplining A-to-Z for cutting margins. A typical statement from one of A-to-Z's competitors was, "George, a lot of the buyers are sore about that smart-aleck New Yorker dropping prices on the Lask line. I can't even open the store in the morning for a 12 percent margin! You'd better tell A-to-Z to get in line or you'll shut off his water! If you don't, lots of us aren't going to buy from Lask any more. It's A-to-Z or us!" Lask's sales to all these southern buyers put together totaled around $350,000 a year and had been slowly increasing for many years.

Mr. Gempler listened carefully to his southern customers, but did not commit himself. He promised that he would look closely into the whole matter and let everyone know shortly what Lask would do.

Questions

1. Should Mr. Gempler worry about this problem very much? Why or why not?

2. Many of the buyers upset by A-to-Z's discount practices are old, established customers who have done business with Lask for thirty years or more. What rights, if any, do they have in this situation? Why?

3. The A-to-Z merchandising idea leads to lower prices for consumers, but less credit availability. What rights, if any, do consumers have here? Why?

4. What should Mr. Gempler do? Why?

Should We Sell to Anyone Who Wants to Buy?

In September, 1984, the most important project at the home office of Michel and Carson, Inc. was arranging to introduce to the trade its new line of filing cabinets. Lars Larson, president of Michel and Carson, felt he had good reasons for optimism about the salability of the new line. Even though extremely expensive, the new cabinets not only were of the highest quality in every way but also included several European-developed features that made them by far the most efficient and convenient filing cabinets ever sold in the United States. They would be, Mr. Larson thought, decidedly the Cadillacs of the office furniture world. According to Michel and Carson's estimates, sales of the new cabinets would account for only about 0.2 of 1 percent of total filing cabinet units sold in the United States but, because of their high prices, they would account for almost 1 percent of total dollar sales of filing cabinets.

Mr. Larson and the Michel and Carson sales people were preoccupied with the problem of whether to introduce the new cabinets on an exclusive franchise basis or offer them to all the retailers to whom Michel and Carson was selling its other items. If they decided on the franchise method, the company would divide the United States into territories and sell the new line to only one retailer in each territory. The chief advantage of franchising seemed to be that any store chosen as the exclusive retailer for a territory would naturally be more eager to push the new line than if every office furniture outlet in his territory also handled it. An exclusive dealer would not be threatened with price-cutting by other stores in his area. Since any advertising or promotion he did on the cabinets would benefit only his store, he would be inclined to advertise them relatively heavily, to feature them in store displays, and to promote them however he could.

The chief disadvantage of franchising was that it would tend to anger any dealer who was not chosen as an exclusive dealer for the new line. An angry dealer might not buy as many other items as usual. Also, among the customers of those dealers not chosen for a franchise would be a number of potential buyers of the new filing cabinets. If the new line were sold on an exclusive franchise basis, some potential buyers might never know that it was available or they might buy competitive top quality cabinets from dealers who were not franchised.

If Michel and Carson decided to franchise, they would have to decide also whether the exclusive territories should each be large enough to cover a population of 3 million to 5 million people or only 100,000 to 200,000 people. Making the territories large would mean that the dealers could be very carefully selected for the size, reputation, and aggressiveness of their business. It would also probably mean, however, that a very large number of important dealers would be angry at not being among the fifty or so chosen. If a great many dealers—say, 1500—were franchised, then franchises could not be carefully selected, there would be some price-cutting and transshipping across territorial lines, and the dealers would not be wildly enthusiastic about pushing the new line. Fewer important dealers would be angry, however, because fewer would be left out.

It was a real problem to decide whether to franchise and, if franchising were chosen, to decide how large the exclusive territories should be.

Questions

1. What groups will be affected and how by Michel and Carson's decision to grant or not to grant exclusive franchises?
2. Suppose that, if exclusive franchises are granted, the average retail price of one of the new filing cabinets will be $18.69 higher than if no franchises had been granted. Would this supposition affect your answer to the preceding question? If so, how would your answer be affected?
3. What rights does an office-furniture dealer currently buying from Michel and Carson have to a franchise for the new line, if the company decides to franchise it?
4. Does U.S. society in general have an interest in the principle of franchising? If so, what interest?

The Big Buyer

A-to-Z Home Furnishings Company is a major buyer from Lask Furniture Company. Since shifting to a discount operation, A-to-Z has steadily increased its purchases from Lask, and they now are running at an annual rate of $900,000.

Recently the head buyer of A-to-Z Company, Mr. Barnes, visited Lask's president, Mr. Gempler. He pointed out that he was now by far the biggest buyer of Lask products. While Lask's home furnishings were excellent and sold well, A-to-Z felt they would sell much better if prices could be reduced a bit. If Lask could get their prices down by 10 percent, say, A-to-Z's purchases from Lask would easily go above $1.3 million a year, Mr. Barnes said.

Mr. Gempler was aware that he had many other buyers in A-to-Z's marketing area, although collectively they accounted for only about $350,000 of Lask's annual sales. If he went along with A-to-Z, he would be giving a special discount to his largest customer—he could not afford to drop his prices 10 percent for all his customers—and he would risk becoming a captive supplier. A-to-Z already accounted for well over 50 percent of Lask's total sales; Mr. Gempler was not sure that he would want to have so much of his production tied up by one customer. If he gave the discounts and A-to-Z's purchases rose as predicted, Lask would be even more a captive producer than it now was. Moreover, he would be in danger of federal prosecution under the Robinson-Patman Act unless he could prove that Lask's cost of sales to A-to-Z was sufficiently lower than to other customers to warrant a special 10 percent discount. Of course, Lask could put out a slightly different line just for A-to-Z, price it differently, and thus probably avoid charges of price discrimination. Mr. Gempler decided to talk to the Household Furnishings Group vice-president before he made a decision about the special discount A-to-Z was requesting.

Questions

1. Should Mr. Gempler give these special prices? Why or why not?
2. If you were the Servex vice-president, would you approve of one of your subsidiaries becoming a captive supplier to an independent discount retailer? Why?
3. Suppose A-to-Z is run by a brilliant but erratic entrepreneur, who is known for his quick reversals of key policies. Does this change your answers to the first two questions? Why?
4. Do other Lask customers have any rights in this situation? If so, what? If not, why not?

New Orders

Westport Brass and Milling's new line of industrial robots, introduced in 1984, was doing extremely well in a highly competitive market. First year sales were over $11.8 million, and Jason Lopata, Westport's president, felt that sales would reach over $50 million by 1986.

In late 1984, Lorna Mitchell, Westport's export manager, received an inquiry from Sweden concerning the possible purchase of about $32 million worth of these robots, to be delivered in 1985–1986. This was by far the largest order inquiry she had ever received, and it came from an unknown distributor in Stockholm. That many robots would staff a quite large factory, and Ms. Mitchell had no idea that anyone in Sweden was in the market for so many industrial robots. It was common in this industry for all suppliers to keep close tabs on any firms that might be seriously interested in placing major orders for domestic or foreign markets.

Ms. Mitchell sent along sales brochures, and at the 1984 European machine tool trade fair in Paris, she met Mr. Larson, who said he was president of this Swedish distributor. Typically for such large orders, the company buying would order directly from the manufacturer. Mr. Larson was charming but evasive when asked about where the robots would be put to use.

On returning to the home office, Ms. Mitchell talked to Jason Lopata about the order. Mr. Larson had said he was ready to place a firm order, accompanied by an irrevocable letter of credit, as soon as Westport gave him a few specifics about some minor technical details and delivery dates.

"Jason, I'm suspicious of this deal. I think the robots are going to the Soviet Union."

"Is that legal, Lorna?" Mr. Lopata asked.

"It depends. If we export to Sweden, it's usually easy to obtain an export license. But anything going to communist countries requires a special export license, and it can be hard to get. The U.S. government is very nervous these days about high-technology exports that might lead to the Soviets' getting an edge."

Mr. Lopata sighed. "And our robots are very, very high-tech, for sure. The microcomputers, all fourteen of them, in our robots have chips that few other companies even know about, let alone use." He thought for a moment. "But Lorna, we don't know that the robots are going to the Soviet Union."

"No, we don't, Jason. But there's no firm in Scandinavia now that would use that many, and I know Larson isn't just building inventory."

"It's an awfully big order, Lorna."

"I know. But some U.S. companies have been caught and fined for shipping to neutrals, when they know, or should have known, what the ultimate destination was."

"What should we do? We really don't know anything for sure."

"I agree," Ms. Mitchell said. "And remember, if this sale goes through, you'll owe me about $85,000 as a bonus for exceeding my sales quota. I could use that. But we could get into some trouble if we're not careful."

"So how do we be careful, Lorna?"

"I can check with the U.S. Department of Commerce before we confirm the order. The feds will let us know, one way or the other, what we should do. If they say no, it's no, and we don't confirm. We'll have to apply for an export license in any case, but if we say nothing, the odds are good that we'll get one."

"Even if you ask in advance, they might say OK, Lorna."

Ms. Mitchell shrugged. "And they might not. We could just go ahead and hope that no one notices. So far, no one in our line has had too much trouble getting export licenses, but then no one has robots as good as ours, either."

Mr. Lopata nodded thoughtfully. "I wonder if I should go to headquarters on this one. It could get all of Servex a bad name."

Questions

1. What should Mr. Lopata do?
2. If you heard about this order at Servex headquarters, how would you answer Mr. Lopata's query? Why?
3. What should Ms. Mitchell do? She's out $85,000 if the order falls through?

10
The Consumers

Consumers, like other participants in the economic game, want the best of all possible worlds: low prices, high-quality goods, and the best service. When consumers fail to get these, as they usually do, they pressure governments and firms to correct the supposed inequities.

What is unfair depends on one's circumstances. Not long ago, people would have considered it a major gain if enough food could be provided for 99 percent of the U.S. population; now people complain about the price of steak. If you lived in a nineteenth-century slum, you would probably welcome almost any shelter; now even a modestly decent house may not seem enough. As people's expectations change about what they want and can get, so does their satisfaction with what is actually available.

Several factors combine to explain why the average person in the United States is dissatisfied with what probably would have been highly satisfactory fifty years ago. Advances in technology and increases in productivity have enabled him to have material possessions and comforts in amounts almost unimaginable early in this century. The media, especially television, and the higher level of education attained by the average person have made him much more aware of just how well the middle and upper economic classes live. Above all, there is no fixed amount of material possessions or physical comfort that satisfies a person. His satisfaction depends on how much he has relative to what other people have, especially those with whom he compares himself. He wants to "keep up with the Joneses"—and to be ahead of them, if possible. Of course, this pursuit of material superiority is probably more a permanent human trait than a modern invention. In the last fifty years, however, the infinite nature of human acquisitiveness and the impossibility of fulfilling all human needs and wants may have ironically become more apparent as opportunities for material satisfaction have increased.

Servex's consumers, like those of most other companies, are a self-selected group. Only when there is a monopoly as in public utilities are consumers forced to use a particular company's products. The seller's doctrine used to be *caveat emptor:* Let the buyer beware. If he was dumb enough to buy something harmful or useless, that was his problem. Now it is increasingly recognized that no consumer can possibly know enough to buy wisely all the complex products he uses. Laws are steadily pressuring manufacturers to provide new warranties and additional information about products so that buyers can overcome their ignorance. Arguments about what is or is not "reasonable" ignorance continue. Few customers would recognize, for example, a poison in the list of ingredients on the label of a modern product; but is a large "poison" warning on the side of a can of insecticide adequate to make the consumer use it with proper care?

Collectively, a company's consumers have unbeatable bargaining strength. If no one buys its products, the company is soon out of business. This happens more frequently than most people realize. Individually, however, consumers usually have negligible bargaining strength, since the typical company has thousands or millions of consumers and one more or less does not matter. As a result, a dissatisfied consumer is likely to try, or threaten to try, to obtain the sympathy and support of additional consumers and of other constituencies such as government and unions.

In recent years, there has been a major consumer movement. It is alleged (and there is considerable evidence to support some of the allegations) that consumers are defrauded, sold poor-quality goods, lent money at exorbitant rates, sold unsafe items, and so on. Such pressures have led to considerable consumer-oriented legislation in the United States, including auto safety rules, a truth-in-lending act, and the formation of the Office of Consumer Affairs. Government is doing more and more to protect consumers from abuses by sellers. Companies are under constant legal and informal pressures to give the consumer a better break, and such pressures seem likely to increase in the future.

The following incidents cover some of the consumer problems a large company is likely to face. As usual, the question of who gets what is very relevant. The seller wants to keep the cost of the product low and to make as much profit as he can; the buyer wants to obtain as much value as he can. Conflict is inevitable.

Honor among Thieves

One of the Lucky Jim discount stores is located in a high-income neighborhood near a major midwestern university. It has consistently been one of the more profitable stores in the Lucky Jim chain. In 1982, shoplifting losses at this store suddenly showed a sharp increase. In 1979, they were the smallest in the chain; by 1983, such losses had reached the level of stores in much less affluent neighborhoods. When they reached $18,000 a month (turning what would otherwise have been a profit into an overall monthly loss of $7000), the manager initiated a get-tough campaign. With the encouragement of the midwestern division manager, he made the following changes:

1. Security surveillance was increased. A detective was hired for $800 a month to be in the store eight hours a day. He was a capable, retired fifty-year-old local police detective; within a week arrests for shoplifting jumped from one or two a week to between fifteen and twenty.
2. All shoplifters were prosecuted. Previously, if the shoplifter offered restitution, the store did not bother to prosecute; now, every shoplifter apprehended was taken to court. Furthermore, the store sought newspaper publicity on these court cases, whereas formerly the store had begged the newspaper to play down the few prosecutions.
3. An additional $5000 worth of special mirrors and other detection devices were installed in the store. After these were installed, the number of arrests for shoplifting jumped to approximately thirty a week.

A study of the shoplifting pattern revealed that by far the largest group of shoplifters were university students. Many of them regarded shoplifting not as a crime, but as a sport that they had a right to engage in. Others, with low incomes, really needed the things they lifted.

Within a month, shoplifting arrests dropped to the former level of one or two, and monthly losses dropped from $18.000 to less than $5000. But the store manager had acquired some new enemies. College student shoplifters often telephoned from the police station to their parents, who seemed very upset that juveniles or teenagers should be accused of felonies (shoplifting was a felony in this state). Both parents and offenders felt that the punishments (which typically ranged from two- to six-month jail sentences, normally suspended for first offenders, plus fines of $100 to $500) were too severe.

In several cases, the person convicted was a second or third time offender. A star basketball player on the university varsity team was one of these; when a judge sentenced him to ninety days in the county jail for his second offense, the university team lost three straight games and the store manager received more than twenty nasty letters. A girl from an upper-middle-class family was given a sixty-day sentence; she tried to commit suicide in jail, and once again many persons felt the store was responsible.

Also, some mistakes were made. The store now faces two false arrest suits in which a person was arrested but turned out (it is alleged) to be innocent. The store's lawyers think they can win one of these cases, since the person is probably guilty; the other case will probably be settled out of court for much less (perhaps $5000) than the $100,000 sought in damages. The legal fees for the two cases are estimated at $7000.

The county prosecutor was less than enthusiastic about the store's policy

144 • *Corporate Social Responsibility*

of prosecuting all shoplifters. The surge of cases had further clogged local courts. Other stores, seeing the success of the Lucky Jim program, were seriously considering doing the same thing. If the number of prosecutions increased much more, the court backlog would become intolerable. Moreover, many students demanded jury trials, which took still more resources and time for many citizens.

Questions

1. Was Lucky Jim's technique of reducing shoplifting a good one? Why or why not?
2. What other options might this Lucky Jim store have tried?
3. Does the punishment fit the crime in this situation? Why or why not?

Product Safety

The Sinbad Paint Company produces a line of high-temperature, special paints for various aircraft uses. Sales are normally made to maintenance bases, military groups, airlines, and aircraft manufacturers. The paints are extremely dangerous to handle, and customers are warned in writing on the cans and in special brochures about how to handle them safely. Sinbad sales-representatives from time to time also comment on the dangers of mishandling paints when they visit places where the paints are used.

Recently (perhaps by accident) part of a large shipment of Sinbad paint that had been delivered to the U.S. Air Force was declared surplus property, and 8240 cases were sold to surplus dealers. The surplus dealers in turn sold the paint to retail dealers serving ordinary consumers. Last week, Mr. Eldridge Jones was using a can of Sinbad's special paint to paint his garage. His young son slipped, fell into the paint tray, swallowed some paint, and died within twenty-four hours.

The story was played up in the local press, and Sinbad was accused of putting dangerous products on the market. An energetic reporter who investigated various Air Force accident reports discovered that often airmen applying these paints were painfully burned when their skin came in contact with the wet paint. In two cases, injuries were serious enough to require that the injured airmen receive medical discharges.

Questions

1. Is it right for Sinbad to market such a dangerous product? Why or why not?
2. You are a Sinbad public relations assistant who is about to be inter-

viewed by the press concerning this accident. Prepare your opening statement and indicate how you will handle questions about the problem.
3. These high-temperature paints are irreplaceable for certain aircraft uses. The next time you fly, your life will depend in part on the quality of these paints around the engines. Does this change your answer? Why or why not?
4. Sinbad's research staff estimates that they could come up with a safer substitute in two years for perhaps $400,000. The researchers define the "safer" paint they think they could develop as one that would do the job of the present paint, but reduce the intensity of skin burns (from contact with wet paint) by 40 to 45 percent. In cases of accidental swallowing, 8 to 10 grams (about ⅓ ounce) of the present paint is ordinarily fatal to a small child, compared to an estimated 12 to 15 grams of the hoped-for safer paint. Of course, development of the safer paint would mean deferring other research interests, including an improved safety belt for autos. Would you order the research people to shift to paint safety research? Why or why not?

There Is Less to This Warranty Than Meets the Eye

"It's simple dollars and cents, George." The accountant's voice was stern as he laid a sheet of figures in front of George Gempler, the president of Lask Furniture. "I *know* we've always advertised 'Now at Lask You Can Be Sure' and 'We at Lask Guarantee Everything We Sell.' It's just that times have changed and Lask has to change with them. Our guarantee policy of paying for transportation and repairs on any Lask product that buyers find fault with has been hitting profits harder each year. For 1984, replacements, repairs by dealers, and transportation under our guarantees took $10.30 of every net $100 of sales! George, Lask has got to either raise prices or drop that company policy of guaranteeing everything."

"Okay, Ed, okay," Mr. Gempler said gloomily. "Leave the figures with me, and I'll see what I can do." Mr. Gempler had reason for gloom. Lask's profit margins had been declining since 1979, and his superiors in the Servex parent company had been increasingly pressuring him to find a way of restoring Lask's profit margins to the industry average, at least. Production costs were up, of course, but the vicious price competition in Lask's best-selling items—folding bridge tables and chairs—kept Mr. Gempler from authorizing an increase in prices. In addition, the famous Lask guarantee cost over 10 percent of Lask's price to the trade. Still, it had been Lask's pride for almost fifty years that "Now At Lask You Can Be Sure," and Mr. Gempler felt consumers were bound to feel that Lask quality was superior.

Maybe people do not care about quality the way they used to, Mr. Gempler thought. Today's consumers seem to want to buy things like folding bridge tables for rock-bottom prices and then throw them away when they break. What does it matter that a bridge table made out of something stronger than staples and cardboard would last longer? An affluent society—the richest in the world—and maybe, Mr. Gempler lamented, all it wants is disposable trash. With that thought he settled down to study Ed's sheet of figures.

Two figures in particular caught Mr. Gempler's attention. Of the total guarantee costs, transportation—getting faulty furniture to the dealer for repair and back to the buyer—accounted for 26.8 percent. Repair or replacement of the Silan simulated leather upholstery on Lask's folding bridge tables and chairs accounted for another 23.6 percent of the total guarantee costs. Silan (a heavily advertised brand name for certain plastic products manufactured by a large chemical company) resists abrasion and staining, but it tears fairly easily under certain unusual circumstances and its color changes somewhat after prolonged exposure to sunlight.

On the basis of these figures, Mr. Gempler drafted a revised warranty for all Lask products. The company's lawyers could look it over and revise it later. Mr. Gempler believed that if the new warranty were substituted for the earlier company policy on guarantees, Lask's before-tax profit margin would rise from about 8 percent to about 13 percent. Mr. Gempler's rough draft of the new warranty read as follows:

> Lask Furniture guarantees full customer satisfaction on all of its products and will repair or replace unsatisfactory merchandise on the following terms: (1) any unsatisfactory product must be returned to the original Lask dealer within six months of purchase; (2) product satisfaction is guaranteed under normal use only; (3) this guarantee applies only to those portions of the product that Lask manufactures (upholstery not included); (4) the customer will arrange both to deliver to the dealer and to pick up from the dealer any product to be repaired or replaced.

Before implementing the new warranty for Lask products on a nation-wide basis, Mr. Gempler wanted to discuss it with his superiors at Servex.

Questions

1. Should Lask put the new warranty into effect? Why or why not?
2. If you were buying a set of bridge table and chairs, how much additional would *you* pay for a "full" guarantee versus the "limited" guarantee Mr. Gempler is considering.
3. What does "full customer satisfaction guaranteed" mean to you? For how long? Under what circumstances? What parts of the product?

The Poor Pay More

One of the smaller (18.000 square feet) stores in Servex's Lucky Jim discount chain is located in a very poor, black section of a major midwestern city. This store, among the first established in the chain, opened in 1953, when the neighborhood was largely middle class. As the neighborhood changed the store's sales volume slipped a little, but it was still a modestly profitable outlet.

In 1979, Lucky Jim opened a major store (42,000 square feet) in a high-volume shopping center in a nearby suburb. At that time, Lucky Jim's management considered closing the old store. Since it was still marginally profitable, however, and the only store of its type within several square miles, they decided to keep it open.

In the past few years, the store has become more of a problem. Because it is a high-cost operation, profits have been below the average for the Lucky Jim chain even though markups have been higher. Petty theft, vandalism, and insurance costs are more than twice as high for this store as for the suburban one. Furthermore, the street pattern around the store prevents large trucks from getting to the back of the store, and so economies of volume deliveries cannot be achieved. During a riot in 1969, the store suffered $82,000 in damages. At that time, Lucky Jim wanted to close the store. However, the mayor asked Lucky Jim to repair the store and keep it open for at least a year or two, because it would not only provide jobs badly needed in the neighborhood but also signify that the white establishment was not abandoning the area. Lucky Jim's managers agreed, although they felt that prices charged in the store would have to reflect real costs, including the riot damage costs. They feared that higher prices would reduce sales volume still further and lead to an overall loss on the store's operation.

In mid-1983, a local black group started a boycott of the store. They alleged (and proved the allegation by comparison shopping at the suburban Lucky Jim's) that prices were from 10 to 25 percent higher at the inner-city store. Moreover, almost 20 percent of the store's personnel were white, although the immediate neighborhood was 95 percent black. Of the store's twenty-seven personnel, there were five whites and twenty-two blacks; both the manager and assistant manager were white.

The black group demanded that prices at the inner-city Lucky Jim's be lowered to equal those at the suburban store and that all employees be black. The leader of the black group told newspaper and television reporters that the group's demands were nonnegotiable: the boycott would be continued until the demands were met. In a dramatic interview on the city's principal television station, he emphasized that it was just about impossible for poor blacks to believe that white businessmen were not exploiting them. "Look," he said, "here you've got a white-owned, white-managed giant chain of stores. When they sell to whites, they charge low prices. When they're the only store in a black area, they use their monopoly to charge poor blacks sky-high prices! Racism—that's what we're boycotting and will always boycott!" During the first week of the boycott, sales dipped 35 percent, and the inner-city store slipped badly into the red, losing over $1900. Normally, the store would earn about $110 a week in net profits, or $5000 to $6000 a year. The suburban Lucky Jim's, with much larger sales volume and lower unit costs, typically netted $100,000 or more a year.

Questions

1. What should Lucky Jim's management do? Be specific.
2. You are the manager on whom a delegation from the boycotting group is calling tomorrow. Prepare a response to its demands.
3. Does Lucky Jim, in the situation described, have any reponsibility besides making money? If not, why not? If so, what is it?
4. Lucky Jim's management needs two seasoned, able employees—a manager and an assistant manager—for a new store nearing completion in a nearby city. If the inner-city store closes, its manager and assistant manager would be ideal for the new store, where they would manage an operation estimated to generate approximately $150,000 in annual net profits. Given this information, what would be the real cost to Lucky Jim of keeping the inner-city store open?

Honesty in Packaging

Under its own label, Servex's Lucky Jim discount store chain very successfully marketed a line of spray paints. The paints retailed for $1.88 for a one-pint (16 fluid ounces) spray can. Most competitive one-pint spray cans retailed for $1.98 to $2.29.

In mid-1984, the supplier of this line raised price quotations to Lucky Jim by 6 percent. Higher labor and materials costs were given as the main reasons for the increase. Lucky Jim had been able to retail the cans of paint for low prices because it bought them in very large volume from one supplier and shaved the ordinary retail margin a bit. Hence, the price increase had to be passed on to the customer—Lucky Jim had no choice.

Lucky Jim chose to raise the price by ordering new supplies of the paint in 14-ounce cans, still retail priced at $1.88. The supplier's price to Lucky Jim for a 14-ounce can remained the same as it had been for a 16-ounce can. (The cost to the supplier of the 14-ounce container was almost exactly the same as for a 16-ounce container; but since the materials cost was lower, the supplier received the 6 percent price increase). As Lucky Jim's president pointed out at a management meeting, virtually no customer ever checks a label to see exactly how much a can contains. Lucky Jim's sales of this line in fact held up very well after the change. Customers who had been getting 16 ounces now received 14 ounces, but they didn't seem to pay much attention and there were only a few scattered complaints in the first six months following the change.

Questions

1. Was it ethical to increase the price to consumers in this particular way? Why or why not?
2. How else might Lucky Jim have dealt with the supplier's increase?
3. Should customers have been told about the change in amount of contents in a more attention-getting way than just changing the small print on the sides of the cans? Why or why not?

Immoral Ads

Vepcoland Mobile Inc. manufactures, among other things, a wide variety of parts for older autos and trucks, including axle shafts, wheel bearings, and transmission parts. Typically it markets these products in volume to various parts distributors, which in turn sell them to parts dealers around the world. Over 80 percent of total sales are in the United States, with about half (some $2.4 million) being auto parts.

As the competition to supply original manufacturers has intensified, Vepcoland has dropped out of this market. It originally planned to phase out all auto parts production by 1980; however, for various reasons, including the rapidly increasing cost of new cars, older cars have tended to stay on the road longer. In 1984, the average age of U.S. cars was about 7.5 years, up over two years from the 1980 average. One result has been that Vepcoland keeps selling mechanical parts for older cars. Since the tooling has long been amortized, this is quite a cash cow for Vepcoland. Only $920,000 of direct cost is incurred in selling those $2.4 million of auto parts.

Vepcoland has never advertised much to sell the parts, with an occasional specialty ad in auto parts dealers' magazines being their only sales effort. Indeed, many of their parts are put in boxes carrying the distributors' brand name.

Recently, Mervin Thomas, president of Vepcoland, was visited by Jack McCann, who represents a group of independent parts distributors. This group has its own Washington lobbyist, who tries to present to congressmen the point of view of these distributors. Mr. McCann showed Mr. Thomas some plans for a new ad campaign that the distributors were planning as a group. The ads would be used on TV during periods when many males might be watching, such as during sports events. Such people tended to own older cars. Mr. McCann wondered if Mr. Thomas might be interested in partially supporting this promotion, to the tune of perhaps $50,000 per year, since Vepcoland benefited greatly from sales of older-car parts.

Mr. Thomas promised to take a look. He was well aware that Mr. McCann had a lot of influence with distributors, and Mr. Thomas was anxious to stay on the right side of this group. Recently there had been heavy new competition from imports, and although the import quality wasn't great, prices were low. Distributors could easily shift orders away from Vepcoland.

The proposed ads had two major themes. One was that older, heavier cars are safer than lighter, more modern, gas-saving cars, both domestic and foreign. Indeed, careful U.S. government studies suggested that by far the safest cars on American roads were big Oldsmobiles, Buicks, Mercurys, Dodges, and similar vehicles manufactured between 1972 and 1974. The safest car of all was the large 1974 Olds station wagon. One suggested theme was, "What's worth more . . . your children's safety or a few gallons of gas?"

The second theme was that by keeping (and carefully maintaining) a ten-year-old car, one could save much money and even save energy. This was based on the fact that if you kept on driving the old car, the energy needed to build a new one was saved, and the extra gas used was trivial compared to this. The ad didn't mention that if people kept their cars a lot longer, new car manufacturers and workers might be in trouble.

A suggested illustration showed a smiling man filling his own gas tank at a self-service station from a pump labeled regular leaded gas. Most cars built before 1974 could use leaded gas, which in 1984 was usually cheaper than unleaded. It also was alleged to be a dangerous pollutant; in late 1984 the federal government was seriously considering banning its sale. Such legislation would possibly have the effect of leading to the early demise of most pre-1974 cars because they were not designed to use unleaded gas efficiently, and often their engine valves burn up after a short time on unleaded gas. One reason why many people keep older cars was just this. They saved from five to fifteen cents per gallon of gas by using leaded regular. Although the ad did not stress this point, the intent was clear.

Mr. Thomas was bothered by this proposed ad campaign. He was well aware of the fact that big, old cars were safer; indeed, he owned an immaculately maintained 1973 Olds wagon, which got about six miles to the gallon of leaded gas. But he had two small children, and with all the wild drivers in his town, he felt much safer with the big tank. But the propriety of subtly pushing older cars in the way the ad suggested bothered him. If everyone really did drive old fuel guzzlers, then where would energy conservation be? And if people continue to use leaded regular gas, then it was possible that considerable pollution would result.

Still, Vepcoland owed a lot to the independent parts distributors, which were his big and very profitable customers. He decided to think about this issue a few more days before calling Mr. McCann.

Questions

1. Should Vepcoland support this ad campaign? Why or why not?
2. It is true that big cars are much safer than small ones. Yet government-mandated fuel mileages for new cars make it necessary to manufacture smaller cars. Is this ad campaign correct in noting by implication that one net result of this government law is the needless killing of many people? Why or why not?
3. It is probably true that leaded gasoline is a potent pollutant. It is also probably true that if the government bans leaded gas, many older cars, typically owned by low-income people, will have to be replaced. Since lower-income persons driving ten-year-old cars won't be able to buy new cars, they may be forced to give up cars. Is this fair? Why or why not?

11
Governments

The traditional role of government has been to preserve life and protect property. In the United States in the twentieth century, especially in the past forty years, other roles of government have grown very rapidly: tax collector, business regulator, social welfare grantor, safety controller and promoter.

As the chief productive agents in society and the major employers, firms often find that their activities are at least partially restricted by some government rule, law, or regulation. Potential conflicts over these restrictions must be resolved. Managers must decide for themselves what the law or regulation means, whether it applies to a particular situation, and whether society really intends that it apply. Government prosecutors must decide these same issues when faced with what at first appears to be at least a technical violation.

Governments can, however, directly or indirectly promote a firm's profitability. Smart firms stand to gain greatly from government contracts, direct subsidies, or indirect subsidies (paid for by consumers) such as duty or quota protection against foreign competition.

Since there are fifty state governments, each with its own laws and prerogatives, as well as the federal government, what is legal in one place or at one level of government may be illegal in another place or at another level. On occasion the laws are in direct conflict. For example, one cannot, under federal law, legally discriminate against women, and yet under some state laws, women cannot perform certain duties or work certain hours. What is legal? The firm is always in the middle on this question. Frequently, the only true answer is: "It depends."

There are also thousands of local governments (cities, towns, counties, and various special districts) with laws and rules that firms in their jurisdictions must observe. Of particular importance to business firms are zoning codes and tax laws; there can be striking differences in law, and hence in costs, between two superficially similar local situations.

In the international arena, there are many situations in which either no laws apply or only ill-structured and often misunderstood rules may or may not be enforced. Since many U.S. firms operate across international boundaries, they often come in conflict with foreign laws and regulations.

In addition to protecting life and property, all governments at all levels determine who gets what and who pays what portion of the costs. A tax levied on a profitable firm reduces the firm's profits by a certain amount of money; a subsidy for a farm product raises the incomes of certain farmers at the expense of taxpayers; a minimum wage law increases the incomes of certain low-paid workers at the expense of firms. Conflict and controversy are certain: those who pay object, and those who receive seek to maintain or increase their gain.

The following incidents suggest some aspects of the conflicts involving a firm's social responsibility. As usual, a person's view of what is the "best" distribution of society's total costs and total income will probably determine which solution he thinks is best.

The Investigation

The Astro Aeronautics Company, a Servex manufacturing subsidiary, is under contract to Lock-American McConnell (L-AM) to build tail surfaces for the X311, the latest supersonic fighter plane for the U.S. Air Force. L-AM worked extremely hard to get the X311 contract, since four other major companies were also trying to get it. Recently, big-ticket contracts have been increasingly hard to obtain, and all aerospace firms are in somewhat wobbly financial condition.

Perhaps L-AM pushed its promises to perform a bit too far: after six X311s were delivered, the crashes began. The first plane exploded in mid-air, killing its two pilots; the second crashed in a California desert. The remaining four planes were grounded and the production line slowed, while accident investigators tried to find the probable cause of the crashes. They discovered that at supersonic speeds, under the stress of sharp turns, the tail surfaces of the X311s developed flutter and tore off.

Senator Poindexter represents a state whose major aerospace facilities lost the multibillion dollar contract for the X311. Senator Poindexter began to follow the news of the accidents and flights of the X311 with great interest. In a speech in his home state, he implied that the real cause of the accidents was probably granting the X311 contract to an out-of-state aerospace firm, whose subcontractors were below par. He referred specifically to the tail group structural failures, noting that clearly someone had badly bungled the design work. If the contract had gone where it properly belonged (that is, to his state), the disasters would not have happened.

After extensive checking, the four remaining X311s were allowed to fly, at subsonic speeds only, so that further tests could be made. A third X311 crashed within a week after renewed flights began. The two crewmen successfully ejected, but the aircraft smashed into a suburban district, wiping out six houses, killing four and injuring eleven people, and narrowly missing an elementary school filled with children. Senator Poindexter demanded a full-scale investigation and scheduled hearings for the investigation in a key Senate committee of which he was a chairman.

Astro Aeronautics was well aware of all the available information on the failures of the tail surfaces. As is the rule in such situations, Astro worked closely with the prime contractor after the initial crashes to try to determine what was wrong. Some very sticky problems were involved. The X311 design was pushing at the current limits of the art, and so even the best engineers were not at all sure exactly what the real problem was. The third aircraft to crash incorporated several modifications suggested by L-AM, but not several further modifications suggested by Astro's engineers. After the third plane crashed, there was a great deal of conferring and some shouting and arguing among the L-AM and Astro engineers involved with the X311 project.

L-AM had for years been a major customer of Astro, and was at present practically its only customer, accounting for $10.7 million of $13.3 million in total Astro sales in 1983. Cancellation of the tail surface subcontract would very nearly put Astro out of business—a fate already suffered by a number of subcontractors in the aerospace industry.

In a speech on the Senate floor just before his hearings convened, Senator Poindexter blasted "stock-manipulating" conglomerates that put profits before human lives. If each firm paid attention to a specific business, he said, so that each knew its business and was really expert at it, such disasters would not happen. He stated that he expected to discover at his hearings who the guilty parties were and to bring criminal indictments against them if negligence could be proved. Both Mr. Bagby, president of Servex, and Mr. Hambling, president of Astro Aeronautics, were subpoenaed to testify at the Senator's hearing.

Questions

1. Mr. Bagby and Mr. Hambling will each be given an opportunity to make a statement at the hearings, after which they will be questioned by Senator Poindexter and other interested senators. Outline the key points they should make in their statements.
2. Should Astro try to put any blame on L-AM in this case? Why or why not?
3. Should Mr. Hambling do anything in addition to giving a statement? If so, why and what?

Protection Needs

Servex's Alpine Fiberboard subsidiary produces a wide line of special four-by-eight fiberboard panels, for use mainly in building construction. Sales of U.S. fiberboard manufacturers have been purely to the domestic market, ever since fiberboard was invented many years ago.

In the late 1970s and early 1980s, imports of competitive fiberboard products increased their share of the U.S. West Coast market from almost nothing to 40 percent and are continuing to expand their sales throughout the country. Most of the imports come from the Philippines and South Korea, where efficient, modern plants have been established, using low-paid local labor and low-cost cellulose fiber from local sources. (In the Philippines, they use *cogon,* a fast-growing tropical grass that grows up to eight feet high.) Although transport costs from the Far East are relatively high, the new competitors are able to deliver fiberboard on the West Coast for slightly less than 80 percent of Alpine's prices. Buyers, after initial hesitation about buying unknown foreign brands, have been delighted.

Mr. Jack P. Jackson, Alpine's president, first tried to compete by emphasizing the quality of his product. However, the argument was not effective, since the imported fiberboard was, if anything, a bit superior in quality. Mr. Jackson then shaved prices as far as he could and even put the whole Alpine operation through a rough cost-cutting campaign that included firing twenty-three staff and eight production people. As a result, Alpine's unit costs were down 8.7 percent in 1984 and were expected to decrease by another 4.2 percent in 1985. Mr. Jackson is still gloomy about the future, however. In a recent letter to Servex headquarters Mr. Jackson frankly expressed his opinion that, given Alpine's fixed and labor costs, his fiberboard would not be able to compete with the Far Eastern fiberboard on the basis of cost and quality.

Servex has always taken a strong free trade position. Mr. Bagby feels that his company can compete on equal terms anywhere in the world—even if plants must be set up abroad to produce goods more cheaply than in the United States. On several occasions the company has formally expressed its opposition to further trade controls. In 1982 and 1983, for example, Servex officials appeared before Congressional committees to give testimony against imposing further quotas on U.S. imports of textiles.

Mr. Jackson is now faced with the prospect of closing Alpine's plant in Michigan if sales do not improve. He has discussed Alpine's competitive problems at length with his boss, Mr. Botts, arguing that the only thing that can save Alpine is to get high tariffs or, better yet, quotas imposed on imports of fiberboard. Otherwise, Alpine's main product line will go down the drain.

Mr. Botts at first felt that Alpine was not controlling costs as well as it should and pressed for more efficient management. After six months of studying Alpine's competitive situation, however, Mr. Botts became convinced that Mr. Jackson is right: the only way to save the Alpine Fiberboard operation in the United States in its present form is to get its product protected from import competition.

Mr. Botts also knows that Servex is examining several potentially very profitable investments in both South Korea and the Philippines. In each country, government permission is needed for a foreign company to make investments. If Servex pushes for U.S. imposition of tariffs or quotas on fiberboard, the repercussions may be serious in the Far East and elsewhere.

Questions

1. Should Mr. Botts press Servex to push for import controls through various connections in Congress? Why or why not?
2. If a firm gets into competitive difficulties, is it right for it to ask the government to change the rules to its advantage? Why or why not?
3. Is is better or worse (or the same) to ask for changes in rules involving foreign countries than in those involving the domestic economy? Why?

Forbidden Fruit

The Luckless Lake Mining Company, a Canadian operation 88.6 percent owned by Servex, produces mainly uranium ore. It also has a small plant that manufactures specialized mining machinery to order. The plant was set up in 1957 to produce special types of ore shakers and sorters used by Luckless Lake, and from time to time outside sales (at very good profits) are made.

In 1981, Luckless Lake received an inquiry from the People's Republic of China (PRC) asking if it were interested in providing certain special mining machinery for export to this country. Canada has recognized the PRC for many years, and there are few trade restrictions between the two countries. Hence, as a Canadian company, Luckless Lake could legally make this sale.

In 1981, however, the U.S. restrictions on trade with the PRC were still very tight. Machinery such as Luckless Lake manufactured was specifically mentioned on the "banned" list prepared by the U.S. State Department. No U.S. firm could legally export such machinery.

Mr. Williams, president of Luckless Lake, was a Canadian, and he shared many of his countrymen's views about the high importance to his country of export trade. Moreover, the deal would be profitable, and the Chinese had an excellent reputation for paying their bills. They were always tough negotiators but, once the deal was made, they invariably carried out their side of the bargain.

Mr. Williams also knew that the machinery specified in the inquiry was normally used only for uranium production. It was fairly certain that if the PRC bought the machinery, it would use it to handle uranium ore. Since in 1981 the Chinese did not, to anyone's knowledge, have atomic power plants, any uranium they produced would undoubtedly go into the production of nuclear weapons.

Business had been poor at Luckless Lake in recent years. An international oversupply of uranium had depressed markets, and Luckless Lake was surviving only through long-term government supply contracts, which were due to terminate in 1988. It was forecast that after 1988, the company would have to close down its mining operations, which now grossed $7.5 million a year, netting $2.7 million. Mr. Williams had been exploring various alternatives to mining, including expanding the manufacture of mining machinery. The Chinese contract, if it came through, would amount to $2.1 million, on which Luckless Lake's gross profit might run as high as $1.0 million.

Although Mr. Williams had complete legal freedom to act, he still felt he should consult his superiors at Servex to see whether Servex had any objections to this deal. He knew that one senator from Servex's home state was a violent opponent of any relations with the PRC. Also, Mr. Williams remembered the uproar caused in the United States and Canada a few years ago by the question of whether Ford of Canada should sell Canadian-made Ford trucks to the PRC.

Questions

1. What should Servex top management do about the proposed deal? Why?
2. The government of Canada is eager to expand its trade with the PRC. Should Servex take this factor into account in its decision? Why or why not?
3. Suppose Canada said "Trade!" while the U.S. government said, "Don't trade!" How could Servex handle relations with both governments?

Equalizing Loads

Servex's Lucky Jim discount stores owe much of their cost advantage over competition to their ability to deliver truckload lots of merchandise from factories directly to each of their stores. The freight rate for a truckload lot (up to 50,000 pounds) to one destination is commonly only one-third to one-fourth the rate for the same 50,000 pounds shipped in ten 5000 pound less-than-truckload lots to ten destinations in the same city. Therefore, much higher transport costs must be included in the prices smaller stores pay for their merchandise.

Lucky Jim occasionally uses common carrier and contract carrier trucks (owned by commercial trucking lines that sell transportation to their customers) in addition to their fleet of twelve heavy tractor-trailer combination units. Lucky Jim has found, as have many other large shippers, that government regulations in trucking have the effect of keeping freight rates well above the actual costs for truckload lots. Therefore, it is economical to operate one's own units full time and rely on commercial carriers only to supplement them at peak periods.

Rules governing truck use differ from state to state in regard to not only speed but also lighting, height, gross weight, axle loading, length, and width. A truck that is legal in Michigan may be illegal in Indiana because it is too heavy, has the wrong lights, or fails to meet some other specification. Ever since the early 1930s the American Trucking Association and other lobbying groups have pushed for uniform laws governing trucks. By now most state laws are more or less in agreement on this issue, but differences persist.

In one midwestern state where Lucky Jim operates, the total gross weight of a truck is limited to 77,000 pounds, which is a relatively standard limit throughout the region. However, this maximum weight applies only to freeways and interstate roads or roads built to similar standards; 77,000 pound trucks are allowed to use local roads only within three miles of the interstate roads.

Lucky Jim has several stores that are four to six miles from major highways in this state. If Lucky Jim is to obey the law, it must have the truck stop, offload a part of the cargo to reduce total cargo weight, and then reload this part into a smaller truck. The offloading and reloading would significantly raise costs and increase the price a consumer must pay. This increase might amount to $3 on a television and $5 to $8 on a refrigerator.

Lucky Jim's trucking manager is Mr. Silas, a very capable trucker who has been with the firm for more than twenty years. He runs the trucking operation so smoothly and at such low cost that only rarely does any of Lucky Jim's top managers pay much attention to trucking. Mr. Silas is fond of beating averages, and the ton-mile costs of his operation ordinarily average about 40 percent less than the average reported by the Interstate Commerce Commission for trucks in this midwestern area.

In the last few years local independent merchants have been hurt badly by chain discount operations such as Lucky Jim. Naturally, these merchants have tried to find ways to lower their own costs, raise the costs of chain discounters, or both. The independent merchants tried to enforce a Sunday closing law in this state, but were overruled in the courts. Then one of their members discovered that Lucky Jim, along with many other mass merchandisers, was not observing the three-mile law: 77,000 pound trucks were going as far as twenty miles on local roads to make deliveries. Pushing their investigation, the independent merchants found that the state and local police rarely enforce the three-mile law, because many counties in the state have heavy coal and grain traffic that requires the use of big trucks on local roads. If the law were strictly enforced, many farmers and coal-using industries would have a serious cost handicap in competing with similar firms in neighboring states.

Further investigation showed that heavy trucks often chewed up local roads badly. State and local highway departments often had to expend more funds than budgeted to keep local roads even in fair repair. In spite of this expense, most officials felt that local jobs and incomes were more important than a few roads.

Nevertheless, the local merchants started a campaign to keep heavy trucks off local roads. In one county where Lucky Jim had a store, they were successful. A number of truckers were arrested, including two of Lucky Jim's drivers. The first case that came to court involved a truck belonging to a local grain dealer. He insisted on a jury trial in the county courthouse and after some delay was granted it. In spite of overwhelming evidence that he was guilty, he was acquitted in less than ten minutes. Apparently the local citizens on the jury believed the grain dealer's defense that if his truck could not haul heavy loads, he would be forced out of business and ten to twenty workers and farmers would be out of jobs.

The county in which the first Lucky Jim case will be tried receives $1.7 million a year from the state for local road repairs. The county road commissioner estimates that overload damage to his roads costs approximately $200,000 a year. The state is responsible for the much better built local state roads, and the cost of overload damage to state roads in the county is estimated at about $50,000 a year. Perhaps the biggest problem with heavy trucks on local two-lane roads is the slowing down of traffic when the trucks grind up steep grades and along winding roads at ten to thirty miles per hour, with long lines of impatient motorists trailing behind.

The first of Lucky Jim's cases is coming up for trial next week. The maximum fine in this state for a violation of the three-mile law is $100. Mr. Silas estimates that Lucky Jim saves about $250 each time he does not have to offload a heavy truck—a saving that largely explains why he has never paid much attention to this law before.

Questions

1. Should Lucky Jim plead guilty or not guilty when the case comes up?
2. Should Lucky Jim ask for a jury trial? Why or why not?
3. Is it right for a big firm to ignore a law, even one that citizens apparently do not care much about? Why?
4. In the future, if the police continue to enforce the law, what should the Lucky Jim truckers do? Should they obey it or ignore it? Why?

Immoral Interest

Servex's Oregon Finance Company operates in seven states. In one of these, the state legislature has recently changed the state usury law. Under the old law, the maximum interest rate chargeable was 7 percent; but no creditor was really constrained by the law to charge only 7 percent, since, by definition, interest was not considered to include service charges. Most companies charged the average credit user from 18 to 24 percent a year, of which 11 to 17 percent covered service charges.

The new state usury law is more carefully drawn than the old law. Although it allows total charges of up to 18 percent a year, no longer will the amount of service charges by uncontrolled. The new 18 percent maximum includes such charges. Oregon Finance, along with other consumer credit companies operating in the state, opposed the new law on the grounds that for many risks (such as financing older used cars) credit cannot profitably be given at 18 percent or less. Under competitive conditions, loans on older used cars often carry financing charges of around 24 percent annually. Risks are high in financing older used cars; and if rates chargeable were limited to a maximum of 18 percent, Oregon would have to give up this part of its business. On loans of $21 million on older used cars, last year Oregon had costs of over $4 million—about $1 million in operating costs plus about $3 million in write-offs on loans that were uncollectible. The previously legal 24 percent rate, however, made this part of Oregon's business profitable.

In studying the new legislation, Oregon Finance's lawyer found what he thinks may be a loophole. Certain kinds of credit insurance are not clearly specified in the new law. The lawyer feels that Oregon can legally charge 18 percent in interest and service charges plus 6 percent for credit insurance. As with any other legal opinion, this is a probability statement. The lawyer estimates that there is one chance in ten that the company could be brought to court and found guilty of violating the law. Until the definition of credit insurance is tested in the courts, no one can really be sure exactly what the law means. Oregon Finance's lawyer did note, however, that the intent of the law was very clear; interest rates including service charges should not total more than 18 percent annually. Only a bit of fuzzy draftsmanship of the law created the potential loophole of extra charges for credit insurance.

In testimony and statements preceding passage of the law, it was clear the legislature felt strongly that borrowers should pay no more than 18 percent interest annually. If some credit applicants were such poor risks that an 18 percent charge did not allow financing companies to make a profit, then those applicants should be denied loans. As Oregon Finance saw it, under the new law, many people would be denied loans, even if they were willing to pay 24 percent rates. Under the federal Truth-in-Lending law, Oregon Finance had to make clear to all prospective borrowers precisely what its rates were,

and past disclosure of 24 percent rates had not to any noticeable extent
deterred people from borrowing.

Questions

1. Should Oregon Finance try to finance older used cars at an annual rate of
   18 percent for interest and service charges plus 6 percent for credit insurance? Why or why not?
2. Many customers obviously are willing to pay 24 percent total annual
   rates. What rights, if any, do they have in this situation? Why?
3. Why would a state legislature vote to restrict high-interest loans? What
   is the public interest here?

Evil Holes in the Ground

Many firms, including Servex's Petersford Copper Mining Company, do
extensive strip-mining, which involves stripping away an overburden of earth
to get at the minerals underground. The great piles of overburden removed
often block creeks, streams, and roads. Exposed mineral-bearing subsoil
erodes and fouls streams and rivers with acidic, discolored water. The strip-
mined land itself is an immense messy hole in the rocky subsoil, which usually
is not good for any possible purpose at any time in the future, not even as
scenery. It is a permanent eyesore.

Petersford Mining has recently built a copper mine in a certain western
state. At present, the state has a very ineffectual law against strip-mining,
passed in 1911 when the ranchers and mining companies were said to "own"
four out of five legislators. The law is full of loopholes and exceptions, and
under it no mines have ever been convicted for illegal strip mining, although
there are over 255 strip mines in the state. Now, local conservationists are
pressing hard to get a really effective law against strip-mining passed. Best
estimates are that such a law might be passed next year, particularly since
twenty-two incumbent state senators and legislators were defeated at the
polls this year by pro-conservationists.

Petersford Mining's operation is probably no better or worse than that of
most other companies in the state. Its copper mine is a highly efficient strip
mine, and each day the company dumps aside thousands of cubic yards of
dirt to get at the copper ore. Unlike many others, it does make an attempt to
reclaim mined-out areas, bulldozing the overburden into smooth piles and
planting a few trees on them. As a result, its overall operation does not look
as bad as many others. Nevertheless, the operation does pour small moun-
tains of dirt and debris into Wells Creek, which used to be a clear mountain
stream visited only by a few fishermen. Now, for more than twenty miles

downstream. Wells Creek is too dirty to support the trout and other game fish that used to be found there. The banks of the creek are marked by broad bands of rotting vegetation, killed by acid and the occasional floods caused when overburden dammed the creek. None of the dirt in the water is harmful to humans. In fact, a town thirty-four miles downstream uses water from Wells Creek for its water supply. At that distance from the pollution source, the dirt has settled out and the acidity is reduced, and so the water is clear and quite potable after minimal chlorine treatment.

Two years ago a brilliant photographer took hundreds of photographs of the damage to Wells Creek near Petersford Mining and offered the pictures free to newspapers in the state. Several of the important newspapers have used the photos to illustrate articles about the "ruin of our state's wilderness through strip-mining," and much of the political heat is directed at Petersford. As a result, Mr. Lorbell, president of Petersford, asked his staff to work out a scheme to reduce greatly the severity of damage to Wells Creek. According to the staff report, for $75,000 the dumping platforms could be shifted so that even the first twenty miles of the stream would once again be clear. Extra costs per year would run about $120,000.

Two weeks ago, Mr. Lorbell attended a state convention of mining engineers. In casual conversations with other representatives of strip mines, he discovered that many of them were deeply resentful of Petersford. The chief reason for their resentment was that they felt the adverse publicity all strip mines were getting as a result of Petersford's activities would help greatly in getting a tough new law passed in the next legislative session.

"You guys know how much it would cost to avoid the problem!" Mr. Lorbell finally snapped at several of his friends, "If you're so hot for Petersford to stop polluting Wells Creek, why don't you guys pay for it?"

Instead of being angry, several of the men looked thoughtful. One said, "It's an idea. After all, we're all hurting from this. If we spread the costs over all of us, it could be a hell of a lot cheaper than that new law. Why, that proposed bill would cost us all at least forty million a year—maybe twice that."

"Relax, Sam," another man said. "See your lawyer first. A deal like that would violate every antitrust law in the country."

"Still, it's worth thinking about," Sam said. "I think I will talk to my lawyer. After all, we aren't even in the same game—I'm working sand and gravel, while Lorbell here is working copper. And you've got a coal mine. Maybe we should think about something like this."

Questions

1. Should the strip miners follow up on this idea? Why or why not?
2. Suppose it turns out that the idea is illegal. What should Mr. Lorbell do? Why?

3. Suppose the new state law is passed and as a result, 15,000 workers are put out of work in the next two years, since many mines will close rather than incur these costs. Would you still favor the law? Why or why not?
4. Strip-mining is much safer than tunnel mining. Virtually no one is ever killed in strip-mining. Moreover, it typically is much less physically demanding than tunnel mining and much more productive. Instead of many miners underground, subject to high danger, a few men operate productive huge shovels and bulldozers. If the mines go back to tunneling, it is likely that perhaps 100 people a year will be killed working as miners to get out the same amount of materials, as compared to an average of one killed every two years with strip-mining. Does this fact change your answer? Why or why not?
5. Strip-mining is less expensive than tunnel mining. Suppose that if the new law forces the mining companies back to tunneling, the electric bill of the average family in the state will rise by about $3.35 a month—$40.20 a year. Does that fact change your answer? Why or why not?

Zoning Codes

Servex's Lucky Jim discount stores have recently purchased an 18-acre tract of land on the outskirts of a midwestern city. The property is ideally suited for a major suburban store: several important highways pass near it, and there is plenty of room for a large building as well as for parking close to it. Two large shopping centers are just a few hundred yards down the road.

The only problem facing Lucky Jim is that the property is currently zoned R-1 (single-family residential dwellings). This zoning was established in 1951 when the city annexed 800 acres of outlying land—including the Lucky Jim property and the land on which the nearby shopping centers are located. When the land for those shopping centers was bought a few years ago, however, the developers easily managed to have the zoning changed to B-1 (ordinary business retailing and office operations). On the assumption that a similar change in zoning would be easy for them to obtain, Lucky Jim bought the land for $25,000 an acre—$15,000 more than what is normally paid for R-1 land in this area (but $5000 to $15,000 less than what attractive land already zoned B-1 normally sells for in this area).

In the last few years, attitudes about land use in this city have changed. The nearby residential property owners, all of whom own nice single-family, upper-income homes, have formed a neighborhood association and hired an attorney to fight further zoning changes that would bring more business and traffic into the neighborhood. When Lucky Jim applied for a zoning variance at the last meeting of the Planning Commission, many citizens attended the meeting and spoke out strongly against allowing another major store to build in the neigborhood: traffic was already too congested; there was no need for the store; and the character of the neighborhood would change for the worse if the store were built. The Planning Commission tabled the proposal for the meeting, agreeing to take it up at the next bi-weekly meeting. It was standard procedure to postpone a decision, to allow time for public discussion, whenever opposition to a zoning change was expressed.

The Planning Commission in this city was made up of seven people, elected by the voters for four-year terms. The Commission held thirty to forty public hearings each year, each one lasting about three to four hours. In addition, each member spent four to five hours a week discussing upcoming requests for zoning variances and studying relevant material. Because the work load of a Planning Commission member was sizable and there was no pay for the job, it was difficult to find able candidates who were also impartial in real estate matters. Most candidates for Commission membership were real estate agents, insurance agents, or persons who were strongly committed to various positions concerning commercial and industrial activity in the city.

Lucky Jim's local attorney tried to analyze how each Planning Commission member would be likely to vote on rezoning the land. It appeared that there would be three votes in favor, two against, and two undecided. From asking around about the two undecided members, the attorney discovered that these two usually were undecided on zoning issues until the last minute. The word around the county courthouse was that "they could be had." The cost would be about $1000 apiece. While no one had ever proved anything or gathered enough evidence to take these men to court, it was fairly sure that they could be persuaded to shift their votes when convenient or useful. One of the men owned a worn-out farm in the county. He could probably be persuaded to sell a few acres of it for about $1000 over its going market value. The other man needed a new heating and air-conditioning system in his home and would probably be delighted to buy it from Lucky Jim at $1000 less than the going market price.

Lucky Jim's management figured that, if the Planning Commission did not approve the zoning variance, they would be out approximately $270,000. They had purchased the land at a price far above its market value as single-family residence lots; if they had to resell it as R-1 land, they would lose an estimated $15,000 an acre. Moreover, another supermarket chain was angling for the site (or one near it), and this company was thought to have few scruples about arranging for the zoning of its land to be changed. Even if Lucky Jim backed out, the local home owners would probably have a huge new shopping center in the neighborhood.

Questions

1. What should Lucky Jim's management do here? Why?
2. Is it always unethical and immoral to do a "favor" for a local official? Why or why not?

3. What can the local home owners do, if they suspect a commission member of taking a bribe? Or can they do anything?

Death, Taxes, and Annexation

In taking over Letson and Baker Chemical Company, Servex obtained eighteen U.S. plants producing a variety of chemical products. One of the plants was located near a small (40,000 pop.) southeastern city and had been acquired in 1980 by Letson and Baker from Mr. James Black, a local millionaire with an intense dislike of taxes. At the time Letson and Baker bought his chemical business, Mr. Black was influential in local politics, to say nothing of being the city's largest employer. Mr. Black had successfully used his political power to avoid having his plant annexed to the city, because paying city rather than county taxes would add approximately $64,000 to his annual property tax bill. Local property taxes in this state are structured in such a way that a factory located on rural land instead of in a city pays much lower property taxes. This is particularly true where a county is highly agricultural, as this one is. The state's farmers are not eager to pay high taxes on their farms, and in most counties they have successfully fought off major tax increases on land outside the cities.

The plant formerly owned by Mr. Black is on land now officially designated as not being in the city, even though it is completely surrounded by the city. Most of the plant's workers use city facilities, such as police and fire protection and schools. The plant even gets something for nothing: when a fire occurred there in 1980, the city fire department quickly put it out, although the factory pays no city taxes.

In the 1984 city election, a new mayor and a slate of other local officials were elected on a tax reform program. They promised to do everything possible to remove all inequities in assessments and in rates of property taxation. On taking office, the mayor promptly investigated the possibilities for annexation of Letson and Baker's chemical plant. He discovered that city annexation of the plant had been tried earlier—in 1970, 1976, and 1978. Each time, legal maneuverings by Mr. Black's lawyers had prevented annexation. Given the very complex nature of annexation proceedings in this state, the city attorney estimated that if Letson and Baker were to fight annexation of their plant, they could delay for at least five years and probably for ten—at an annual cost of not over $5000. At those rates, delaying tactics might seem like a good bargain to Letson and Baker and its parent company, Servex.

The city's new mayor wrote to Servex to inquire about their policy on this matter. Mr. Bagby, who received the mayor's letter, turned it over to his assistant to check. Mr. Bagby's assistant found that Servex really did not have a policy, at least not one specifically concerned with possible annexations of their plants. In the tremendous pre-merger work load, no one had looked very carefully at local tax bills for the Letson and Baker plants, and the annexation issue had not come up at Servex headquarters.

Servex did have a company policy concerning local taxes. It reads as follows:

> Servex believes that it should pay its fair share of local taxes in political jurisdictions in which it operates. A fair share is construed to be reasonable payments, given existing tax rates, payments made by similar taxpayers in the jurisdiction, and other relevant factors. Servex will not hesitate to question any tax rates or payments that appear to be discriminatory, nor will it hesitate to take legal action where tax rates or payments are levied in an unlawful or discriminatory manner.

Mr. Bagby's assistant wrote to ask Mr. John Letson II for comment and advice on the proposed annexation, attaching a copy of the mayor's letter. Mr. Letson replied within a week. He noted in his letter that the plant concerned was very old and marginal, and it produced a minor chemical subject currently to ruinous price competition because of excess capacity in the industry. Severe price competition was expected to continue for many years, and Letson and Baker had begun a study to decide what action to take to improve the plant's profitability. Profits were marginal—about $25,000 in 1984 (as compared to $52,000 in 1982 and $46,000 in 1983). Table 11–1 shows the condensed financial statements for the plant.

Table 11–1
Condensed Financial Statements for Letson and Baker Plant No. 7, 1984
(millions of dollars)

Balance Sheet			
Current assets	5.3	Current liabilities	2.8
Land (at cost)	.4[a]	Long-term liabilities	1.4
			4.2
Buildings and equipment	3.5	Earned surplus and equity	5.0
	9.2		9.2

Income Statement	
Total sales	8.5
Cost of goods sold	5.4
Administration[b]	3.0
Miscellaneous	.1
Net profit	$25,003

[a]Estimated 1984 market values, $2.7 million.
[b]Payments to Letson and Baker and to Servex for administrative services rendered.

Mr. Letson's letter closed with a statement of the principal alternatives being considered. In brief, these alternatives were:

1. Close the plant, terminate the workers, sell the land. Meanwhile, stall off annexation because lower taxed land will bring a higher price. Move production of the minor chemical to the new plant near Erie, Pa.

2. Build a new modern plant on farmland two miles outside the present city limits, next to a major highway. When the new plant is built, shift the present plant's workers and production there and add production of the rapidly growing new product Z-Z7. Close the old plant and sell the land on which it is situated. Meanwhile (estimated two and one-half years), stall annexation.

3. Ask the city to buy the land and to build at the city's cost a new plant. The city then to lease the plant long-term to Letson and Baker at a lease rental low enough at least to let the company pay city taxes and still have plant costs no higher than under the second alternative. Use the new plant to produce the present minor product and Z-Z7. Promise the city to accept annexation.

Questions

1. Are there any alternatives more attractive than those Mr. Letson has listed? If so, what are they, and why are they more attractive? Also, if so, to whom are they more attractive?

2. Mr. Bagby's assistant has to recommend to Mr. Bagby what should be done. Give him some advice and tell him what he should do in this case.

It's All Tax Free

Wadman and Wadman, a division of Servex, manufactures a line of steel furniture for offices and institutions. The market for steel furniture has begun to improve recently, causing the company to consider expanding its manufacturing capacity to handle the potential increases in business.

Mr. Nicolas Adams, president of Wadman and Wadman, has been thinking of placing a new factory somewhere in the New England—New York–New Jersey area, which is currently the company's largest market. To date, nothing has been done about the project except to take cursory looks at two possible plant sites in western Massachusetts. Nevertheless, word is beginning to get around the furniture trade that Wadman and Wadman may be interested in building an additional plant.

Recently, Mr. Adams received a carefully drafted letter from a small town in the Deep South. The letter stated that the town was anxious to obtain more industry; local workers were willing and eager to work for going wage rates; unions were nonexistent in the area (in part because there were so few industries); finally, the town was willing to issue and sell tax-exempt bonds and to build with the proceeds a factory to Wadman and Wadman's specifications, which it would lease to the company at a very low rental.

On investigation, Mr. Adams found that everything the letter promised was true. The town was the county seat of a depressed agricultural area. Local businessmen, convinced that the only way to get economic growth was to attract new industry, were solidly behind a plan to find a firm that would lease a plant once it had been built with the proceeds from a municipal bond issue. Since the industrial payroll would be spent locally, the jobs and increases in population and property values would more than pay for the plant (the local businessmen hoped). Many small towns in areas otherwise unattractive to industry had been doing this for years.

Mr. Adams estimated that the lease-back arrangement proposed might save Wadman and Wadman about $1.5 million in capital investment. The rent to be paid would amount to close to $150,000 a year. One major reason why the town could afford to do this is that investors receiving interest paid on local government bonds do not have to pay income tax on the money. Naturally, wealthy investors in high income tax brackets are willing to buy tax-exempt bonds that have lower interest yields than do nonexempt corporate bonds. The town could easily sell twenty-year tax-exempt bonds that paid only 9 percent interest, whereas Wadman and Wadman (or Servex) would have to pay 13 to 14 percent interest on their twenty-year bonds, in order to make them salable.

Unfortunately, the town was otherwise poorly suited for a factory. Roads and railroad service were poor; the town's schools were dismal; labor would be unskilled and would require a great deal of training. Adams figured that extra costs (above those at a Massachusetts location) for transport alone might range up to $200,000 a year. Also, it might take six months more to get this plant up to an efficient level of operation than it would for a new plant in a more economically developed section of the country. The total payroll would be lower, though. Mr. Adams estimated that a northeastern plant would have an annual payroll of $2.2 million, the southern plant $2.1 million. State taxes for a southern plant would be about $18,000 a year lower than in Massachusetts, and there would be another $18,000 saved because of lower power costs (principally due to less need for heating). Gross sales of product from a new plant, in either the Northeast or the South, were estimated at $2.9 million a year.

Wadman and Wadman was having problems negotiating with its union in the present plant, and this difficulty made the idea of ducking unions attractive. Mr. Adams was, however, well aware that union ducking normally was successful for only a short time. If the southern town attracted much industry, union organizers would not be far behind.

The proposed southern plant would be within reach of Wadman and Wadman's main markets, it was thought. Mr. Adams believed that he could serve most of his major customers efficiently and quickly—although at higher cost—from this plant.

Questions

1. Should Wadman and Wadman seriously explore further the possibilities of building a southern plant? Why or why not?
2. Is there anything wrong with an economically backward area trying to attract new industry through the use of its tax-free bonding powers? Why or why not?
3. Suppose that a Massachusetts town Wadman and Wadman looked at became aware of the southern town's offer. What, if anything, should it do about the southern competition? Why?
4. Mr. Adams senses that his firm might play off one town against another to get the best deal. Would this be proper? Why or why not?

The Un-Taxpayer

A small but very profitable bit of the business of SPECwerke, Servex's German chemical subsidiary, is in exporting several types of polyethylene plastics to Jordan. Plastics imported into Jordan must pay duty at the rate of 19 percent *ad valorem* (imposed at a rate percent of the value as stated in an invoice). SPECwerke's sales to Jordan in recent years have ranged from $165,000 to $300,000 a year. Mr. Ali Mohammed, a Jordanian citizen, is the exclusive distributor for SPECwerke's products throughout Jordan. It is customary in the export-import trade for the exclusive distributor of a foreign manufacturer to be the only customer in that country to whom the manufacturer sells his goods. The exclusive distributor orders from the manufacturer, takes title to the goods somewhere outside the country, arranges clearance of the goods through customs and payment of customs duties, then resells the goods to wholesalers and perhaps retailers throughout his country.

Dr. Otto Holshen, general manager of SPECwerke, rarely paid any attention to the minor market of Jordan which caused no special trouble and was growing steadily if unspectacularly. Late in 1983, he visited several countries in the Middle East, including Jordan, on a business trip, during which he paid courtesy calls on each of SPECwerke's exclusive distributors. In Amman, Mr. Mohammed entertained and dined Dr. Holshen in the lavish Middle Eastern style. In the course of their evening's conversation the two men took up the usual problems—competitive pricing, goods damaged in shipment, late delivery, and the like—connected with their business. Nothing seemed out of the ordinary.

The following day, as Dr. Holshen was preparing to check out of the hotel and go to the airport, he had a visitor. The man identified himself as Abdul Shariff, a dealer in polyethylene imports. Dr. Holshen recalled vaguely that a man with this name had been mentioned in recent correspondence with Jordan as a sharp competitor. He was distributor in Jordan for several competitive English and U.S. chemical companies.

Mr. Shariff apologized for interrupting Dr. Holshen, explaining he felt it was very important that Dr. Holshen should know what was happening to SPECwerke's reputation in Jordan. Mr. Mohammed was, said Mr. Shariff, systematically falsifying customs documents in a way which undervalued SPECwerke's products by over 70 percent. Mr. Shariff knew that Dr. Holshen's company produced very high quality, very expensive polyethylene products, but so far the customs officials had not recognized their true value. SPECwerke's quality products were being declared for customs at prices typical of the lowest quality plastics. Since only experts knew the difference in the materials, so far Mr. Mohammed had gotten away with it, Mr. Shariff said. Paying lower customs duties gave SPECwerke's products a significant price advantage in the Jordanian market, which of course, made it more difficult for Mr. Shariff to sell the English and U.S. plastics he imported.

Mr. Shariff explained that in order to carry out this fraud, Mr. Mohammed had to counterfeit invoices from SPECwerke in Germany, to say nothing of various consular stamps and seals. It was possible that under Jordanian law SPECwerke might be liable for damages if the fraud were discovered. They were clearly a party to the fraud, even though they might not be aware of it. Mr. Shariff stated he fully intended to expose this fraud, since it was hurting his business. He had first called to warn Dr. Holshen of what was happening, he said, since he felt from his experience in the Jordanian trade that SPECwerke was a very honorable company. While he objected to losing business through a competitor's cheating, Mr. Shariff said he did not feel a foreign company should be penalized for its distributor's dishonesty.

Mr. Shariff left his card with Dr. Holshen, saying that he would be happy to be of service in the future if he could be.

Questions

1. What, if anything, should Dr. Holshen do as a result of Mr. Shariff's conversation? Why?
2. Why do you suppose that Mr. Shariff took the trouble to visit Dr. Holshen?
3. Suppose Dr. Holshen investigated and found out that Mr. Shariff's accusations were true. What should he do then? Why?

4. Suppose Mr. Shariff's accusations are true. List all the parties who are benefited, or might be benefited, by Mr. Mohammed's deception of Jordanian customs, and how. List all the parties who are injured, or might be injured, and how.

Beating the Local Exchange Control Laws

In a certain small, poor country where a subsidiary of Servex's Northeastern Insurance and Auto Claimants Group has an operation, the government has imposed very tight exchange control laws. The local currency is officially overvalued in comparison to major currencies such as the British pound sterling and the West German deutsche mark, because the local citizens want to buy from abroad goods with more total value than the total value of the goods they can sell abroad. The result of the official overvaluation is a severe shortage of foreign exchange, including dollars: through exchange controls, the government rations scarce dollars and other hard currencies to those who seem to qualify best to receive them. This exchange control system involves a clumsy bureaucracy that checks, double-checks, and triple-checks cash requests for foreign exchange before approving or disapproving them.

Northeastern's subsidiary has been profitable each of the past five years, with the profits, of course, in the local currency, not dollars. The subsidiary has repeatedly requested exchange control permission to remit its profits to its parent company in the United States in dollars, but permission has not been given. At present, Northeastern's subsidiary has a backlog of $300,000 worth of profits (at the current official exchange rate) that it cannot remit.

Since all official forms of transfer of funds abroad are carefully controlled, a lively black market for foreign currencies has grown up. While the local currency is officially valued at twenty to the U.S. dollar (which means that Northeastern's profits are worth 6 million locally), the black market rate is sixty to the dollar. At this rate, Northeastern's backlog of profits is worth only $100,000. Northeastern's local manager has suggested in desperation that the firm resort to the black market to remit profits, but Servex headquarters has vetoed the idea, on the grounds that Servex companies should observe all local laws. Moreover, if Northeastern can ever get permission to remit at the official rate, Servex will, of course, receive many more dollars.

Recently Northeastern's lawyer discovered what he thinks is a loophole in the regulations. There is a local company whose shares are traded on the local stock market. This company, which processes cottonseed for export, has consistently been very profitable. More important, many of its shares are held in the United States, where they are traded on the American Stock Exchange. There is no law that prohibits buying shares of this company locally, sending the share certificates to New York, and reselling the shares for dollars. Because this old and well-established company has managed to get exchange control permission to remit some profits to foreign owners, its shares are in demand by U.S. investors and can be sold at relatively good prices. The lawyer estimates that if Northeastern's profits of 6 million locally were used to buy these shares, which were then resold in New York, the net effect would be to obtain about $210,000 in dollars. Although this method of exchange would yield $90,000 less than at the official rate, it results in more than double the black market yield. Furthermore, this share transaction would be completely legal. The lawyer urges immediate action.

The country concerned is currently having a food crisis, along with its other troubles. Its president has called on the people to use all possible foreign currency to import food to help keep the people alive, develop the local economy, and safeguard the republic.

Question

1. Should Servex allow its Northeastern subsidiary to take advantage of the loophole, which would allow it to circumvent the publicly stated policy of the country? Why or why not?

The Partner

When Servex Consolidated Industries acquired the West Coast Steel Company many years ago, it also obtained Acierro de Santiago, a small metal fabricating subsidiary set up in 1941 by West Coast. This firm in Chile performs such work as the fabrication of steel sheets into tanks and construction of girders from steel stock. It was set up originally to avoid the high Chilean customs duties on prefabricated steel materials. Sales have always been relatively small ($385,000 in 1983), but profits have been quite satisfactory, ranging from 15 to 20 percent on sales in recent years.

Late in 1983, Mr. Manfield B. Foster, president of West Coast Steel, received information from his Chilean manager that the Chilean government wished to purchase 51 percent of Acierro de Santiago. They would pay $148,000 (based on the small book value of the company) in government fifty-year Chilean peso bonds yielding 3 percent. Since inflation in Chile in the past twenty years has ranged from 10 to 50 percent annually, Mr. Foster felt the government's offer was tantamount to confiscation. He instructed Acierro de Santiago's local Chilean manager to refuse the offer.

Very shortly thereafter, the local Chilean manager frantically cabled that if West Coast did not accept the offer, the government would take over the company anyhow. Steel apparently had a mystique all its own in Chile, and the government was interested in controlling all steel production. The local manager had emphasized to no avail that Acierro was not a steel maker but a steel fabricator. If West Coast were to accept the government's original offer, there was at least a chance that the company could salvage something of value out of the deal.

Mr. Foster discussed the problem with his boss, Mr. Botts, whose first reaction was that, as both of them well knew, Servex had a policy of 100 percent ownership in all overseas ventures. If Servex could not do it alone, it would not do it. Even private foreign partners were not allowed under the policy, let alone a government.

Mr. Botts also noted that the company had been farsighted enough to obtain expropriation insurance from the U.S. Agency for International Development several years earlier. If the Chilean government did expropriate Acierro de Santiago, Servex would simply collect the AID insurance, call its resident manager home, and invest the insurance money in the new Mexican venture, Suerte y Suerte. While rates of return were reasonably high in Chile, the possibilities of their staying high under the present government were very dim.

Mr. Foster was less optimistic. In his personal opinion the Chilean government was crazy but not stupid. A previous Chilean government had signed a treaty with the United States whereby Chile would make good to the U.S. government any compensation that AID paid an expropriated Chilean company. Rather than straight expropriation, Chile would undoubtedly force Acierro de Santiago to "sell" 90 percent, 80 percent, or some majority percentage to the Chileans and "pay" with fifty-year 3 percent peso bonds. Under these circumstances, Mr. Foster felt, AID would be very slow indeed to pay off on the expropriation insurance. As a matter of fact, Mr. Foster went on, he had heard that AID practically never paid off on expropriation insurance.

Also, Mr. Foster was worried that Acierro might, under Chilean ownership, use West Coast's technology. Mr. Botts pointed out that on the day of nationalization, all licensing and technical agreements with West Coast would end. Acierro would be without any source of advanced technological know-how, and within a year or two would be unable to compete. He suggested that Mr. Foster fly to Chile as soon as possible to consult with the local manager and destroy or bring back any records, files, blueprints, and similar materials that might be of use to the new owners.

West Coast was well known for its innovative technology in welding and heavy plate cutting. Much of Acierro's recent sales had come from applications of such steel fabricating techniques. The resident manager, a very higly skilled technician, was the key man in both selling and applying these techniques in Chile. With him gone, there would be left an inventory of steel, a small shop, some skilled welders, other metalworkers, and not much else.

Mr. Foster still felt that something should be done to try to stave off a government take-over. He agreed to go to Chile, but he felt that at least Acierro should make its case to the Chilean government. Perhaps the company could do better than currently forecast. But while in Mr. Botts' office, he received a phone call from his office. His Chilean manager had cabled that a take-over was imminent and asked for immediate instructions.

Questions

1. What should Mr. Foster do? Be specific.
2. Is it right for West Coast to remove all plans, technical materials, and other know-how from the Chilean subsidiary, even though they will be repaid for the takeover?
3. Chile has a per capita income of about $1000 per year (compared to about $12,000 in the United States). For many years, Acierro de Santiago has helped Chile technically and economically. If the Chilean government does take it over, does Acierro owe the country anything? Does Servex? Why or why not?
4. Is it right for Servex to sit back, be taken over, and then collect on its expropriation insurance? Why or why not?

Noble Pollution

Alpine Fiberboard owns a small plant in central Maine, which produces a high-quality fiberboard from wood chips. In the 1970s, this plant, which needs a great amount of steam for its production process, burned fuel oil to generate steam. With the sharp rise in oil prices beginning in 1974, the plant rapidly became uneconomic, but Jim Burns, the plant manager, figured out in 1976 a way of burning wood chips to get steam. Since there is a lot of wood in central Maine and it is very cheap, the plant continued to operate with even lower energy costs than it previously had.

Other Maine citizens and companies also got tired of paying high fuel oil bills, so they also shifted to wood burning, to the point where a high percentage of energy used in Maine now comes from wood. Ecologists, energy planners, and conservationists have eagerly supported this shift since oil was a major air pollutant in the past. Coal pollutes the air even worse, so avoiding this fuel was also a benefit. In other parts of the country, most notably the industrial Midwest, there is now serious concern that coal burning causes acid rain, which ruins forests all over the northern United States and Canada.

Mr. Burns, however, whose hobby is conservation and who loves to hunt and fish, has now seen another problem: wood pollutes the air too. Burning green, seasoned, and trash wood sends up various materials that might be harmful to human health. Ironically, few conservationists or ecologists have worried much about wood smoke pollution, perhaps because, in some mystical sense, wood is noble, while coal and oil are nasty. Wood brings images of sturdy frontiersmen struggling honestly and nobly on small farms; coal and oil bring images of rapacious firms despoiling the environment.

But Muriel Larsen, a close friend of Jim who is a chemist at the local college, has done a bit of research and is seriously concerned. She recently told Jim that at the current rate of wood burning in Maine, the state's air would probably be rapidly polluted. She analyzed some of the smoke from the fiberboard plant and discovered that it was full of particulates and dirt that could cause considerable harm.

Servex's corporate policy on environmental problems is to observe fully all laws and regulations concerning pollution levels. Plants are expected to do whatever necessary to keep pollution levels (in air, water, and otherwise) below federal and state requirements. Mr. Burns' problem is that to date there are no federal or state standards for wood burning so his plant is legal. Wood burning may be dangerous to its workers and the surrounding population, but it is not against the law.

Mr. Burns is also aware of problems some companies have had with lawsuits about damages done long ago. Companies using or processing asbestos have been particularly harmed since it is now proved that asbestos can be harmful to human health. The Manville Company, which had produced asbestos for over fifty years, went bankcupt in 1982, staggered by lawsuits by ex-workers and their heirs. Perhaps Servex could get into the same kind of trouble if, in ten or fifteen years, it turns out that the company was doing something that was legal now but seriously harmed people.

Mr. Burns was worried about the problem but wasn't sure what to do. He felt that this issue was important, but to date he didn't have much hard evidence as to potential problems.

Questions

1. What should Mr. Burns do, if anything? Why?
2. Is it enough for a company to observe current pollution control laws, even when it knows (or suspects) that something it is doing, though legal, could be harmful to people?
3. Should government do something here? If so, at what level of government? What action should it take?

12
The Suppliers

Every firm buys many items from individuals and other firms: machinery, raw and packing materials, supplies of all kinds—importantly—intangible items in the form of advice and specialized services. Unless the items it purchases are available in the quantities and qualities required, at the time they are needed and at generally competitive prices, a firm is certain to have trouble.

In addition to counting on its suppliers to furnish necessary items, a firm ordinarily tries to obtain from its suppliers advance information on new developments in their special fields. Expert suppliers can, if they want to, greatly extend the research and development capabilities of a company, giving it considerable competitive advantage at little or no direct cost to the company. When a capable advertising agency or a large television network offers its best new ideas first to a particular advertiser, that advertiser has a small but definite advantage over competition. Similarly, if a major chemical company knows that one of its big customers is trying to find a lower-cost substitute for a certain chemical ingredient, it may assign its own research people to work with the customer's research people on the project, thus reducing the customer's research cost and increasing the chances of success. Or the chemical company's research people might happen to find a new compound, say to themselves, "This would be a great lower-cost substitute for one of the ingredients in that Servex product!"—and the chemical company might offer the new substitute first to Servex.

In such cases, there is usually unspoken agreement between the supplier and the purchaser that, if the purchaser accepts the new idea, he will buy his supplies of the new item—for at least a short time—exclusively from the supplier who helped him.

Naturally, firms try to buy from the suppliers that have an optimal combination of reliability, capacity, quality control, price, expertise, and willingness to help good customers obtain competitive advantages. When a well-managed firm finds a good supplier, be it a law firm or a manufacturer of office machines or anything else, it tries to cultivate good relations with the supplying firm by being aware of the supplier's desires and catering to them as far as seems profitable.

All companies are both customers of some firms or individuals and suppliers to other firms or individuals. This dual role helps them understand thoroughly the business needs and desires of both sides in the supplier-customer relationship.

Conflict between the wishes of a supplier and the wishes of his customers is inevitable, of course. The low price the customer wants, or the increased costs he wants the supplier to incur on his behalf, would mean lower profits to the supplier and higher profits to the customer. Who wins in a particular conflict between a supplier and a customer? It depends on the relative bargaining strength and skill of each. A customer who buys large quantities regularly at reasonable-to-high prices and pays promptly can demand more expensive services from a supplier than can a less valuable customer, but there is a limit. A supplier with great expertise and reasonable-to-low prices (or other characteristics desirable to a purchaser) has real bargaining strength in dealing with his customers, but once again there is a limit.

The results of any bargaining agreement reached by a supplier and a customer affect all the other constituencies of the two firms. Stockholders, managers, employees, the public, creditors, the trade, consumers, and even governments gain or lose something from the terms of bargains made by firms and their suppliers.

Back Scratchers

The Mammoth Corporation is a major buyer of many of Servex's products, particularly from the Plastics and Petrochemicals Group, where goods worth $26.7 million were purchased in 1983. Mammoth's purchases from Servex's other groups amounted to $9.4 million.

Recently, Mr. James Poindexter, executive vice-president of Mammoth, asked for an appointment with Mr. Alexander Botts, vice-president of Servex. At the meeting, Mr. Poindexter presented data showing that Servex had purchased only $7.2 million worth of Mammoth products in 1983. "Alex," said Mr. Poindexter, "I frankly am puzzled as to why Servex doesn't buy more of Mammoth's products. We make all sorts of things you need to buy, but we can't seem to persuade your purchasing people to give us a fair share of Servex's orders. My own people at Mammoth are even more puzzled than I am. They've figured out that we bought over $36 million worth of Servex products in 1983 and you bought only $7 million from us. My people are asking why, if Servex doesn't want to buy from Mammoth, should Mammoth buy so much from Servex?" Mr. Poindexter then gave Mr. Botts a list of possible Servex purchases from Mammoth worth about $30 million. The items ranged from light bulbs (to be sold through the Servex Retailing Group) through bearings for the Machine Tools Group to special retorts and piping for the Petrochemicals Group.

Mr. Botts promised to look into the matter and discuss it further with Mr. Poindexter shortly. As he was leaving, Mr. Poindexter cordially reminded Mr. Botts that he hoped their next meeting would be productive. His own people were pressing him, he said, and he would like to get the problem resolved quickly.

Mr. Botts did some telephoning to various group presidents, who in turn checked with their buyers. Normally, Mr. Botts discovered, the groups followed Servex's policy of buying the best items they could at the best prices. The major reason for not buying more from Mammoth was that Mammoth often failed to meet competitive prices or qualities or delivery times. An example was light bulbs. The Retailing Group in 1983 purchased over $4 million worth of bulbs. Less than $100,000 worth of light bulbs were bought from Mammoth because experience had shown that Mammoth bulbs caused many more customer complaints—leading to returns and refunds—than did the leading brand the group was selling. (Servex's own laboratory tests more or less agreed with findings published in consumer magazine that Mammoth bulbs produced fewer total lumens per 1¢ of average retail price than did any other leading brand. Also, the useful life of Mammoth bulbs varied more widely than for other brands; some Mammoth bulbs lasted two or three times normal expectancy while others burned out very quickly.) Moreover, Mammoth often failed to deliver to Servex's stores on time, causing inventory problems. Breakage in transit also was higher than with other brands, because of Mammoth's sloppier packing practices. In short, although Mammoth's price was fully competitive, product quality and service from Mammoth to Servex were not.

Questions

1. What should Mr. Botts say to Mr. Poindexter at their next meeting? Why?
2. Is it ethical for Mammoth to take a "you scratch my back, I'll scratch yours" approach to selling? Why or why not?
3. Suppose that, if Servex does not increase its purchases from Mammoth, Mammoth will decrease its purchases from Servex by about $30 million a year. Who will be hurt by the decrease? Who will be helped? List the parties affected.

Fishing for Better Contract Terms

Each July for many years, J. Baxter Bagby, the chief executive officer of Servex, has arranged for one of the Servex corporate jet airplanes to fly him to Milwaukee and then to Toronto, Ontario. In Milwaukee Mr. Frederick Vierson, the chief executive officer of Braunschweiger Corp., brewers of one of the best-selling beers in the United States, joined Mr. Bagby for the flight to Toronto. From Toronto, the two friends would drive to Sudbury, Ontario, where a chartered light float plane would be waiting to fly them straight north across 350 miles of wilderness to a small lake. On the shore of the mile-long lake were three or four simple log cabins. Much more important, in the lake were the world's largest and most aggressive brown trout. Mr. Bagby and Mr. Vierson looked forward from one year to the next to a July week of fighting those magnificent fish all day, and swapping stories each night over a beer or two.

Among the many pleasurable features of the annual trip was the fact that the cost was tax deductible for each of them as a business expense. Braunschweiger was in 1984 the largest volume customer of Almont and Sons, a Servex subsidiary. Naturally, the Internal Revenue Service could not object if the two executives each charged off as business expenses any costs of their meeting to discuss problems arising from their customer-supplier relationship.

In 1984, there was more justification than usual for claiming that Mr. Bagby and Mr. Vierson were meeting on the little lake just below the Arctic circle primarily to talk business. Mr. Bagby had suggested to Mr. Vierson that this time Mr. John Maxwell, president of Servex's Almont subsidiary, should accompany them on the annual fishing trip. When Mr. Vierson showed some surprise at the suggestion, Mr. Bagby said, "Fred, this time I do have a little business to talk, if you don't mind, and John ought to be in on it. Anyway, John's good company, and you and I can take some of his money at gin rummy." In the end, the three men made the trip together.

After the first night's dinner at the fishing camp, the three men settled down in front of the wood fire.

"John," said Mr. Bagby, "I told Fred I'd like to talk a little business on this trip, and what I'd like to talk about is that cost situation on the self-destruct beer bottles."

"You mean those special bottles you make for us?" Mr. Vierson was surprised. "I thought Braunschweiger and Almont had a long-term contract that covered every conceivable angle of cost. Isn't that right?"

"Fred, that's right—and that's what's *wrong*! I'm really not bitching to you about the contract. When we signed in 1980, we were happy, even if your negotiators did squeeze our forecast profit margin so thin you could read the contract through it. And it's a clean contract—covers everything clearly, just as you say. I'd better start back at the beginning and recapitulate the whole deal, so we're all together on what we're talking about."

The story Mr. Bagby recapped was a simple one. In 1972 at an international conference, one of Braunschweiger's research chemists heard about a chemical compound with unique properties that the Germans had newly developed. It seemed to Braunschweiger's researcher that the new compound offered the possibility of packaging beer for the first time in plastic throwaway bottles, at a cost even lower than cans or glass bottles. What is more, the new plastic could perhaps be molded into box-like shapes, with flat sides and square corners. Box-like bottles would save enormous amounts of space in the brewer's warehouse, on the grocer's shelves, and in the consumer's refrigerator and might also be a highly marketable distinction. In brief, the use of the new chemical compound in plastic beer bottles was an exciting idea that Braunschweiger management was eager to pursue.

Having no expertise in plastics themselves, Braunschweiger took the idea to Almont and Sons, from which for many years they had bought plastic promotion items and molded dummy display bottles. After formal letters had been exchanged, promising that Almont would keep the idea secure as a trade secret (the idea was not patentable) and that both Almont and Braunschweiger would share completely the results of any research either did on the idea, Almont began what became five years of intensive research. It was quickly apparent that Almont's substantial expertise in extruding and molding plastics was not going to be enough to deal with research in the formulation of plastics. Therefore in 1975, with Braunschweiger's agreement, EPIC Corporation (then an independent firm, now a Servex subsidiary) was brought into the research project because of EPIC's experience with the kinds of plastics that tolerate extreme temperatures.

The three-company research project was unusually successful. As early as March, 1976, an EPIC researcher made a real breakthrough. With only slight modification of the original formula, the new plastic would now self-destruct when discarded! About six months after manufacture of a batch of the new plastic, a crystalline change took place. As a result of that change, any portion of the plastic sheet that had both sides exposed to air with less than 70 percent relative humidity would begin to disintegrate to powder. Disintegration would be complete after cumulative exposure to low humidity for from 1200 to 1300 hours. The advantages of self-destructive plastic containers for beer were obvious. No longer would litter live forever to shame the brewer—and subject him to probable future legislative penalties.

By 1979, the three companies had sunk about $3,200,000 into research on self-destruct plastic bottles, and had whipped all the practical problems of producing a high-quality product in the laboratory. The companies also believed they knew how the product could be produced in volume in a factory. The companies recognized, of course, that it was one thing to have highly trained laboratory technicians produce small batches of product from carefully checked and scientifically measured raw materials, in laboratory glassware, with someone watching the process every second—and quite another thing to produce plastic for tens of millions of bottles on a continuous basis, on factory machined controlled and maintained by skilled factory workers, from carload lots of raw material.

In early 1980, Braunschweiger and Almont signed a 122-page contract under which Almont would build in Milwaukee a new plant specially to produce self-destruct bottles exclusively for Braunschweiger. The contract was for seven years after plant completion. The agreed price for the agreed quantities of bottles was sufficient, according to Almont's estimates, to let Almont during the seven-year period recover 100 percent of Almont's and EPIC's $2,900,000 share of the research cost, plus 100 percent of the installed cost of all special factory machinery, plus 100 percent of all direct and indirect factory costs and still make a small profit (estimated at 7.3 percent of sales, before tax).

"The trouble," J. Baxter Bagby went on after summarizing the history to date, "is that inflation has driven costs up so much faster than we allowed for, while the price Braunschweiger pays us for bottles has of course been fixed. In late 1979, when we were estimating costs, we allowed for an average 5 percent annual inflation over the 1981–1987 period. We were even careful to allow, in our contingency costs, for an *extra* 0.35 percent inflation. But, inflation since the plant was built has run about 8 percent a year. Compounded, 5 percent inflation amounts to a 35 percent increase in seven years, while 8 percent inflation amounts to a 70 percent increase. When you add the fact that we've had to give our workers increases that are higher than the rate of inflation, while their productivity in the new plant stays about the same, not only is all our profit on the bottles we sell you wiped out, but already in 1984 we're losing money on every bottle. Last month we lost about $35,000 and by the end of the year we'll be losing about $40,000 a month. The contract has over three years to run and each month we'll be losing more!"

"Now, Bax," Fred Vierson said soothingly as Bagby paused for breath, "calm down. Look, self-destruct bottles have been a big success—bigger each year. You provided in the contract for Servex and Almont to get back almost $4,000,000 of research and special machinery cost, over the life of the contract. Actually, if you and we had known for sure the bottles would be a success on the market, you could have capitalized at least the research part of cost—about $3,000,000 wasn't it?—instead of charging it off in seven years. If you look at it that way, you're still making a profit. Smaller than you like, maybe, but an operating profit."

"Fred, that's changing the rules after half the game's played!" J. Baxter Bagby was intense, leaning forward in his chair. "We took a risk, sinking about $3,000,000 into research that we weren't sure would amount to any-

The Suppliers • 183

thing. Well, it did amount to something, but don't tell me that just getting back part of the money we've already spent—and worse, getting it back in inflated dollars years after we spent it—is making a profit!"

"Just suppose, Bax," asked Mr. Vierson, "just suppose I accepted your point of view. What do you think we ought to do?"

"That's more like you, Fred," said Mr. Bagby, calming down. "We've been doing business together for years now, and that's more what I expected from you. What *I* think we ought to do is to tear up the old contract and write a new one with all the same terms as the old *except* for recognizing that past costs have inflated faster than was originally expected and that future inflation will probably run closer to 8 percent than to 5. We'll still settle for a 7.3 percent profit margin, on that basis. My figure boys have run some numbers—what it will amount to is an increase in bottle costs of about $14.17 a thousand—1.4¢ a bottle."

"Tear up the contract and give you 1.4¢ a bottle more from her on? Ooof! What with inventory costs, plus my profit margin, middlemen's and retailers' margins, that's going to mean a 2¢ increase in the retail price per bottle. My competitors are going to love to see Braunschweiger raise prices. Tear up a valid contract with three years still to run? I wonder if my stockholders could sue me for throwing away company money?"

"Fred," Mr. Baxby said firmly, "Almont is a supplier to you, but Lord knows that to lots of companies Almont and Servex are customers, so I can see your side of this. But I tell you this, Fred—in all my years in business I've come to believe that a good supplier—one who's running an efficient operation and giving you good service—deserves to make a profit. I hope and believe Almont and Braunschweiger are going to do business for many, many years in the future, and that both sides will find it reasonably profitable. Right now, though, Almont is in a bind, through no fault of its own. Let's tear up the old contract."

Questions

1. In Braunschweiger's position, what would you do about the current arrangement with Almont? Why?
2. What rights do other groups have, concerning the future price Braunschweiger pays Almont for self-destruct bottles? What action, if any, should an affected group take?

When Is a Bad Debt Bad?

There was an argument going on in the office of Mr. William W. Williams, president of Oregon Finance Company. All three of the men there were a little tense, and the voice of the young man directly in front of Mr. Williams wavered a bit as he tried to control himself.

"Well, it *is* a fact that your balance sheet overstates Oregon's assets by over a million dollars, Mr. Williams. As an independent auditor, I can't ask my firm to just kindly and conveniently overlook that fact, and sign the balance sheet. Pickwick, Pickwick and Radebaugh doesn't play games like that!"

"Young man," Mr. Williams said sternly, "you're making four serious mistakes. In the first place, your sarcasm is out of place in a business discussion. Second, you're confusing facts and opinions. It is *your opinion* we're overstating assets. Your opinion does not make it a fact. Third and most important, you're forgetting that a balance sheet is primarily intended to show management's valuation of assets and liabilities. If I say the receivables you're talking about are worth a million dollars to Oregon, and you see the receivables exist, then they are worth one million dollars and that's what goes on the balance sheet! Fourth and last, I think you'll find when you talk to your bosses that Pickwick, Pickwick and Radebaugh *does* play the game—as you call it—like that."

The question that had brought the young auditor into Mr. Williams's office along with Larry Sanders, Oregon's controller, was whether the reserve for uncollectible loans on Oregon's 1984 balance sheet was sufficient. On the 1984 balance sheet, outstanding loans were shown as an asset and the reserve for uncollectible loans as a liability. The young auditor had seen an interoffice memo breaking down the reserve by various classes of outstanding loans. A low percentage reserve was established for loans being paid off promptly, a higher percentage for loans on which payments were ten to thirty days overdue, a higher percentage still for loans on which payments were thirty-one to sixty days overdue, and so on up to a 33 1/3 percent for loans on which payments were twelve months or more overdue. The interoffice memo showed $1,560,000 in outstanding loans more than twelve months overdue, and $520,000 of the total reserve for uncollectable loans was assigned to these loans.

The interoffice memo also broke down reserve and outstanding loan totals for several previous years (table 12–1). Examination showed the young auditor that the total of twelve-months-overdue loans was declining year by year, while Oregon Finance's business was growing. Apparently—definitely, to the auditor's mind—Oregon had at some time failed to write off some bad debts, in order to make its earnings and assets appear larger than they really were. Since then, Oregon seemed to have bit by bit reduced the twelve-months-overdue category by yearly write-offs somewhat exceeding yearly additions to the category.

Still, in the auditor's opinion, a reserve of only $520,000 against long overdue loans of $1,560,000 was absurdly low. He had learned from office gossip that in fact Oregon eventually collected only a small percentage of

Table 12-1
Excerpts from Interoffice Memo, Oregon Finance Company to Servex Consolidated Industries, July 3, 1984: Receivables and Reserve Positions (End June)

| | Outstanding Loans (000's) | | | Reserves for Uncollectible Loans (000's) | | | | |
| | | 12 Months Overdue | | Total | | 12 Months Overdue | | |
Year	Total $	$	% of total	$	% rate	$	% rate	% of total
1984	76,449	1560	2.0	2764	3.6	520	33	18.8
1983	68,915	1746	2.5	2597	3.8	582	33	22.4
1982	66,268	2011	3.0	2599	3.9	671	33	25.8
1981	53,755	2480	4.6	2365	4.4	827	33	35.0
1980	42,334	2879	6.8	2155	5.1	960	33	44.5

loans that went twelve months with no payment. If so, the Oregon balance sheet was overstating the asset value of Oregon's outstanding loans.

The young auditor said as much to Mr. Williams.

"Mr. Williams, the value of those twelve-months-overdue loans is, I believe, overstated. If you insist that the balance sheet show the reserve figure you want, I shall have to recommend to the home office that the Servex consolidated balance sheet show a footnote that explains just how low your reserve is against those loans and that says further that Pickwick, Pickwick, and Radebaugh feels the reserve is inadequate. I'm sorry, sir, but that's what I feel I must do."

Mr. Williams stared at him for a moment, then laughed and shook his head.

"Son," he said, "you must be a little pompous and a little naive, but I surely have to credit you with persistence. Good sense? No, you don't have that—and your bosses will make that clear to you when and if you report on this conversation—but persistence, yes, you've got it."

"Do you know what will happen if you recommend that a footnote explain this reserve situation in the Servex balance sheet? I'll make a list for you again. First and least important, they'll tell you that even if they did insert a footnote, it couldn't say that Pickwick, Pickwick and Radebaugh felt the reserve was inadequate. How in hell could they say such a thing? That's a management-type opinion and they're not finance company managers—they're auditors. The most they could say is that Pickwick, Pickwick and Radebaugh didn't know whether the reserve was adequate. That language would imply, of course, that they thought the reserve was inadequate—but it doesn't say it. Second, your bosses will tell you that there are dozens of similarly disputable items—maybe even hundreds or thousands of them—on the balance sheet of a company as big as Servex. Most of the disputable items are tiny, some are medium-sized, a few are big. What that means is that PP&R has to decide which items, if any, are big enough and also disputable enough to be worth footnoting—which items are, in fact, 'material' to the balance sheet. On the Servex balance sheet, with over a half-billion dollars in assets, no mildly disputable item of a net million dollars in outstanding consumer loans is going to be considered 'material'. We aren't misleading anybody about our total net worth. Oregon understates—and you auditors are delighted to agree with the understatement—the market value of our real estate by more than $3,000,000. That ought to take care of any shortfall in our reserves for bad debts, right?"

Mr. Williams paused to light a cigarette and then went on.

"Lastly, son," he said, "if you're fool enough to recommend to your bosses that they footnote this bit about reserves, they're going to explain to you carefully but maybe brutally that clients don't like footnotes on their balance sheets, that clients are people who pay Pickwick, Pickwick and

Radebaugh money that lets them hire you and that clients—even great big desirable clients like Servex—have been known to change auditors. In brief, young man, I'd suggest for your own sake that you forget this whole question about increasing the reserve against uncollectible loans."

Questions

1. What should the young auditor do? Why? To whom are public auditing firms really responsible?
2. Should Mr. Williams take any action in this matter? If so, what and why?
3. What rights do other groups have in this matter?

What Have You Done for Me Recently?

Soon after Richard S. Richards was made president of what was in the early 1970s the small and faltering Northeastern Insurance and Auto Claimants Group, he became convinced that the company should concentrate on consumer advertising as its main competitive advantage.

Any company that is to survive in a competitive business needs to have an advantage over its competitors in at least one aspect of the business. Thinking over the various aspects of the insurance business, Dick Richards felt that his relatively tiny regional company could not realistically expect to have an edge over established giant companies in the size and average quality of sales force or the availability of capital at low interest or the promptness and low cost of claim adjustment. Sales people, capital, and claim adjusters would have to be obtained through middlemen, and so costs per $1000 of premium income would be much higher than those incurred by larger companies; no possible competitive advantage to Northeastern in those areas. If, however, Northeastern could use intelligent planning and creative imagination to develop a unique advertising message that made thousands of the right people ask their local insurance agent specifically for a Northeastern policy, consumer advertising could be a real and profitable advantage.

As it turned out, Richards's basic thought had been correct. With much careful planning and hard work—and some luck—Northeastern and its advertising agency, Harry Lee Associates, developed an advertising campaign that provided the basic impetus for Northeastern's rapid rise in premium income and profits throughout the 1970s, In 1981, Servex acquired Northeastern, principally because of Northeastern's outstanding growth record but also in large part because J. Baxter Bagby, operating head of Servex, thought Dick Richards was an unusually able and promising executive who would strengthen Servex's management team. Many of the executives that Bagby knew in other insurance companies were stodgy, bureaucratic types. He liked

Richards's flair for planning and his imaginativeness, when Richards told him how Northeastern's advertising campaign had been created.

Richards's story was that, after he tentatively fixed on consumer advertising as a probable area in which Northeastern could have a competitive advantage, he realized that he needed expert advertising brains to help develop the campaign. He went first, naively, to the large and plush offices of several big, famous Madison Avenue advertising agencies, but quickly found out that none of them had the faintest interest in taking on his small (an estimated $70,000 a year) account. Next, he talked to several one-man agencies in New York and in the small New England city where Northeastern was headquartered.

"I've since found," Richards told Bagby, "that there are some fine and reputable one-man agencies that do excellent jobs for the small accounts they handle. But the ones I saw in 1974 were either sharks—very nearly out-and-out crooks—or jellyfish. They all talked flamboyantly about how creative they were and how many different wonderful services they would provide. In the end, though, it seemed to me that all any of them had to offer was a rebate on the costs of advertising space or time. If Northeastern buys a television commercial spot for $1000, say, the station bills the advertising agency for $850 and the agency should bill Northeastern for $1000. The $150 difference is supposed to be an agency commission, which is an advertising agency's main source of income. The one-man operations I talked to that were jellyfish offered to put together a routine television commercial at cut rates and also to bill Northeastern for only $925 or $900 or $940, depending on which jellyfish was talking. That is, instead of a standard 15 percent agency commission they'd take only 7.5 percent or 5 percent or 9 percent and let the company keep the rest. If they were sharks, they offered in roundabout language to give *me* personally, the rebate—maybe in money, maybe in trips to Hawaii and Europe for Mrs. Richards and me. Ugh! I didn't want lousy advertising at supposedly cut-rate prices. I figured that lousy advertising is expensive advertising, at any price. What I wanted was superior advertising at regular prices. Anyway, I finally was lucky enough to find Harry Lee."

Harry Lee Associates was a small firm with total annual billings of about $1,500,000, when Northeastern first became a client in 1974. Lee, an able and conscientious businessman, had had fifteen years of experience with two giant advertising agencies, as account executive for intangible goods such as insurance, before he set up his own agency. His associates consisted chiefly of a brilliant middle-aged woman (she was creative director of the agency) and a suave gray-haired man in his fifties, whose movie-star looks concealed from most people his computer-like mind (he was media and production director of the agency). These two associates had been hand-picked by Harry Lee as among the three or four ablest people in their specialties in New York, but battle-weary after more than twenty years in the Madison Avenue trenches. It was important that they be battle-weary, for Harry had to convince them to leave $90,000 salaries and the big-time agencies and throw in with him on the risky and back-breaking venture of starting a new advertising agency in a medium-sized New England city.

Harry Lee Associates was delighted to take on Northeastern as a client. There was the money, of course; the $10,500 agency commission on the tentative $70,000 advertising budget would be very welcome. Even more important, perhaps, was that Dick Richards and the other Northeastern people seemed intelligent and genuinely interested in working out a good advertising campaign; they would be fun to work with. Finally, there seemed to Lee and his associates an excellent chance that, provided they could find the right advertising ideas, the Northeastern account would grow from $70,000 billing a year to hundreds of thousands and eventually millions a year—and 15 percent of millions would be a great deal of money, some of which would go to each of them as salaries, bonuses, and dividends.

To put it briefly, Northeastern under Richards and Lee Associates under Lee put together an advertising campaign that affected, to at least a small extent, the marketing of the entire insurance business, as one after another of the larger insurance firms changed somewhat their marketing thinking to cope with the obvious success of the small Northeastern company.

Richards and Lee agreed on the overall objective of the Northeastern campaign: at minimum cost per 100 serious inquiries, to persuade the largest possible number of persons who represent the lowest possible insurance risks in their categories and who are resident in states where Northeastern is licensed to sell insurance to inquire either directly from Northeastern, or from their local insurance brokers for additional information on the various policies Northeastern offers and to presell the inquirers on the special advantages of insuring with Northeastern.

Moving toward the stated objective involved careful investigation, deep thought, and precise definition of many of its terms. It became clear that both a statement of long-term strategy and a statement of shorter-term tactics were needed. Together, Northeastern and Lee Associates developed these statements. The long-term one spelled out the image Northeastern would always want to present to the public. This permanent image would direct and limit in various ways what short-term tactics should be used. For example, "friendly dignity and integrity, such as President Reagan as a person represented to many Americans" was a part of the desired permanent image, as were descriptions commonly sought by insurance companies: "sympathetic to policyholders in difficulty" and "able to help, and to help quickly, policyholders in difficulty." Lee Associates suggested also that Northeastern work to establish its initials—NIAC-as its logotype and generally accepted company name, since Northeastern Insurance and Auto Claimants Group was so long and clumsy a name as to be eminently forgettable by the general public.

The most valuable recommendation on long-term strategy that Lee Associates made to NIAC was that "innovative" should be an important part of NIAC's permanent image. The general public, Lee pointed out to Richards, tended to think of insurance companies as authoritative, bureaucratic, unwilling to bend to meet the desires of their customers.

"As you know," Lee argued to Richards, "it's vital to create a friendly image—we've already got that written into the strategy. But, Dick, a true friend is willing to adjust his actions a bit to meet your wishes. Let's tell the people that NIAC is willing and eager to change to give people the insurance they want. Let's say things like 'times change and NIAC changes with them.' Better, let's say 'NIAC offers you, for the first time, the insurance you've wanted.' People like novelty—look at the way the detergent companies keep putting 'New!' on their packages."

Eventually, strategy and tactics were settled and the first NIAC campaign launched. It aimed at a market scorned by most insurance companies—the youthful auto driver. At the time the NIAC campaign appeared, many parents were angered and concerned because insurance companies were cancelling insurance policies on autos that might be driven by sixteen to twenty-five year olds or raising premium rates on such autos to fantastic heights. NIAC understood why other companies were cancelling or raising rates: youthful drivers accounted for a shocking percentage of all auto accidents and an even more shocking percentage of the most serious and costly accidents. In total, the statistics showed that youthful drivers as a group were poor insurance risks; it seemed natural to most insurance companies to try to avoid insuring them. NIAC, however, studied the statistics a little more closely and thought about them a little more. It was found that only a small percentage of total youthful drivers accounted for 85 to 90 percent of accidents involving youthful drivers. The great majority of youthful drivers were no more accident-prone than other age groups. Why not, Lee argued to NIAC's management, direct your advertising effort toward the great majority of reasonably careful youths?

"You get the careful youthful driver market now," Lee said, "and you'll not only have most of them as policyholders ten years from now when they're twenty-six to thirty-five, but you will also get many of their parents as policyholders, because of your second-car-discount plan and because many parents will like and insurance company that doesn't think their kids are uninsurable."

The youthful driver advertising was responsible for much of NIAC's spectacular growth throughout the 1970s and is still an important element in the company's overall advertising and promotion, which by 1982 was running at over $1 million in annual billing by Harry Lee Associates. Harry Lee Associates had done well, too. By 1982 they were billing a total of $12 million to $13 million a year and had grown to over sixty full-time employees in addition to the original three partners.

In March, 1982, about six months after Servex completed the acquisition of NIAC, Dick Richards received a strong sales pitch from Alan Flowton, vice-president of K. Thomas Johnson, Inc., the giant New York agency that handled the Servex corporate advertising account. Mr. Flowton made a very impressive, carefully organized presentation of the reasons the NIAC advertising account should be moved to the Johnson agency. He showed Mr. Richards many award-winning print advertisements and television commercials created by his agency for its clients. Furthermore, he emphasized that the great importance of the Johnson agency to television networks and individual stations enabled Johnson clients to get the "cream" spots (the spots next to the most popular programs) for their commercials, and so their cost of delivering a message to an average 1000 viewers was less than at non-"cream" times. Mr. Flowton also mentioned tactfully that while Mr. Lee and his chief associates had without doubt done an outstanding job for NIAC in the past, they were all well along in years and well fixed financially so that, perhaps, they were now lacking in some of their original drive and creativeness. Lastly, Mr. Flowton pointed out that it would be desirable to have all of Servex's national advertising under one agency roof: the account would be large enough to warrant putting some of the agency's best and most creative young people on it.

Dick Richards thanked Mr. Flowton warmly for his presentation, but said that, before coming to a decision, he would have to discuss with his top management and with Servex management any possibility of shifting the NIAC account.

Questions

1. Should Servex and NIAC agree to keep the NIAC account with Harry Lee Associates? Why or why not?
2. Suppose that Servex and NIAC decide that in their managers' best judgment the Johnson agency would probably do a somewhat better job for NIAC over the next few years than would Harry Lee Associates. Does that supposition change your answer to the preceding question? Why or why not?
3. What groups, other than the two competing advertising agencies, will be affected by Servex's and NIAC's decision? How will they be affected?

13
The Public

Many people have no direct relationship with a given company, but they are concerned about the company's operations and affected by them. If a firm pollutes, everyone in the area is or may be a victim of the pollution. By expanding its business, a firm may increase employment opportunities; or its business may decline, thus decreasing the number of jobs available. These changes in a firm's employment also affect the livelihoods of the people who sell to the firm's employees. A company that pays heavy taxes reduces the burden on other taxpayers. A company that is inefficient and must therefore raise the prices of its products to cover excessive costs contributes to inflation. In short, if a firm helps or hurts your neighbor, in the end it may well help or hurt you.

Major corporations are watched carefully by the general public. Television programs, newspapers, and magazines cover business news and gossip and add their own editorial comment. For example, if a corporate action is distasteful to a consumer directly affected by it, he may use the media to draw public attention to the action and sway public opinion in his favor. An opinion that is held strongly by much of the general public affects the opinions and actions of the various groups dealing directly with the company. In particular, a strong negative feeling against a corporate activity frequently leads to the passage of laws or regulations prohibiting it. General public opinion in favor of a corporation can have profitable consequences. A generally favorable public reputation helps a company obtain a larger number of high-quality applicants for positions. A company with a good PR department may be able to raise prices without incurring much adverse public reaction.

There is potential conflict between the general public and the corporation whenever their views differ. Many actions that the public wants will cost the company money it cannot recover. Actions such as paying high taxes and contributing heavily to charity may in fact be unprofitable for a company. To optimize its profits, however, a company needs to create and maintain at least a minimally favorable public image. It must weigh the costs and benefits of satisfying the desires of the public against the costs and benefits of satisfying its other constituencies. The skill with which the corporation balances these opposing demands will determine how much freedom it has to pursue its own goal of maximizing profits.

The following five incidents illustrate some of the potential conflicts between a company and the public in general.

Better Dead Than Red

Because of general declines in capital spending, Westport Brass and Milling has had a disastrous profit record in the past few years. Recently Westport received an inquiry for the purchase of over $98 million worth of machine tools to be delivered over two years to Armtog, the Soviet Union's foreign trading agency. The tools specified in the inquiry are to be used in a new truck plant near Moscow, now under construction by a French firm.

Westport's president, Mr. Lopata, is a very conservative man. He dislikes the system under which the Russian domestic economy operates and deeply distrusts Russian intentions in their dealings with other countries. Mr. Lopata also likes his job, however, and pressure from the Servex home office to improve profit performance has been high for over a year. Mr. Lopata figures that Westport's gross profit would be increased by over $18 million in two years, if the proposed Russian contract were obtained. It seems likely that Westport will get the contract since it makes several types of machines with special patented features that are ideal for the new Russian plant and unavailable from competitors.

Under U.S. law, any exports of a long list of critical items (including machine tools) to the Soviet Union must be specifically licensed. After a few days of hesitation, Mr. Lopata arranged for Westport to apply for the appropriate licenses. The Armtog representative had assured him that, if the licenses could be obtained, the deal would go through. When Mr. Lopata checked on Armtog's past performance with regard to foreign contracts, he found that they observed them faithfully. He felt sure that Westport could count on prompt payment if it delivered the machinery as specified in the contract.

Shortly after applying for the U.S. government licenses, Mr. Lopata received the following letter from an organization called the Sons of American Freedom:

Dear Commie fink:

We hear you are about to help to kill American boys by
selling machinery to the commies. We all know the
only good red is a dead red. We're disgusted to see
a good American firm like Westport selling out to the
commies for a quick lousy buck.

The Executive Council of the Sons of American Freedom
has met and decided to make an example of Westport if
Westport sells to commies. Anti-American behavior
will not be permitted by the Sons of American Freedom!
If Westport makes this rotten Russky deal, every piece
of machinery for the damn commies will be sabotaged
by some good Americans in your own plant. (Yes, there
still are a few real Americans around!) We also will
boycott your products and tell all your customers what
you really are so that they will do the same. We can
do this. We have done it, as lots of sick, anti-
American firms have discovered. Our good friends in
Congress will hear the truth about you too--don't you
forget it.

Everyone knows commies have killed over ten million
Americans in the past twenty-five years. We know who
the enemy is, even if you don't. Watch out, you
commies, because we are going to get you and your kind!
No deals with commies!

Yours,

Although Mr. Lopata did not know whether this organization was big and
powerful, he was not used to such threats and thought he should consult the
Servex home office before going further.

Questions

1. Should Servex and Westport push the Soviet deal? Why or why not?
2. How might they evaluate the potential power of the Sons of American
   Freedom? Is it worth worrying about this power?
3. Take the stand you feel Westport should take, and write an answer to the
   Sons of American Freedom.

4. Would the United States get anything out of this deal? If not, why not? If so, why?

Slander

For the current television season, Servex is sponsoring a series, called "Westward," about the U.S. West in the 1870s. Servex's commercials on this series rarely promote any specific product; instead, they try to put across the idea that the whole Servex company is a most useful part of American life. For this rather diffuse and general message, buying relatively cheap time (Monday night at a poor hour) for a wholesome show seemed more appropriate than paying very high rates for the most popular hours and shows. By sheer luck, "Westward" turned out to rank among the top five programs in terms of number of viewers. Servex's cost per thousand viewers of its commercials on the show is amazingly low—only $1.97 a minute. Over 40 million people watch "Westward" every Monday night.

Recently, Servex received a letter from Mr. Paco Gomes, who identified himself as the president of the Chicano Society of the United States.

"We feel that your program "Westward" is a slander against all Chicanos. Most of the scripts portray Latin Americans (usually Mexicans) as villains. Adding insult to injury, the villains are crude, vulgar, sadistic, and ugly. All your villains have Latin surnames. The clear implication is that all Chicanos are ugly, mean, villainous, and untrustworthy. Please cease such slander against millions of decent, law-abiding American citizens immediately, or we will be forced to take further steps."

A quick check showed that Mr. Gomes is indeed president of the Chicano Society, which represents the interests of millions of U.S. citizens of Latin descent.

Questions

1. What should Servex do? Why?
2. Suppose Servex replies to Mr. Gomes's letter. Draft this reply. Say whatever seems to you best to say.
3. Should Servex put pressure on the writers and producer of the series to change the images of the villains? Why or why not?
4. The two writers of this series have finally made it to the big time, after years of trying. One of them, José Alvarado, is a Chicano. He argues that one major reason for the success of the show is the wonderful villains he can create from his own experiences and from the tales his grandfather told him years ago. If these villains are eliminated, the show may lose some of its appeal. Do these writers have any rights here? Why or why not?

Rights to Life

Recently J.B. Bagby had dinner with an old friend. His friend's son, Dr. Sam Baily, had started a high-tech pharmaceutical research laboratory, financed by an astute group of Boston venture capitalists to the tune of $4.5 million. Dr. Baily was an able biochemist, and he and his research team were working on a pill that would induce abortion. At dinner, J.B. and Dr. Baily spent much time toying with the idea of how such a pill might be marketed. Dr. Baily noted that they had the pill now and that it was undergoing tests on laboratory rats, a first step in a long and time-consuming process necessary to obtain FDA (Food and Drug Administration) approval. He estimated that if all went well, approvals might be obtained by 1988. The pills would be expensive. He figured he would need about $6 million more than his company now had to get the drug approved and ready for market.

J.B. knew that in the United States about 2 million legal abortions are performed annually. Potential markets in other countries with legalized abortion could be enormous. This pill might be sold at perhaps $50 per total dosage of five pills, and if it were as safe and efficient as Dr. Baily thought, it might gain half the total U.S. market in a short time. Sam felt that it would be perfectly safe if used within the first three months of pregnancy and probably safe in the fourth month.

J.B. spent some time giving young Dr. Baily marketing advice, along with some ideas about how to get more capital. Then Dr. Baily smiled and said, "J.B., you're a major entrepreneur yourself. Why don't you buy a piece of our company? We could have a new stock issue, and you could put in $6 million or $7 million for Servex. It would give you a lead into a market that could double Servex's size in ten years!"

J.B. laughed this suggestion off, but when he got to his office on Monday, he asked one of his assistants to check out Dr. Baily's company. Dr. Baily had been very honest; the company was just about what he said it was. But J.B. saw some problems. First, Servex had never bought part of any company, preferring to take over smaller firms completely. But perhaps he could buy out Sam's firm if the offer were right.

Second, there were real risks in getting FDA approval. Many drugs were never approved or took ten or even fifteen years of testing before they got to market. Dr. Baily was optimistic, but he was young and a scientist, not a businessman or bureaucrat. There were many steps to approving any drug, and this one would be dynamite in terms of its possible harmful side effects and damage.

Third, J.B. was aware of the intense emotional and religious struggles going on in terms of the right-to-life movement. He knew that this abortion issue cut across many ethical and religious beliefs of many Americans. If Servex marketed the drug, he could expect a lot of political and religious heat from many quarters.

Still, Dr. Baily was right; the profit possibilities were mind boggling. This one product could literally double Servex's size in a few years.

Finally, Dr. Baily claimed that the drug was safe. Although modern abortion techniques are quite safe, they involve surgical procedures that can be dangerous. Avoiding these might save some women's lives. J.B.'s niece had been raped a few years ago, and she had become pregnant. She had an abortion. The whole experience had scarred her emotionally. Perhaps the simple act of taking a pill instead of going through an elaborate and emotionally charged hospital procedure would save women in a similar plight much mental damage.

Questions

1. What should J.B. do? Why?
2. Suppose this drug finally gets approved and gets to market by Servex. What kinds of public reactions might the company expect as a result, if any? Why?

Visual Pollution

Letson and Baker is expanding its production of a relatively new type of fertilizer that seems likely to be particularly useful in areas where soils are very poor. The fertilizer shows great promise for unindustrialized countries where annual incomes often average less than $200 per person, population is expanding rapidly, and starvation and malnutrition are widespread. Mr. W. John Letson II, Letson and Baker's president, is enthusiastic about the new fertilizer. He estimates that within ten years this one product may save as many as ten million lives a year in poorer countries, as well as slightly raising dietary standards among the poor in the United States by bringing food costs down a trifle.

To make sure that the fertilizer formula is the best possible for various types of marginal farmland, Letson and Baker decided to build a pilot plant in the United States to make experimental batches of varying qualities and compositions for use on test plots of land. It will take a year to build the pilot plant, which is planned to be in full operation within two years. As a pilot manufacturing operation only one step above a laboratory, the plant was designed to be as clean and small as possible.

In 1984, Letson and Baker selected a site near San Francisco, principally because of the large number of highly trained researchers and technicians in the area. Operation of the pilot plant would demand much expertise. Also, Letson and Baker thought the many colleges and universities in the Bay Area would provide a valuable source of talent for consultative services.

A suitable site, atop a small hill north of San Francisco, was selected and acquired. Before building the plant, a number of redwood trees had to be cut down, and access roads had to be built. When the contractor's men arrived with their chain saws, they found the site occupied by a group called Save Our World. This group blocked efforts to start cutting down the trees.

The contractor's crew withdrew, and the story was featured in the newspapers and on local television. Save Our World's lawyer obtained a temporary court injunction stopping further work, on the grounds that construction and operation of the plant would both damage the environment and irreparably ruin the natural beauty of the site. After two months of legal maneuvers, Letson and Baker was able to obtain the court's permission to begin again to clear the site. This time, more than five thousand protesters showed up to block the work. There was some shoving and pushing and a scuffle started. Television cameramen were well placed to tape the action, which was aired on the evening news programs. By showing only the two-minute scuffle plus a closeup of one of the hard-hatted contractor's men taking an enraged full swing at the beaded and bearded protester, one television news program gave the impression that a sizeable riot had occurred.

The next day, a front-page newspaper story and a strong editorial characterized Letson and Baker as a company that would willingly cut down every redwood in California for the sake of its selfish profit. From the letters to the editor concerning the incident, it seemed that most people in the Bay Area felt Letson and Baker should build its fertilizer factory elsewhere—preferably at least a hundred miles away.

Letson and Baker had already invested over $300,000 in land acquisition and preparation. The land was zoned for light industry. If buildings could not be put on the land and it had to be resold as parkland, it would bring perhaps $40,000. There are about 150 mature redwoods on the site, forty-five of which would have to be cut down to make way for the plant and access roads.

Questions

1. Should Letson and Baker continue to try to build the pilot plant on the controversial site? Why or why not?
2. Fifty construction men in the Bay area might lose over 3000 man-days of work as a result of this hassle. Do they have any rights? Why or why not?
3. Suppose that there is a 25 percent chance that this new fertilizer, when developed, will save about 10 million lives a year—over 800,000 a month—in the poor parts of the world. Do these foreigners have any rights in this matter? Why or why not?
4. The supply of redwoods is steadily dwindling. There is real concern in California and elsewhere that rapidly spreading industry, highways, and

urbanization will eventually make these giant trees almost extinct. Who
has rights to the existing redwoods? Why?

5. Suppose that if the new pilot plant is not built on this site, fifty highly
    skilled chemists in the Bay Area will not obtain work. There currently is
    major unemployment in California among people with such expertise,
    and jobs that utilize their specialties are very difficult to find. Do these
    people have any rights? Why or why not?

Black Protests

New African News, a large black-owned newspaper in a major midwestern
city, has been running a series of articles exposing Servex and its operations.
The paper has made several allegations: Servex does not hire a fair percentage
of blacks, and the few hired almost invariably end up in dead-end, low-level
jobs; Servex has a lucrative, growing export business to South Africa; Servex
is moving its plants and stores out of the inner cities as fast as it can, and low-
income blacks cannot afford to commute to jobs they might get with the company; and Servex is undeniably racist, since its president, Mr. J.B. Bagby, is
from the Deep South. The paper has been running the anti-Servex articles for
a number of months and shows no signs of letting up on its attack.

Servex's public relations staff has clipped these articles. Such attacks on
major corporations are common in most of the black press in the United
States. What seems uncommon is for one black paper to mount such a con-
centrated attack on one corporation. *New African News* is now featuring
news of threats of black boycotts of Servex operations and black demonstra-
tions against the company. Sales are down a bit in the inner-city Lucky Jim
discount store in this city, to no one's surprise since the store's volume has
been slipping for several years, and already its closing is planned for a few
months from now when a new suburban store will be completed.

As Servex sees the situation, the true facts about the allegations are as follows:

1. Servex has been trying for five years to hire more blacks. It has increased
    its percentage of black employees from under 1 percent in 1977 to about
    5 percent now. (Blacks form about 12 percent of the total U.S. popula-
    tion.) Servex has discovered, as have many other American companies,
    that finding qualified blacks for many kinds of jobs is very nearly impos-
    sible. As a result, Servex's minority hiring campaign has gone more
    slowly than desired.

2. Black workers often end up in low skill, dead-end jobs because they do
    not have the training needed for better jobs. For several years Servex has
    had a small training program to upgrade black workers, but it is low key,

expensive, and not particularly effective. Also, many of the blacks successfully trained in the program have left the company for better-paying jobs elsewhere.

3. Servex has closed four plants in the last five years. These plants were built many years ago and were very high cost operations. Transportation facilities and security provisions necessitated expenditures that were far above average. No blacks lost jobs when these plants closed, although some white workers were terminated. (In earlier years almost no black workers were around, nor were they hired if they were available.) All the newer plants not only hired some blacks, but also expanded both output and employment because of lower operating costs in outlying, suburban plants. These black workers were typically not low-income blacks, but skilled middle-class blacks, many whom lived in the suburbs rather than in the inner city.

    Servex is slowly but steadily closing its Lucky Jim discount stores in inner city locations. The reason, once again, is the high operating costs in the older, poorer neighborhoods compared to those in the suburbs. An average suburban Lucky Jim store nets twice as much per square foot as an average inner city store, and the suburban stores are much bigger. As with the plants that were closed, no blacks have lost jobs as a result of these moves, and some have been hired.

4. Servex exports about 0.1 percent of its total sales to South Africa. The figure is indeed growing. Five years ago, exports to South Africa were 0.05 percent of total sales. Servex does not own any South African plants or other facilities.

5. Mr. Bagby was born and raised in Alabama. In fact, he comes from a distinguished old Southern family.

The PR department noted that the anti-Servex articles in *New African News* are being picked up and reprinted in black-owned papers in other cities. Servex's PR chief, Mr. Wallen, suggested recently in a memo to Mr. Bagby that it might be useful to invite the editor of *New African News,* or possibly one of its reporters, to visit Servex and listen to a presentation of the true facts concerning the paper's allegations. Perhaps if a visit from a representative of the paper were arranged, Servex might be treated somewhat more fairly in *New African News* than it now is.

Questions

1. Should Mr. Bagby invite the editor of *New African News* to visit Servex? Why or why not?
2. What else, if anything, should Servex do? Why?
3. Do facts matter much in this situation? Why or why not?

4. What obligations, if any, does Servex have to black Americans? Why?
5. What obligations, if any, do black Americans have to Servex? Why?

14
Conclusion:
Living in the Real World

The incidents in this book have tried to show what the world is like. Some things are going badly, and changes are necessary. Unfortunately, neither Servex nor anyone else can make decisions that give everyone a better deal and make everyone happy. If a plant is closed down because it pollutes, someone loses his job and livelihood; if more blacks are hired, perhaps fewer women are; if one group gains an advantage, others may lose; and on and on. If Servex could miraculously have all the resources in the world, it still could not do everything right. Human demands are infinite; resources are limited.

This is an imperfect world. No institution, no organization, no person is perfect. Complaining that such-and-such is less than perfect is a waste of time. What we need is to push for improvement, to move toward perfection, rather than resenting the fact that perfection is nowhere achieved.

Profits and Survival

Servex has to make profits to survive. It would do little good to liquidate Servex. To do so would either transfer the profits to someone else or make everyone poorer by the amount of real goods and services the company produces. Even if Servex were a state-owned firm, it would need new equipment, new training programs, new research and development facilities. Without any profit or surplus, who provides all this? If no one does, Servex is left with an aging plant and equipment, mediocre employees, and decay.

A state-owned firm has more difficulties than a private one in solving the problems suggested in the incidents. A private firm at least has some clear idea of what its goals are. We could have presented, in only slightly modified form, similar sets of incidents for the British State Railway System, the Tennessee Valley Authority, or Amtrak—all good government-owned firms. The problems would be the same, and the solutions would be no better (and possibly, given confused goals, a lot worse) than for Servex.

204 • *Corporate Social Responsibility*

The Value of Human Life

There is no such thing as a completely safe, free, happy world. Always we are trading off benefits against costs. Painfully, we are driven to determine just what human life is worth. The problem cannot even be meaningfully discussed among decent people in our society. The usual answer—infinite value—is meaningless. If we really believed that each human life is of infinite value, society could not function at all. No one could move because airplanes, autos, buses, and other modes of transportation (including bicycles and walking) result at times in human deaths. Since we do not have either the technical or managerial ability, let alone the resources, to make travel absolutely safe, we accept some loss of life as an inevitable part of moving around. Otherwise, society would immediately collapse. The problem is not whether to move but at what level of deaths, at what level of financial costs, do we find the system acceptable.

It does not matter whether you dislike the question or whether you refuse to think about it. Every time you take a walk, fly, ride in a car, or step across a room, you are ipso facto answering the question. If you do not like the answer that a certain number of accidental deaths are inevitable, try to reduce the number. Pressure legislators to enact new safety laws, or pressure businesses and government to build safer roads and bicycle paths. At the point of trying to decide what to do, however, you are stuck with the problem posed throughout the incidents in this book: What are your priorities, since you cannot do everything at once? Is auto safety more important than pedestrian safety? Should all airline customers be forced to accept more safety costs to avoid loss of life? Should some types of travel and some types of vehicles be banned on the grounds that they are too dangerous? Suppose that, as an all-powerful transportation czar, you ban something that other people are willing and even eager to use in spite of the risks involved. What rights do they have?

Who Should Decide—Individuals or Society?

Historically, individuals have had certain rights (such as owning property and doing what they wanted with it). The state, however, has prevented individuals from exercising other potential rights (such as having an abortion). The content of these rights, obligations, and bans is constantly changing. Since these changes deeply affect many people, there are likely to be violent disagreements both among people and between the state and individuals concerning the exercise of authority.

Ten years from now, many of the incidents in this book may seem silly, since by then the problems they represent will probably have disappeared; most (but never all) persons will agree that one solution is preferable. Other things now seen as trivial or irrelevant (such as sex mores in a spaceship) may assume great importance. We keep changing our collective mind about what is significant and what is not, and about what questions the whole society should decide and what should be left to individuals.

No Absolutes

There are no right answers to problems of corporate social responsibility. There are only evaluations of what impact the various solutions might have on various individuals or groups. In the end, all of the choices are ethical, because there is no criterion other than morality on the basis of which to decide who should bear what costs. Since your ethics are as good as ours, anyone has a right to decide what is right in such situations—right, that is, for him as an individual. Who, except for a majority of members of a society, knows what is right for society?

A consensus is sometimes difficult to reach, however, because not all people see a problem from the same perspective. We might feel that Mexican braceros have as many rights as other people and hence should be freely admitted to the United States. Of course, if they are, they might get jobs that otherwise would go to Americans. You might feel that a bracero's rights are irrelevant and should not be considered. We are each "right" in our own eyes; but because we see the same problem from different perspectives, our answers may be quite different.

Small World

It may seem reasonable to make a copper mining company spend lots of money to diminish air pollution in its copper smelting operation. However, this expenditure raises the price of copper quite a bit, and as a result electrical machinery made in Los Angeles cannot profitably be exported and someone there loses his job. If a reformer considers the problem at all, the usual answer he gives is that pollution should be stopped and people in Los Angeles should also keep their jobs. This answer assumes that there is such a thing as a free lunch, that costs can be passed clear out of the system to no one at all.

There can be no such thing as a free lunch, however. For everything we do and for everything we receive, good or bad, there is a cost that someone must pay. It would be nice never to do anything that might conceivably harm another person, but this is no utopia—just a messy planet full of confused people trying somehow to get along.

Of course, there is nothing wrong with shifting the burden of costs. Much of human history is one of trying to get someone to bear the costs now borne by others. But the costs are there, and they will not go away and they cannot be avoided. If they are high enough, as in the case of air or water pollution, it may well turn out that everyone has to bear his share—which means that everyone's money income and material wealth decreases.

What most people want, however, is to have someone else pay all the costs. If social responsibility efforts were to cost $1500 billion a year, when current national income was $4000 billion, then "someone else" becomes you—and me. No one can escape sharing in the payment of such high costs. Some of the incidents in this book suggested how this might work out. If you stick Servex with all costs, they close down the operation and we are worse off. If you make someone else produce the goods Servex produced, he will insist on charging higher prices for the product to cover the costs—and you and I are the ones who pay. A simple electric lamp requiring the use of copper might have cost $9.95 when copper was made under polluting conditions, but it costs $49.95 when copper is produced under pure and very high cost conditions—or $499.95 if the price of copper takes into account the irreplaceability of the metal.

Much of what we call thought about corporate social responsibility is composed of opinions, ethical beliefs, and just plain guesses about what might happen. We stick Servex with a cost, and we hope that the company will bear it. That is, we make a guess that, given the facts (which we are not really sure of), something we consider useful will happen: the big corporation and its stockholders will bear the costs, not you and me. Maybe, but if our guesses are wrong, it may turn out that we are the ones who must pay the bill.

As Pogo once said, "We have met the enemy, and they is us." In the end, whatever happens affects us all—not someone else out there, those rich companies, those enemies, or whatever. In the end, the world is us, and we have to make the painful choices about what to do based on what we can do, and what happens to us, not on what happens to everyone else.

Bibliography

Benson, George C.S., *Business Ethics in America*. Lexington, Mass.: Lexington Books, 1982.

Braybrooke, David. *Ethics in the World of Business*. Totowa, N.J.; Rowman & Allanhead, 1983.

Bunke, Harvey C. *The Liberal Dilemma*. Englewood Cliffs, N.J.: Prentice Hall, 1964.

Business Leadership in Social Change. New York: The Conference Board, 1971.

Corporate Organization for Pollution Control. New York: The Conference Board, 1970. Pp. 26–34.

Corporations and Their Critics. Ed. Thornton Bradshaw and David Vogel. New York: McGraw-Hill Book Company, 1981.

DeGeorge, Richard T. *Business Ethics*. New York: Macmillan Publishing Co., Inc., 1982.

Donaldson, Thomas. *Corporations & Morality*. Englewood Cliffs, N.J.; Prentice-Hall, Inc., 1982.

Ethical Issues in Business. Ed. Thomas Donaldson and Patricia H. Werhane. Englewood Cliffs, N.J.: Prentice-Hall, Inc., 1983.

Ethical Theory and Business. Ed. Tom L. Beauchamp and Norman E. Bowie. Englewood Cliffs, N.J.: Prentice-Hall, Inc., 1979.

Garrett, Thomas M. *Business Ethics*. New York: Appleton-Century-Crofts, 1966.

Greenwood, William T. *Issues in Business and Society*. Boston: Houghton Mifflin, 1971.

Halm, George N. *Economic Systems: A Comparative Analysis*. New York: Holt, Rinehart and Winston, 1951.

Luthans, Fred, and Hodgetts, Richard M. *Social Issues in Business*. New York: Macmillan, 1972.

McFarland, Dalton E. *Management and Society*. Englewood Cliffs, N.J.: Prentice-Hall, Inc., 1982.

Sethi, S. Prakesh, and Swanson, Carl L. *Private Enterprise and Public Purpose*. New York: John Wiley & Sons, 1981.

Social Responsibilities of Business Corporations. New York: Committee for Economic Development, 1971.

Steiner, George A. *Issues In Business and Society*. New York: Random House, 1972.

Sturdivant, Frederick D. *Business and Society*. Homewood, Ill.: Richard D. Irwin Inc., 1981.

Tanzer, Michael. *The Sick Society.* New York: Holt, Rinehart and Winston, 1971.

Walton, Clarence C. *Corporate Social Responsibilities.* Belmont, Calif.: Wadsworth, 1967.

Case Index

About the Authors

Richard N. Farmer is professor of international business at the Graduate School of Business, Indiana University. He has also taught at the American University of Beirut, U.C.L.A., and the University of California at Davis. In addition, he has managed a transportation company in Saudi Arabia and has written numerous business- and economics-related articles, as well as books dealing with international business, comparative management, economic development, and management. His latest book is *Business: A Novel Approach.*

W. Dickerson Hogue has spent most of his business life in senior management positions with Procter & Gamble. His last management position was as president and general manager of Procter & Gamble A.G., Geneva, Switzerland, and of fourteen other Procter & Gamble subsidiaries throughout the world, which developed new markets and activities in over one-hundred countries. On retiring in 1966, he became senior lecturer and research associate in business at the Graduate School of Business, Indiana University. He has written a number of articles dealing with top-level management problems, both domestic and international. He is now retired for the second time and lives in California.